# Federated Learning - A Systematic Review

*Edited by Sultan Ahmad,*
*Meshal Alharbi, Sudan Jha, Aleem Ali*
*and Robertas Damaševičius*

Published in London, United Kingdom

Federated Learning - A Systematic Review
http://dx.doi.org/10.5772/intechopen.1003284
Edited by Sultan Ahmad, Meshal Alharbi, Sudan Jha, Aleem Ali and Robertas Damaševičius

Contributors
Ahmad Al Badawi, Aleem Ali, Briana Wan Nee Toh, Carol Anne Hargreaves, Geng Deng, Gorli L. Aruna Kumari, Jiangchao Yao, Lucas Nunes Barbosa, Luwei Li, Madhavidevi Botlagunta, Mahdi Morafah, Mahendran Botlagunta, Majid Morafah, Meshal Alharbi, Pranjali Malviya, Qiang Fu, Robertas Damaševičius, Sudan Jha, Sultan Ahmad, Viktoria Sheshukova, Xindong Wang, Yaoguo Xie, Zeba Khan, Ziqing Fan



First published in London, United Kingdom, 2025 by IntechOpen
IntechOpen is the global imprint of INTECHOPEN LIMITED, registered in England and Wales, registration number: 11086078, 167-169 Great Portland Street, London, W1W 5PF, United Kingdom

For EU product safety concerns: IN TECH d.o.o., Prolaz Marije Krucifikse Kozulić 3, 51000 Rijeka, Croatia, info@intechopen.com or visit our website at intechopen.com.

British Library Cataloguing-in-Publication Data
A catalogue record for this book is available from the British Library

Federated Learning - A Systematic Review
Edited by Sultan Ahmad, Meshal Alharbi, Sudan Jha, Aleem Ali and Robertas Damaševičius
p. cm.

This title is part of the Artificial Intelligence Book Series, Volume 33
Topic: Machine Learning and Data Mining
Series Editor: Andries Engelbrecht
Topic Editor: Marco Antonio Aceves-Fernández

Print ISBN 978-1-83634-212-0
Online ISBN 978-1-83634-211-3
eBook (PDF) ISBN 978-1-83634-213-7
ISSN 2633-1403

IntechOpen Book Series

# Artificial Intelligence

Volume 33

## Aims and Scope of the Series

Artificial Intelligence (AI) is a rapidly developing multidisciplinary research area that aims to solve increasingly complex problems. In today's highly integrated world, AI promises to become a robust and powerful means for obtaining solutions to previously unsolvable problems. This Series is intended for researchers and students alike interested in this fascinating field and its many applications.

# Meet the Series Editor

Andries Engelbrecht received the Masters and Ph.D. degrees in Computer Science from the University of Stellenbosch, South Africa, in 1994 and 1999 respectively. He is currently appointed as the Voigt Chair in Data Science in the Department of Industrial Engineering, with a joint appointment as Professor in the Computer Science Division, Stellenbosch University. Prior to his appointment at Stellenbosch University, he has been at the University of Pretoria, Department of Computer Science (1998-2018), where he was appointed as South Africa Research Chair in Artifical Intelligence (2007-2018), the head of the Department of Computer Science (2008-2017), and Director of the Institute for Big Data and Data Science (2017-2018). In addition to a number of research articles, he has written two books, Computational Intelligence: An Introduction and Fundamentals of Computational Swarm Intelligence.

# Meet the Volume Editors

Dr. Sultan Ahmad has been associated with the Department of Computer Science, College of Computer Engineering and Sciences at the Prince Sattam Bin Abdulaziz University in Alkharj, Saudi Arabia. He is also an Adjunct Professor at Chandigarh University in Gharuan, Punjab, India. He received his Master of Computer Science and Applications from Aligarh Muslim University in India in 2006 and his Ph.D. in CSE from Glocal University in Saharanpur, India. He has more than 18 years of teaching and research experience. He has around 130 accepted and published research papers and book chapters in reputed SCI, SCIE, ESCI, and SCOPUS-indexed journals and conferences. He also serves as Guest Editor for SCIE/ESCI/SCOPUS indexed journals. He has an Australian, a Chinese, an Indian and two UK design patents. He has authored and edited 5 books on cutting-edge topics. His research has also secured funding from national and international projects. He also took up the roles of resource person and technical panel member and headed several international conferences. He has presented his research papers at many national and international conferences. He has been integral to the university's accreditation processes, such as the ABET and NCAAA. His research interests include intelligent computing, data science, machine learning, and the Internet of Things. He is a member of IEEE, IACSIT and the Computer Society of India.

Dr. Meshal Alharbi received the M. Sc. degree in Computer Science from Wayne State University in the USA in 2014 and the Ph.D. degree in computer science from Durham University, U. K., in 2020. He has ten years of experience in teaching, research, and the industry. He is currently an Assistant Professor of Artificial Intelligence at the Department of Computer Science at the Prince Sattam Bin Abdulaziz University in Saudi Arabia. He is dean of the College of Computer Engineering and Sciences. His research interests include artificial intelligence applications and algorithms, agent-based modeling and simulation applications, disaster/emergency management and resilience, optimization applications, and machine learning.

Dr. Sudan Jha is a Senior member of IEEE and a Professor in the Department of Computer Science and Engineering at Kathmandu University in Nepal with over 23 years of combined teaching, research, and industrial experience. He is a lead researcher in the IoT R&D lab at Kathmandu University. His previous affiliations include KIIT University, Chandigarh University, Christ University, etc. He was 'Technical Director' at Nepal Television, 'Principal' at Nepal College of IT, and 'Individual Consultant' at Nepal Telecom Authority. He is dedicated to advancing higher education quality and actively works on smart platforms. His extensive research portfolio comprises 85+ SCI and SCIE-indexed research papers and book chapters in international peer-reviewed journals and conferences. He serves as a Co-Editor-in-Chief of an international journal. He also serves as Guest Editor for SCIE/ESCI/SCOPUS indexed journals. With three patents to his name, he has authored and edited 7 books on cutting-edge topics in IoT, 5G, and AI, published by Elsevier, CRC, and AAP. His research has also secured funding for two international projects. Additionally, he has contributed as a keynote speaker at more than 40 international conferences. In addition, he has also delivered faculty development programs, short-term training programs, and workshops at national and international conferences and universities. He holds Microservices Architecture, Data Science, and Foundations of Artificial Intelligence certifications. His primary research interests encompass Quality of Services in IoT-enabled devices, Neutrosophic theory, and Neutrosophic Soft Set Systems.

Dr. Aleem Ali is an accomplished Professor and Research Coordinator in the Computer Science & Engineering Department at Chandigarh University, Punjab, India. With over 15 years of rich teaching and research experience, Dr. Ali has emerged as a prominent figure in the field. He holds a B. Tech degree from Kumaon University (A State Govt. University), an M. Tech from Hamdard University (Deemed to be a University funded by the Central Government), and earned his Ph.D. from Gautam Buddha University (A State Govt. University), in Noida, U. P., India. His doctoral research, titled "Delay Aware QoS in MANET by Using Queueing Theoretic Approach," reflects his expertise in addressing complex challenges within IoT, AI, ML/Deep Learning and network security. His contributions extend beyond the classroom and lab. Dr. Ali has been integral to university accreditation processes such as ABET, NAAC, and NBA. His commitment to maintaining rigorous academic standards underscores his dedication to quality education. As a Professor, DAAC member, and a key faculty member at Chandigarh University, Dr. Ali plays a pivotal role in shaping the future of computer science and engineering.

Prof. Robertas Damaševičius received a Ph.D. in Informatics Engineering from Kaunas University of Technology, Lithuania, in 2005. He is currently a professor in the Department of Applied Informatics at Vytautas Magnus University, Lithuania, and an adjunct professor at the Faculty of Applied Mathematics at Silesian University of Technology, Poland. He lectures software maintenance, human-computer interface, and robot programming courses. He is the author of more than 500 articles and one book. His research interests include sustainable software engineering, human-computer interfaces, assisted living, and AI explainability. He is the editor-in-chief of Information Technology and Control. He has served as a guest editor of several invited issues of international journals, such as BioMed Research International, Computational Intelligence and Neuroscience, Journal of Healthcare Engineering, IEEE Access, Sensors, and Electronics.

# Contents

# Preface

The digital revolution has transformed how we interact with technology, with data-driven solutions increasingly becoming the backbone of modern innovations. As the demand for data privacy and security grows, Federated Learning (FL) has emerged as a groundbreaking approach to distributed machine learning, offering a path forward that respects privacy while delivering powerful, scalable, and intelligent models.

Federated Learning enables multiple clients to develop machine learning algorithms collaboratively without sharing their local data, preserving privacy and ensuring compliance with regulations. It eliminates the need for centralized cloud storage, offering reduced latency, energy efficiency, and enhanced data security. However, adopting FL brings significant algorithmic and computational challenges that researchers and practitioners must address.

This book serves as a comprehensive resource, offering a deep dive into FL's architecture, classification, and development. It bridges the gap between theoretical exploration and practical applications, providing a clear understanding of FL's distinctions from traditional distributed learning. The book showcases the breadth and depth of FL's capabilities by carefully examining topics such as Federated Neural Networks, Federated LSTM, Federated Reinforcement Learning, and more.

The chapters in this book explore key issues such as data heterogeneity, algorithmic efficiency, and scalability while presenting novel methods and applications. Researchers will also find detailed discussions of advanced federated learning algorithms and their implementation in real-world scenarios, enabling them to contribute to the field's evolution.

This work is a collaborative effort of experts in machine learning, deep learning, and artificial intelligence committed to advancing privacy-conscious technologies. We hope this book inspires further exploration, innovation, and practical adoption of Federated Learning in diverse domains.

We extend our gratitude to the contributors, reviewers, and editors who made this project possible. Their expertise and dedication have resulted in a volume that reflects the current state of the art and lays the foundation for future advancements in Federated Learning.

**Sultan Ahmad and Meshal Alharbi**
Department of Computer Science,
College of Computer Engineering and Sciences,
Prince Sattam Bin Abdulaziz University,
Alkharj, Saudi Arabia

**Sudan Jha**
Department of Computer Science and Engineering,
Kathmandu University,
Dhulikhel, Nepal

**Aleem Ali**
Department of Computer Science and Engineering,
University Institute of Engineering,
Chandigarh University, Punjab, India

**Robertas Damaševičius**
Department of Software Engineering,
Kaunas University of Technology,
Kaunas, Lithuania

Section 1

# Federated Learning and Applications

Chapter 1

# Introductory Chapter: Federated Learning – Bridging the Gap between Privacy and Collaboration in Machine Learning

*Sultan Ahmad, Meshal Alharbi, Sudan Jha and Aleem Ali*

## 1. Introduction to federated learning: A paradigm shift in data privacy

A distributed machine learning (ML) framework is called federated learning (FL). Under the control of the central server, several clients work together in FL to solve traditional distributed machine learning tasks without disclosing their local private information to third parties. Federated learning functions without requiring cloud storage of user data. Federated learning guarantees privacy while enabling smarter models, reduced latency, and less power use. Numerous algorithmic and computational challenges had to be solved before federated learning could be implemented. This book mostly uses machine learning and deep learning to classify federated learnings. This book first describes the definition, architecture, classification, and development process of FL and provides an explanation of the concept through a comparison with traditional distributed learning. After that, it lists common FL issues that must be resolved. Several federated machine learning algorithms, with a focus on deep learning and classification, are briefly explained and compared, building upon the foundation of classical federated learnings algorithms. Lastly, the breadth of FL based on deep learning and potential future advances are covered in this book.

In the age of AI, collaborative learning, particularly the exchange of data among various institutions, can significantly enhance the development of robust AI models. In standard machine learning, models are trained in centralized, isolated sites, causing communication between them to be challenging. Conversely, X-rays, CT scans, and MRIs constitute personal data related to particular patients, necessitating protection against the danger of unauthorized disclosure to third parties. Moreover, although data sharing is feasible, the centralized storage, processing, and analysis of data remain challenging endeavors. In this circumstance, data encryption and decryption may serve as a viable option for information sharing among participants; nevertheless, the process could be intricate, time-consuming, and unsustainable. Rather than transporting data to the model's training site, it is more efficient to transport the model to the data sources, such as institutions and hospitals, for in-house training. This approach facilitates collaborative learning without the need to centralize the dataset, a method known as federated learning (FL). Initially released in 2016, it has garnered significant attention in the healthcare sector over the past few years. It tackles the issue of privacy and data protection, a significant challenge in the advancement of medical AI. In FL, participants can locally train models and estimate various parameters for their particular models, thereafter sharing these values with a centralized server for aggregation. Consequently, the emphasis is not on the specific data utilized or the algorithms that might be developed but rather on managing the data in a manner that preserves data privacy.

The exponential growth of data generation (estimated at 2.5 quintillion bytes daily) has fueled advancements in machine learning (ML) but also intensified concerns about data privacy and security. By 2025, global data volumes are projected to exceed 180 zettabytes, with healthcare, finance, and IoT sectors contributing significantly to this surge. However, stringent regulations like the General Data Protection Regulation (GDPR) and the California Consumer Privacy Act (CCPA) have made centralized data aggregation increasingly impractical. Enter federated learning (FL), a decentralized ML framework that enables collaborative model training without exposing raw data. This approach ensures privacy, enhances security, and allows institutions to benefit from collective intelligence without regulatory conflicts.

### 1.1 Definition and architecture

FL, introduced by McMahan et al., allows multiple clients (e.g., smartphones, hospitals, or IoT devices) to train a shared model under the coordination of a central server [1]. Unlike traditional distributed ML, where data is pooled into a central repository, FL keeps data localized. Clients compute model updates on their devices, transmitting only these updates (not raw data) to the server, which aggregates them into a global model (**Table 1**).

### 1.2 Historical context and motivation

The concept of FL emerged from the need to address data silos, isolated datasets trapped within organizations due to legal or competitive barriers. For instance, healthcare institutions generate 30% of the world's data volume but share less than 5% due to privacy laws. FL's development was further accelerated by the rising cost of data breaches, which averaged $4.45 million per incident in 2023. By enabling privacy-preserving collaboration, FL unlocks insights from otherwise inaccessible data.

| Feature | Traditional machine learning | Federated learning |
|---|---|---|
| Data storage | Centralized | Decentralized |
| Privacy risk | High | Low |
| Communication overhead | Moderate | High |
| Computational load | Server-heavy | Distributed |

**Table 1.**
*Traditional ML vs. federated learning architecture.*

## 2. Key challenges in federated learning

Despite its promise, FL introduces unique challenges that demand innovative solutions:

### 2.1 Communication efficiency

FL systems often involve resource-constrained devices (e.g., smartphones) with limited bandwidth. Transmitting large model updates (e.g., deep neural networks) can be prohibitive. Studies show that communication overhead accounts for 70–80% of total training time in cross-device FL [2]. Techniques like model compression and sparse updates have reduced communication costs by up to 60%.

### 2.2 Statistical heterogeneity

Data across clients is typically non-IID (non-independent and identically distributed). For example, wearable devices from different demographics may capture varying activity patterns. This heterogeneity degrades model accuracy, with experiments showing a 20–30% drop in performance compared to centralized training [3] (**Table 2**).

## 3. Algorithmic innovations in federated learning

### 3.1 Foundational algorithms

The Federated Averaging (FedAvg) algorithm, the cornerstone of FL, aggregates client updates via weighted averaging. FedAvg reduces communication rounds by 10x compared to naive methods, achieving 98% accuracy on MNIST benchmarks [1]. Subsequent adaptations, like FedProx, address heterogeneity by allowing variable client participation.

### 3.2 Deep learning in FL

Deep neural networks (DNNs) dominate FL applications, from natural language processing (e.g., Google's Gboard) to medical imaging. However, training DNNs in FL settings requires balancing model complexity with resource constraints. For instance, split learning partitions models between clients and servers, reducing computational load by 40% [4].

| Challenge | Impact | Solution |
|---|---|---|
| Non-IID data | Model divergence, reduced accuracy | Personalized FL, meta-learning |
| System heterogeneity | Stragglers delay training | Asynchronous aggregation |
| Privacy threats | Model inversion attacks | Differential privacy, encryption |

**Table 2.**
*Common FL challenges and solutions.*

## 4. Real-world applications and impact

### 4.1 Healthcare: Collaborative diagnosis without data sharing

FL enables multi-institutional medical research while complying with HIPAA. For example, the COVID-19 Open AI Consortium used FL to train models on chest X-rays from 20 hospitals, improving diagnostic accuracy by 15% without sharing patient data [5].

### 4.2 Finance: Fraud detection across banks

Major banks like JPMorgan Chase employ FL to detect fraudulent transactions. By pooling insights from 50+ institutions, their FL system reduced false positives by 25% [6].

## 5. Future directions: The road ahead for FL

### 5.1 Cross-silo vs. cross-device FL

While cross-device FL (millions of smartphones) dominates current applications, cross-silo FL (collaboration among enterprises) is gaining traction. The latter is projected to grow at a CAGR of 25% from 2023 to 2030.

### 5.2 Integration with emerging technologies

Combining FL with blockchain enhances auditability, while quantum computing could solve encryption bottlenecks. Startups like Owkin and Secure AI Labs are already pioneering these integrations.

## 6. Conclusion

Federated learning represents a transformative approach to ML, reconciling the dual imperatives of data utility and privacy. As industries grapple with escalating data volumes and regulatory pressures, FL's role will only expand. However, overcoming its technical and ethical challenges requires sustained innovation.

**Author details**

Sultan Ahmad[1,2]*, Meshal Alharbi[1], Sudan Jha[3] and Aleem Ali[4]

1 Department of Computer Science, College of Computer Engineering and Sciences, Prince Sattam Bin Abdulaziz University, Alkharj, Saudi Arabia

2 University Center for Research and Development (UCRD), Department of Computer Science and Engineering, Chandigarh University, Mohali, Punjab, India

3 Department of Computer Science and Engineering, Kathmandu University, Kathmandu, Nepal

4 Department of Computer Science and Engineering, University Institute of Engineering, Chandigarh University, Punjab, India

*Address all correspondence to: s.alisher@psau.edu.sa

## References

[1] McMahan B, Moore E, Ramage D, Hampson S, Arcas BA. Communication-efficient learning of deep networks from decentralized data. In: Artificial Intelligence and Statistics. Ft. Lauderdale, FL, USA: PMLR; 2017. pp. 1273-1282

[2] Kairouz P, McMahan HB, Avent B, Bellet A, Bennis M, Bhagoji AN, et al. Advances and open problems in federated learning. Foundations and Trends in Machine Learning. 2021;**14**(1-2):1-210

[3] Li T, Sahu AK, Zaheer M, Sanjabi M, Talwalkar A, Smith V. Federated optimization in heterogeneous networks. Proceedings of Machine Learning and Systems. 2020;**2**:429-450

[4] Agbley BL, Li JP, Haq AU, Bankas EK, Mawuli CB, Ahmad S, et al. Federated fusion of magnified histopathological images for breast tumor classification in the internet of medical things. IEEE Journal of Biomedical and Health Informatics. 6 Jun 2024;**28**(6):3389-3400

[5] Rieke N, Hancox J, Li W, Milletari F, Roth HR, Albarqouni S, et al. The future of digital health with federated learning. npj Digital Medicine. 2020;**3**(1):1-7

[6] Yang Q, Liu Y, Chen T, Tong Y. Federated machine learning: Concept and applications. ACM Transactions on Intelligent Systems and Technology (TIST). 2019;**10**(2):1-9

Chapter 2

# Advancements in Machine Learning and Deep Learning for Breast Cancer Detection: A Systematic Review

*Zeba Khan, Madhavidevi Botlagunta, Gorli L. Aruna Kumari, Pranjali Malviya and Mahendran Botlagunta*

## Abstract

Breast cancer is a significant transnational health concern, requiring effective timely detection methods to improve patient's treatment result and reduce mortality rates. While conventional screening methods like mammography, ultrasound, and MRI have proven efficacy, they possess limitations, such as false-positive results and discomfort. In recent years, machine learning (ML) and deep learning (DL) techniques have demonstrated significant potential in transforming breast cancer detection through the analysis of imaging data. This review systematically explores recent advancements in the research of machine learning and deep learning applications for detecting breast cancer. Through a systematic analysis of existing literature, we identify trends, challenges, and opportunities in the development and deployment of ML and DL models for breast cancer screening and diagnosis. We highlight the crucial role of early detection in enhancing patient outcomes and lowering breast cancer mortality rates. Furthermore, we highlight the potential impact of ML and DL technologies on clinical procedure, patient outcomes, and healthcare delivery in breast cancer detection. By systematically identifying and evaluating studies on machine learning and deep learning applications in breast cancer detection, we aim to provide valuable insights for researchers, clinicians, policymakers, and healthcare stakeholders interested in leveraging advanced computational techniques to enhance breast cancer screening and diagnosis.

**Keywords:** breast cancer detection, machine learning, deep learning, diagnostic accuracy, biomarkers

## 1. Introduction

Breast cancer continues to be a major global public health issue, representing one of the most commonly diagnosed cancers among women. Early detection is crucial in enhancing patient outcomes and lowering mortality rates associated with breast cancer. Conventional breast cancer screening techniques, like ultrasound, mammography, and magnetic resonance imaging (MRI), have demonstrated efficacy in detecting breast abnormalities; however, these methods are not without limitations, including false-negative and false-positive outcomes, discomfort, and cost constraints [1]. Recently, the incorporation of Machine learning (ML) and Deep learning (DL) methods into breast cancer detection has yielded encouraging results, revolutionizing the field of medical imaging and diagnostic radiology. The main aim of the systematic review is to comprehensively evaluate the current state of research on ML and DL applications in breast cancer detection [2]. By systematically analyzing and synthesizing existing literature, we aim to identify trends, challenges, and opportunities in the development and deployment of ML and DL models for breast cancer screening and diagnosis. Additionally, we seek to provide insights into the potential impact of these technologies on clinical practice, patient outcomes, and healthcare delivery in the context of breast cancer detection [3]. Identifying early-stage breast cancer on screening mammograms is challenging because tumors are small compared to the overall breast image. A full-field digital mammography (FFDM) image usually measures around 4000 × 3000 pixels, while a potentially cancerous region of interest (ROI) might be as tiny as 100 × 100 pixels. Consequently, many studies focus solely on classifying manually annotated lesions. However, for a fully automated system to be effective, it must analyze the entire mammogram, providing additional insights beyond identified lesions to aid clinical interpretations [4]. The machine learning process relies on three primary strategies: preprocessing, feature selection or extraction, and classification. Feature extraction is a crucial step within this process, particularly assisting in the diagnosis and prediction of cancer outcomes [5]. Through this process, cancer datasets can be analyzed to distinguish between benign and malignant tumors effectively. Ongoing research in this field aims to develop a tumor outcome that is highly conclusive and broadly recognized, serving as a reliable recommendation for breast cancer screening. This effort seeks to achieve consensus among a broad audience and enhance the effectiveness of screening protocols [6]. Furthermore, we investigated the performance of the system across different patient subgroups and studied instances where the deep learning (DL) system did not yield accurate diagnoses. Lastly, we assessed a particular clinical situation focused on tailoring patient management for those with BI-RADS (Breast Imaging Reporting and Data System) 4 findings, resulting in a decrease in avoidable biopsies. Significant progress has been made in analyzing health data using machine learning algorithms, especially in the context of breast cancer. In order to predict cancer susceptibility, recurrence, survivability, and treatment outcomes, Algorithms, such as random forest, extreme learning machine, naive Bayes, artificial neural networks (ANNs), and support vector machines (SVMs), have been utilized on the Wisconsin Breast Cancer Data Set. Notably, progress has been achieved in the identification and diagnosis of breast cancer, leading to better patient outcomes via early intervention and customized treatment plans [7]. Early-stage breast tumor malignancy and survival have been predicted by ML algorithms with some degree of promise [8]. Precision healthcare is driving a revolution in cancer treatment, made possible by the increasing accessibility and combination of many data kinds, including genomic, histopathologic, and transcriptomic data [9]. Analyzing and assessing different high-dimensionality data types for clinical or translational research projects requires a great deal of work and skill. Moreover, integrating several data types calls for more resources than just understanding individual data types because it necessitates modeling algorithms that can learn from a vast amount of complex information [10]. The application of machine learning algorithms to automate these processes and support cancer diagnosis—which involves characterizing the cancer—and detection—which determines whether cancer is present—has grown in popularity.

Breast cancer is a complex disease defined by various molecular subtypes and different clinical manifestations [11]. Early detection of breast cancer is critical for timely intervention and improved prognosis. Mammography, the gold standard for breast cancer screening, has been instrumental in reducing breast cancer mortality rates; however, its sensitivity and specificity are limited, particularly in women with dense breast tissue or high-risk populations. Supplementary imaging modalities, like MRI and ultrasound, are often employed to complement mammography, but they may also yield false-positive results and increase healthcare costs.

### 1.1 Role of machine learning and deep learning

ML and DL techniques have emerged as powerful tools for analyzing medical images and improving diagnostic accuracy in various healthcare domains, including breast cancer detection [12]. Machine Learning techniques can identify patterns and features from large-scale datasets and make predictions or decisions based on learned knowledge. DL, a subset of ML, employs artificial neural networks with multiple layers to automatically extract hierarchical features from raw data, enabling more accurate and robust image analysis. Hybrid approach was utilized to segment the data, aiming to enhance processing efficiency and improve overall performance [13]. This approach combined intuitionistic fuzzy c-mean and possibilistic fuzzy c-mean. It keeps the benefits of both approaches and grows more resilient to coincident cluster problems, noise, and outliers. These days, convolutional neural networks (CNNs) and deep learning (DL) are gaining popularity due to their superior performance in semantic and medical picture segmentation. The [14] deep learning-based approach's primary advantage is its capacity to autonomously learn from unlabeled raw data [15]. These techniques provide a range of capabilities for breast cancer detection. Analytical confounders, such as batch effects, institutional or site-to-site heterogeneity in sample collection, and pre-analytic processing techniques, are especially common in machine learning approaches. Commercial kit comparisons have revealed varying extraction efficiencies and preferences for different fragment sizes, making it difficult to consistently and comparably identify circulatory tumor DNA (ctDNA) across investigations, especially those that depend on fragmentomics or nucleosomics. There can be additional biases towards longer or shorter fragments due to variations in sequencing platforms and library preparation techniques, such as double-strand (ds)DNA versus single-strand (ss)DNA protocols. Consequently, inconsistent fragment size profiles produced by various laboratories could make the broad application of fragmentomics techniques more difficult. CNN-based algorithms have also been [16] employed in numerous research to classify lesions. But in these articles, the region of interest was extracted by experts or by using conventional image-processing techniques, rather than with the aid of a deep learning system [17]. To be more precise, the authors employed a random forest classifier to select suitable candidate patches for their CNN approach after first dividing MM pictures into patches and extracting the characteristics from the patches using a traditional image-processing algorithm [18]. The main obstacle to deep learning models' excellent performance in medical image processing is their insatiable appetite for training datasets. Data labeling and collection are relatively expensive tasks in the medical industry [19]. Transfer learning was employed in several research as a solution to this issue. The authors of the study created a two-stage transfer learning method to categorize digital breast tomosynthesis (DBT) pictures as normal or mass [20]. First, the authors used FFDM pictures to fine-tune a pretrained AlexNet. Next, they used the refined model to train a DBT image model. For DBT pictures, the CNN model was utilized in the second stage as a feature extractor. The extracted features were then classified as mass or normal using the random forest classifier. They achieved 90% area under the curve (AUC) [21] on their test set of data. In a different study, the authors classified malignant and benign FFDM and DBT pictures using a VGG-19 network that had been trained on the ImageNet dataset as a feature extractor. An SVM classifier was given the collected features in order to determine the likelihood of malignancy. On the DBT images in craniocaudal (CC) and mediolateral oblique (MLO) views, their technique yielded an AUC of 98 and 97%, respectively. These approaches demonstrate that deep learning models can function well when they use transfer learning strategies and a short training dataset. The majority of the previously stated research contrast their DL algorithms with conventional computer-aided diagnosis (CAD) techniques [22].

### 1.2 Importance of systematic review

Given the proliferation of research on ML and DL applications in breast cancer detection, a systematic review is essential to comprehensively evaluate the existing evidence, evaluate the methodological rigor of studies, and identify gaps in knowledge [23]. By synthesizing findings from diverse studies and critically appraising their methodologies and outcomes, this systematic review aims to provide an evidence-based overview of the current landscape of ML and DL applications in breast cancer detection. Additionally, this review will serve as a valuable resource for researchers, clinicians, policymakers, and healthcare stakeholders interested in leveraging ML and DL technologies to enhance breast cancer screening and diagnosis.

### 1.3 Objectives of the review

The primary objectives of this systematic review are:

- To systematically identify and evaluate studies on ML and DL applications in breast cancer detection.

- To analyze the methodologies, algorithms, and performance metrics used in ML and DL models for breast cancer detection.

- To assess the diagnostic accuracy, reliability, and clinical utility of ML and DL models compared to conventional imaging techniques.

- To identify challenges, limitations, and future directions for the integration of ML and DL technologies into clinical practice for breast cancer detection.

- By addressing these objectives, this systematic review aims to provide valuable insights into the current state of research on ML and DL applications in breast cancer detection, informing future research directions and clinical implementation strategies. Additionally, this review will add to the expanding body of evidence that supports the use of advanced computational techniques in improving breast cancer diagnosis and patient outcomes.

### 1.4 Significance and distinctiveness of a thorough literature review in comparison to existing systematic literature reviews in breast cancer

The significance and originality of an extensive literature review (systematic literature review (SLR)) in Breast cancer stem from its special contribution to comprehending the applications and methodologies of machine learning in Breast cancer classification. In contrast to existing SLRs, this review provides various unique characteristics [7]:

- *Extensive coverage*: This systematic literature review (SLR) encompasses a broad spectrum of ML and [24] DL applications and methodologies specifically tailored for breast cancer classification. It offers a comprehensive perspective on the area, incorporating diverse data sources, such as imaging, genetic markers, and clinical information, and leveraging them to effectively classify various types of breast cancer.

- *Comprehensive scope:* This systematic literature review (SLR) covers a wide range of ML and DL applications and techniques specifically designed for breast cancer classification [25]. It offers a comprehensive perspective on the area, incorporating diverse data sources, such as imaging, genetic markers, and clinical information, and leveraging them to effectively classify various types of breast cancer.

- *Comparative evaluation:* Comparison tables are provided, enabling readers to compare this systematic literature review (SLR) with existing ones [26]. This analysis highlights the distinctive aspects and contributions of the current review, including its focus on specific breast cancer applications, extensive coverage, or new insights, setting it apart from previous studies.

- *Implications for readers:* The review's main findings and implications provide important insights for those interested in breast cancer. It emphasizes how machine learning can enhance breast cancer detection, personalize treatment plans, and predict patient outcomes. This knowledge enables individuals to make informed choices about incorporating machine learning techniques in breast cancer diagnosis and treatment.

In conclusion, the importance and uniqueness of this systematic literature review (SLR) in breast cancer prediction stem from its extensive scope, practical examples, comparative analysis, and actionable insights. These qualities make it a valuable resource for researchers, practitioners, and stakeholders engaged in applying machine learning and deep learning for breast cancer classification [27–30].

### 1.5 Different mathematical equations and statistical formulations utilized in various evaluation processes

In this section, we will discuss key mathematical equations and statistical formulations employed in evaluating the diagnostic accuracy and performance of machine learning (ML) and deep learning (DL) models in breast cancer detection. These metrics are critical for assessing the effectiveness of these computational techniques in clinical practice. We will explore the following equations: Sensitivity, which quantifies the true positive rate (Eq. (1)), and Specificity, which measures the true negative rate (Eq. (2)). Additionally, we will define overall Accuracy (Eq. (3)) and the F1-Score, which combines precision and recall (Eq. (4)). We will also address the region of interest (ROI) in clinical practice (Eq. (5)), followed by a discussion on K-fold cross-validation, a widely used data analysis technique for model validation (Eq. (6)). These equations serve as foundational tools for evaluating the performance and utility of ML and DL methodologies in enhancing breast cancer diagnosis.

### *1.5.1 Evaluation of diagnostic accuracy*

Sensitivity (True Positive Rate)

$$\text{Sensitivity} = \frac{TP}{TP + FN} \tag{1}$$

Where TP = True Positive
FN = False Negative
Specificity (True Negative Rate)

$$\text{Specificity} = \frac{TN}{TN + FP} \tag{2}$$

Where TN = True Negative
FP = False Positive
Accuracy:

$$\text{Accuracy} = \frac{TP + TN}{TP + TN + FP + FN} \tag{3}$$

F1-Score:

$$\text{F1} = 2 \times \frac{Precision\ x\ Recall}{Precesion + Recall} \tag{4}$$

Where Precision = $\frac{TP}{TP + FP.}$

### *1.5.2 Future directions for integration of ML and DL*

Return of investment (ROI) in Clinical Practice:

$$ROI = \frac{Net}{Cost\ of\ Investment}\ \text{x}\ 100 \tag{5}$$

### *1.5.3 Data analysis techniques*

(a) K-fold cross-validation: If D is the dataset and k is the number of folds then:

$$\text{Cross} - \text{Validation Error} = \frac{1}{k} \sum_{i=1}^{k} E(D_i) \quad (6)$$

Where $D_i$ is the ith fold and $E(D_i)$ is the error for the fold.

## 2. Related work

The authors proposed a computer-aided diagnosis approach for breast cancer classification using deep neural networks (ResNet 18, ShuffleNet, and Inception-V3Net) with transfer learning, achieving binary classification accuracies of 99.7, 97.66, and 96.94%, respectively. In multiclass classification, ResNet 18 reached 97.81%. Additionally, Moloud Abdar et al. introduced uncertainty quantification (UQ) methods (Deep Ensemble (DE) and Ensemble MC (EMC)) for skin cancer classification, achieving accuracies of 88.95 and 90.96% on two datasets. The findings indicate the effectiveness of the Three-Way Decision-based Bayesian Deep Learning (TWDBDL) model in medical image analysis [31]. Mahmoud Ragab et al. developed the Ensemble Deep-Learning-Enabled Clinical Decision Support System for Breast Cancer Diagnosis and Classification (EDLCDS-BCDC) using ultrasound images. Their approach includes a two-stage preprocessing with Wiener filtering and contrast enhancement, followed by image segmentation using the Chaotic Krill Herd Algorithm and Kapur's entropy. Feature extraction employs an ensemble of VGG-16, VGG-19, and SqueezeNet models, while classification is done using Cat Swarm Optimization (CSO) with a Multilayer Perceptron. Simulations show that EDLCDS-BCDC outperforms recent methods [32]. Ruxandra Stoean introduces an efficient method for tuning convolutional layers of a deep neural network (CNN) and ranking hyperparameters. The approach uses three surrogate models—random forests (RFs), support vector machines (SVMs), and Kriging—along with Latin hypercube sampling for generating configurations. CNN accuracy predicts hyperparameter fitness in an evolutionary algorithm. The method ranks variables for each surrogate model and assesses their impact through response surface methodology. It is experimentally tested on histopathological images for colorectal cancer diagnosis [33]. Shallu Sharma et al. developed two machine learning approaches for magnification-dependent multi-classification of breast cancer using the BreakHis (Breast Cancer Histopathological Database) dataset. The first uses handcrafted features with traditional classifiers, while the second employs transfer learning with pretrained networks (VGG-16, VGG-19, and ResNet50). VGG-16 with linear SVM achieved the highest accuracy: 93.97% at 40× and 93.25% patient based. The "Fibroadenoma" and "Mucous Carcinoma" classes were the most challenging to classify [34]. The DLCAL-SLDC (Deep Learning with Class Attention Levels for Detecting and Classifying Skin Lesions) model is an automated deep learning approach for skin lesion detection and classification using dermoscopic images. It preprocesses images by removing hair and noise, segments lesions with a Tsallis entropy technique, and extracts features using a Capsule Network with a class attention layer. Classification is done with a Convolutional Sparse Autoencoder optimized by the Swallow Swarm Optimization algorithm. Validated on the International Skin Imaging Collaboration (ISIC) benchmark dataset, the model achieved 98.50% accuracy, 94.5% sensitivity, and 99.1% specificity, outperforming other methods [35]. Maad M. Mijwil developed a deep learning network using a Convolutional Neural Network (ConvNet) model trained on over 24,000 skin cancer images from the ISIC archive. Three architectures—InceptionV3, ResNet, and VGG-19—were tested, with InceptionV3 yielding the best results: 86.90% accuracy, 87.47% precision, 86.14% sensitivity, and 87.66% specificity [36]. Nonita Sharma et al. propose a snapshot ensembling technique to aid in disease diagnosis, using t-SNE (t-distributed stochastic neighbor embedding) for enhanced scatter plots and cost optimization. Their deep learning framework combines predictions from multiple models, achieving 86.6% accuracy on the Wisconsin Breast Cancer Dataset, outperforming models like averaging (81%), weighted averaging (81.7%), stacked ensemble (84.7%), and Polyak Ruppert (82.2%) [37]. Savita Kumbhare et al. proposed a breast cancer detection model utilizing Federated Learning (FL) and mammogram images from the Digital Database for Screening Mammogram (DDSM) dataset. The model employs DenseNet for feature extraction and Enhanced Recurrent Neural Networks (E-RNN) for classification, optimized by a Hybrid Dragon-Rider Optimization (HDRO) algorithm. This approach achieves high accuracy and Mathews correlation coefficient (MCC), outperforming conventional methods [38]. Amin ul Haq et al. proposed a breast cancer identification method that integrates machine learning with clinical data. Their approach utilizes the Relief algorithm for supervised feature selection, along with Autoencoder and principal component analysis (PCA) for unsupervised selection. The features selected through these methods are used to train a Support Vector Machine (SVM) classifier. They employ K-fold cross-validation for model validation, achieving an impressive accuracy of 99.91%, which enhances its suitability for dependable breast cancer diagnosis in healthcare systems [39].

## 3. Methodology

We focused our research on breast cancer (BC) detection utilizing ML and DL methods. We reviewed approximately 80 recent papers concerning breast cancer diagnosis and treatment. Some of these studies focused exclusively on deep learning methods, while others examined a combination of ML and DL approaches. To ensure a systematic and thorough approach, we utilized the PRISMA (Preferred Reporting Items for Systematic Reviews and Meta-Analyses) guidelines for reporting items, which encompasses four key stages: identification, screening, eligibility, and inclusion. During the identification phase, we performed searches using pertinent keywords, such as "Breast cancer with deep learning" [35]. Additionally, we used a snowballing method to discover additional relevant literature by reviewing the references of the selected articles. Following identification, we conducted a screening process to assess the relevance of each article based on predetermined inclusion criteria, excluding duplicates and those not meeting our criteria. During the eligibility stage, we assessed the quality and relevance of each eligible article based on scientific rigor and methodology, excluding those that did not meet our quality standards. Finally, during the inclusion phase stage, we chose the final set of articles that fulfilled all inclusion criteria to be included in our review.

We employed the PRISMA (Preferred Reporting Items for Systematic reviews and Meta-Analyses) methodology to guarantee a thorough and methodical examination of various types of Machine Learning systems [36]. This approach facilitated the identification and assessment of a top-tier collection of articles, offering valuable and pertinent insights into the realm of machine learning. **Figure 1** shows the diagrammatic view of this PRISMA methodology.

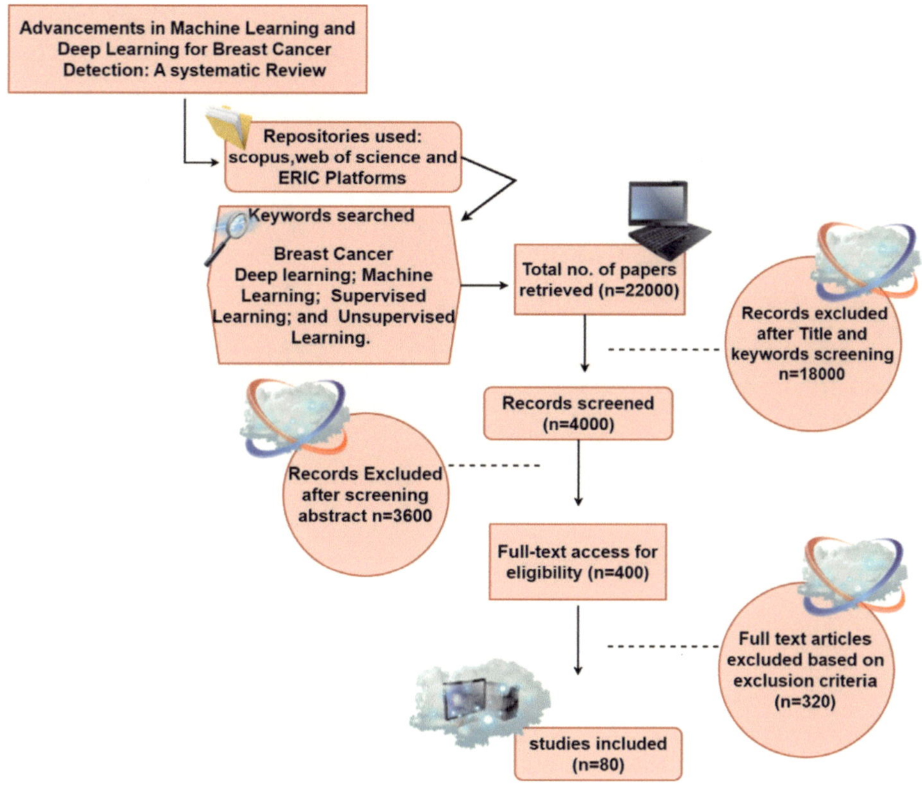


**Figure 1.**
*The figure depicts the systematic process employed for conducting a literature review.*

**Figure 2** illustrates the publication distribution of papers during the specified period of 2015–2024, indicating peaks in publications on breast cancer research around 2020 and 2023. To streamline our analysis, we reduced the selection of papers to 80 by focusing on those that specifically used genetic expression and imaging methods, and by concentrating exclusively on journal and conference papers [37]. The imaging techniques taken into account encompassed ultrasound, radiography, mammography, magnetic resonance imaging (MRI), along with various gene expression and sequencing methods [38].

## 4. Which models achieve the highest effectiveness?

**Table 1** provides a summary of the algorithms utilized and their performance, with an emphasis on both genetic and imaging data.

The research in this field can be divided into two main groups: Binary classification (identifying whether breast cancer is present or not) and multiclass classification (distinguishing between different types of breast cancer). It has been observed that binary classification generally achieves higher accuracy compared to multiclass classification. For instance, in paper [39], the backpropagation neural network (BPNN) algorithm was used with great effectiveness. Many papers that employed binary classification demonstrated strong performance across various evaluation metrics.

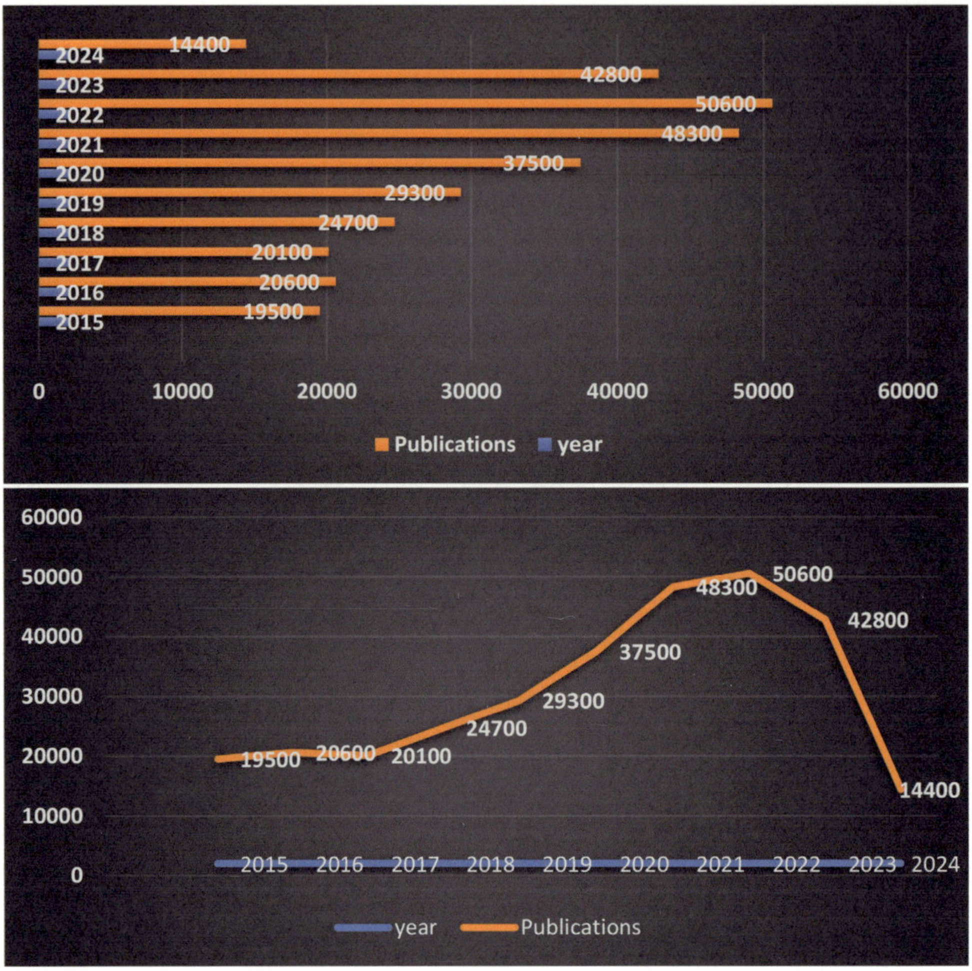


**Figure 2.**
*Publication from the year 2015–2024 based on breast cancer with deep learning.*

However, the best performance for multiclass classification achieved an accuracy of 97%, as reported in a study comparing ML and DL approaches for breast cancer subtype classification [75]. A notable limitation is that most papers focused solely on accuracy, often neglecting other important metrics, such as precision, recall, and AUC, which are crucial in medical projects. Various models were used, including CNNs, deep neural networks (DNNs) with attention mechanisms, feedforward neural networks (FFNNs), and other deep learning methods. Due to the irregular reporting of confusion matrix parameters, our graphs will only show accuracy.

**Table 1** shows that the CNN model is the most frequently utilized for both binary and multiclass classification, as well as hybrid models that integrate machine learning and deep learning. Approaches, such as multilayer perceptron (MLP) with logistic regression (LR) and the SVM algorithm from ML, were frequently employed in the studies reviewed.

For detecting breast cancer with imaging data, binary classification models generally performed well. However, when classifying types of breast cancer, imaging data did not provide results as accurate as those from gene expression data.

| Paper reference | Model | Classification | Classes | Accuracy | Task |
|---|---|---|---|---|---|
| [40] | IABC-EMBOT, IHM-FFNN, PSORM, ABCO-BCD, and DNN-BCD | Binary | Negative, positive | 0.975 | BC detection |
| [41] | FNN, ANFIS, and ANNFIS | Binary | Negative, positive | 0.92 | BC detection |
| [42] | DNN | Multiclass | 4 classes—Basal-like, HER2-enriched, luminal A, and luminal B and binary (basal, nonbasal) | 0.83 | Identify risk categories |
| [43] | DNN + attention mechanism (hybrid) | Binary | — | 0.87 | BC detection |
| [44] | Deep type, state-of-the-art | Multiclass | Normal, luminal A, luminal B, basal, and HER2 | | Identifying cancer subtypes |
| [45] | CNN | Multiclass | — | 0.956 | BC subtype classification |
| [46] | DA | Multiclass | — | 0.95 | BC detection |
| [47] | GCN | Multiclass | Combinations | 0.919 | Synergistic drug |
| [48] | DNN + SVM (separately) | Multiclass | Binary, mitotic/non | 0.94 | Detection |
| [49] | RF, ANN | Multiclass | 7 classes | | Gene prediction |
| [50] | SVM, NB, RF | Binary | ER−− and ER+ | 0.85 | Cancer subtypes (ER+ and ER−) |
| [51] | CNN + HASHI | Multiclass | — | | BC detection |
| [52] | AP + ANN | Binary | Malignant/benign | 0.983 | Feature selection method |
| [53] | CNN, Autoencoder | Binary | Positive/negative | 0.986 | BC diagnosis |
| [54] | KNN, ANN, SVM, and LS-SVM | Binary | Positive/negative | 0.953 | BC image classification |
| [55] | CNN | Binary | Normal/tumor | 0.987 | BC tumor classification |
| [56] | DL + ML (separately) CNN, SVM, random forests, boosting | Multiclass | Axillary lymph node status, binary, cancer or not | 0.97 | Cancer subtype classification |
| [57] | DL + ML (hybrid) Genetic algorithm (GA)-based MLP, multilayer perceptron (MLP), logistic regression (LR) | Multiclass | Binary, cancer or not | 0.84 | Prediction of axillary lymph node status in breast cancer |
| [58] | CNN | Multiclass | 7 cancer types | 0.846 | BC subtypes' identification |

| Paper reference | Model | Classification | Classes | Accuracy | Task |
|---|---|---|---|---|---|
| [59] | CNN | Both | Binary and (epithelium, stroma, and fat) | 0.92 and 0.95 | Identify and classify tumor-associated stroma in diagnostic breast biopsies. |
| [60] | PNN | Binary | Malignant/ benign | 0.963 | BC early diagnosis |
| [61] | DL + ML (hybrid) Model 1: DBN-ELM-BP Model 2: DBN-BP-ELM Model 3: DBN + GA | Binary | Positive and Negative | 0.9975 | BC detection |
| [62] | 2CNN, 3CNN | Binary | Positive and Negative | 0.705 | BC detection |
| [63] | DL + ML (hybrid) Logistic regression, random forest, and deep neural network | Binary | Positive and Negative | 0.98 | BC detection |
| [64] | CNN | Binary | Positive and Negative | 0.873 | BC detection |
| [65] | CNN | Multiclass | Luminal A Luminal B HER2 | 0.70 | BC subtype classification |
| [66] | CNN | Multiclass | Complete, partial, no response | 0.88 | Predict breast tumor, Response to chemotherapy |
| [67] | Meta + SVM, meta-logistic regression, integrative deep learning | Multiclass | — | — | BC gene identification |
| [68] | CNN | Binary | Normal/tumor | 0.987 | BC tumor classification |
| [69] | CNN, SVM | Binary | Low risk, high risk | | BC risk outcome |
| [70] | CNN, SVM | — | — | 0.840 | BC lymph node detection |
| [71] | SVM, CNN, SLIC | Binary | Epithelial and nonepithelial | 0.942 | BC image classification |
| [72] | CNN | Multiclass | 7 cancer types | 0.846 | BC subtypes' identification |
| [73] | Single-output Chebyshev-polynomial neural network (SOCPNN), and the modified SOCPNN | Binary | Malignant/ benign | 0.994 | BC tumor detection |
| [74] | RF, CT, LR, MLP, LSTM, GRU | Multiclass | — | — | Tumor subclass detection |

**Table 1.**
*Models, categories, and performance for gene sequencing data in the chosen papers.*

*DOI: http://dx.doi.org/10.5772/intechopen.1008207*

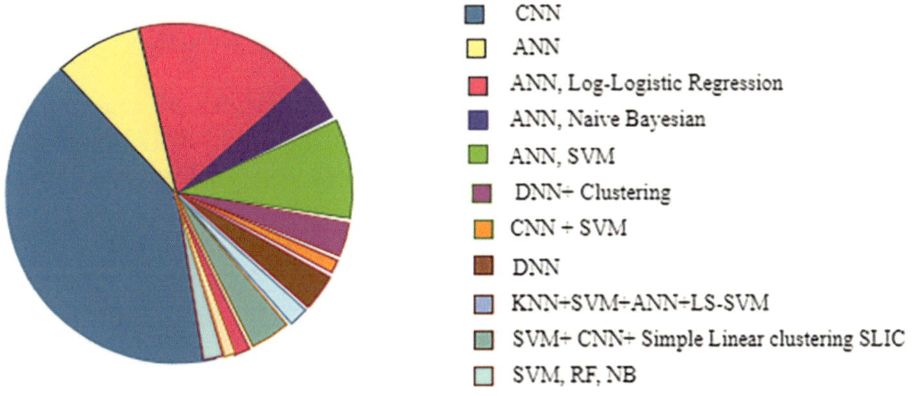


**Figure 3.**
*The algorithms most frequently utilized in research papers.*

Notably, paper [64] reported very high accuracy using a hybrid model combining DL and ML for breast cancer detection.

**Table 1** indicates that the CNN algorithm is the most frequently used for detecting and classifying breast cancer subtypes. This is expected, given that our data consist of MRI images and CNNs are well suited for computer vision tasks.

In summary, the studies employed a range of algorithms. Some papers used multiple models in succession, while others depended on a single model. As shown in **Figure 3,** ANN and CNN were the most frequently utilized algorithms for both gene sequence and image data. Although other algorithms like DNN and SVM were also applied, most papers concentrated on CNN and ANN, each with varying parameters and features.

**Figure 3** shows that the models with the highest accuracies are Single-Output Chebyshev-polynomial neural network (SOCPNN) and CNN, in that order.

## 5. Results and discussion

The identification of breast cancer has entered a new phase of innovation in recent years, due to advancements in machine learning (ML) and deep learning (DL) methods. Despite their effectiveness, traditional screening techniques like mammography, ultrasonography, and MRI have drawbacks that include false positives and discomfort for the patient. The goal of this systematic review was to conduct a thorough assessment of the state-of-the-art in the field of ML and DL applications for breast cancer diagnosis. By means of a thorough examination of the extant literature, we have identified significant patterns, faced obstacles, and discovered auspicious prospects in this emerging domain. These sophisticated computational models are faster and more accurate than humans in processing large volumes of imaging data, and they can identify small abnormalities that may be signs of breast cancer. Healthcare professionals can improve the accuracy and efficacy of breast cancer screening and diagnosis, allowing for early detection and intervention, by utilizing the power of ML and DL. Additionally, [76] ML and DL models may be able to lessen the drawbacks of conventional screening techniques. These algorithms have the capacity to continuously learn and adapt, which allows them to improve their diagnostic abilities over time and minimize false positives and needless interventions. Furthermore, because

ML and DL-based diagnostics are non-invasive, they may reduce patient discomfort related to traditional screening methods, increasing patient satisfaction and routine screening compliance.

One of the main conclusions emphasizes how crucial early detection is to enhancing patient outcomes and lowering the death rate from breast cancer [77]. By utilizing computational methods to examine complex patterns in medical imaging data, ML and DL models present a fresh way to accomplish this goal and may improve the precision and effectiveness of breast cancer screening and diagnosis.

## 6. Conclusion

In conclusion, the integration of machine learning (ML) and deep learning (DL) techniques into breast cancer detection holds significant promise for improving patient outcomes and reducing mortality rates [78]. Our systematic review highlights the potential of ML and DL algorithms to complement conventional screening methods and enhance diagnostic accuracy. Moving forward, Balaji et al. [79] continued research and collaboration that are essential to address challenges and translate these technologies into clinical practice. By leveraging advanced computational techniques, we can make significant strides in early detection, treatment optimization, and ultimately, saving lives in the fight against breast cancer.

## 7. Challenges and limitations

Despite the promising results, several challenges and limitations were identified in the application of ML and DL techniques for breast cancer detection. These included data heterogeneity, limited interpretability of deep learning models, and the need for large annotated datasets for model training and validation. Additionally, concerns regarding model generalizability and clinical implementation were raised, underscoring the importance of robust validation studies and real-world clinical trials.

## 8. Future directions

Looking ahead, future research directions in ML and DL applications for breast cancer detection include addressing the aforementioned challenges, developing interpretable models, and conducting large-scale prospective studies to validate the clinical utility of these technologies. Moreover, efforts to integrate ML and DL models into clinical decision support systems and workflow integration are crucial to facilitating their adoption in clinical practice and improving patient outcomes.

## Acknowledgements

We would like to express our sincere gratitude to all those who contributed to the completion of this research. We thank our colleagues and mentors for their invaluable guidance and support throughout the study.

## Authors' contribution

All the authors have contributed equally.

## Funding

This research did not receive any specific grant from funding agencies in the public, commercial, or not-for-profit sectors.

## Declaration

Competing interests: The authors declare that they have no competing interests.

## Ethical approval

This article does not contain any studies with human participants or animals performed by any of the authors.

## Consent to participate

Not applicable. This study does not involve human participants requiring consent.

## Consent to publish

Not applicable. The manuscript does not include any individual person's data in any form requiring consent.

## Acronyms and abbreviations

| | |
|---|---|
| ML | machine learning |
| DL | deep learning |
| CNNs | convolutional neural networks |
| DNA | circulatory tumor DNA |
| AUC | area under curve |

## Author details

Zeba Khan[1], Madhavidevi Botlagunta[2], Gorli L. Aruna Kumari[3], Pranjali Malviya[4] and Mahendran Botlagunta[1*]

1 School of Bioengineering and Technology, VIT Bhopal University, Sehore, India

2 Department of Computer Science and Engineering, Institute of Aeronautical Engineering, Hyderabad, Telangana, India

3 Department of Computer Science and Engineering, Gitam School of Technology, Gitam Deemed to be University, Visakhapatnam, India

4 School of Computer Science and Engineering, VIT Bhopal University, Sehore, India

*Address all correspondence to: bmnchowdary@gmail.com

## References

[1] Din ud NM, Dar RA, Rasool M, Assad A. Breast cancer detection using deep learning: Datasets, methods, and challenges ahead. Computers in Biology and Medicine. 2022;**149**(January):106073. DOI: 10.1016/j.compbiomed.2022.106073

[2] Rao KS, Terlapu PV, Jayaram D, Raju KK, Kiran Kumar G, Pemula R, et al. Intelligent ultrasound imaging for enhanced breast cancer diagnosis: Ensemble transfer learning strategies. IEEE Access. 2024;**12**(February):22243-22263

[3] Madani M, Behzadi MM, Nabavi S. The role of deep learning in advancing breast cancer detection using different imaging modalities: A systematic review. Cancers (Basel). 2022;**14**(21):1-36

[4] Datasets AR, Directions F. Harnessing Deep Learning for Early Breast Cancer Diagnosis. 2024;**1**(1)

[5] Albitar M, Zhang H, Pecora A, Waintraub S, Graham D, Hellmann M, et al. Homologous recombination abnormalities associated with BRCA1/2 mutations as predicted by machine learning of targeted next-generation sequencing data. Breast Cancer Basic Clinical Research. 2023;**17**:1-17

[6] Abo-El-Rejal A, Ayman SE, Aymen F. Advances in breast cancer segmentation: A comprehensive review. Acadlore Transactions on AI and Machine Learning. 2024;**3**(2):70-83

[7] Yaqoob A, Musheer Aziz R, Verma NK. Applications and techniques of machine learning in cancer classification: A systematic review. Human-Centric Intelligent Systems. 2023;**3**:588-615

[8] Chugh S, Goyal S, Pandey A, Joshi S. Morphological and Otsu's technique based mammography mass detection and deep neural network classifier based prediction. Traitement du Signal. 2022;**39**(4):1283-1294

[9] Solanki YS, Chakrabarti P, Jasinski M, Leonowicz Z, Bolshev V, Vinogradov A, et al. A hybrid supervised machine learning classifier system for breast cancer prognosis using feature selection and data imbalance handling approaches. Electronics. 2021;**10**(6):1-16

[10] Jin S, Liu G, Bai Q. Deep learning in COVID-19 diagnosis, prognosis and treatment selection. Mathematics. 2023;**11**(6):1-17

[11] Elsadig MA, Altigani A, Elshoush HT. Breast cancer detection using machine learning approaches: A comparative study. International Journal of Electrical and Computer Engineering. 2023;**13**(1):736-745

[12] Botlagunta M, Botlagunta MD, Myneni MB, Lakshmi D, Nayyar A, Gullapalli JS, et al. Classification and diagnostic prediction of breast cancer metastasis on clinical data using machine learning algorithms. Scientific Reports. 2023;**13**(1):1-17. DOI: 10.1038/s41598-023-27548-w

[13] Mandair D, Reis-Filho JS, Ashworth A. Biological insights and novel biomarker discovery through deep learning approaches in breast cancer histopathology. NPJ Breast Cancer. 2023;**9**(1):1-11

[14] Cui L, Li H, Hui W, Chen S, Yang L, Kang Y, et al. A deep learning-based framework for lung cancer survival analysis with biomarker interpretation. BMC Bioinformatics. 2020;**21**(1):1-14

[15] Binsaif N. Application of machine learning models to the detection of breast cancer. Mobile Information Systems. 2022;**2022**:1-8

[16] Samala RK, Chan HP, Hadjiiski LM, Cha K, Helvie MA. Deep-learning convolution neural network for computer-aided detection of microcalcifications in digital breast tomosynthesis. Medical Imaging 2016: Computer-Aided Diagnosis. 2016;**9785**(February):97850Y

[17] Huynh BQ, Li H, Giger ML. Digital mammographic tumor classification using transfer learning from deep convolutional neural networks. Journal of Medical Imaging. 2016;**3**(3):034501

[18] Plastiras G, Kyrkou C, Theocharides T. Efficient convnet-based object detection for unmanned aerial vehicles by selective tile processing. The ACM International Conference Proceedings Series. 2018;**18**:1-6

[19] Yaqoob A, Verma NK, Aziz RM, Shah MA. RNA-Seq analysis for breast cancer detection: A study on paired tissue samples using hybrid optimization and deep learning techniques. Journal of Cancer Research and Clinical Oncology. 2024;**150**(10):455

[20] Krizhevsky A, Sutskever I, Hinton GE. ImageNet classification with deep convolutional neural networks. Communications of the ACM. 2017;**60**(6):84-90

[21] Yaqoob A, Verma NK, Aziz RM, Shah MA. Optimizing cancer classification: A hybrid RDO-XGBoost approach for feature selection and predictive insights. Cancer Immunology, Immunotherapy. 2024;**73**(12):261

[22] Romero-Martín S, Elías-Cabot E, Raya-Povedano JL, Gubern-Mérida A, Rodríguez-Ruiz A, Álvarez-Benito M. Stand-alone use of artificial intelligence for digital mammography and digital breast tomosynthesis screening: A retrospective evaluation. Radiology. 2022;**302**(3):535-542

[23] Carvalho ED, da Silva Neto OP, de Carvalho Filho AO. Deep learning-based tumor segmentation and classification in breast MRI with 3TP method. Biomedical Signal Processing and Control. 2024;**93**(March):106199. DOI: 10.1016/j.bspc.2024.106199

[24] Shorten C, Khoshgoftaar TM, Furht B. Deep learning applications for COVID-19. Journal of Big Data. 2021;**8**(1):1-54. DOI: 10.1186/s40537-020-00392-9

[25] Deo RC. Machine learning in medicine. Circulation. 2015;**132**(20):1920-1930

[26] Rentiya ZS, Mandal S, Inban P, Vempalli H, Dabbara R, Ali S, et al. Revolutionizing breast cancer detection with artificial intelligence (AI) in radiology and radiation oncology: A systematic review. Cureus. 2024;**16**(4)

[27] Yaqoob A, Aziz RM, Verma NK, Lalwani P, Makrariya A. A Review on Nature-Inspired Algorithms for Cancer Disease Prediction and Classification. 2023;**11**

[28] Yaqoob A, Mir MA, Jagannadha Rao GVV, Tejani GG. Transforming cancer classification: The role of advanced gene selection. Diagnostics. 2024;**14**(23):2632

[29] Yaqoob A. Combining the mRMR technique with the Northern Goshawk Algorithm (NGHA) to choose genes for cancer classification. International Journal of Information Technology. 2024:1-12

[30] Yaqoob A, Verma NK, Aziz RM, Saxena A. Enhancing feature sele selection through metaheuristic hybrid cuckoo search and Harris Hawks optimization for cancer classification. In: Metaheuristics for Machine Learning: Algorithms and Applications. 2024. pp. 95-134

[31] Sharma S, Mehra R. Conventional machine learning and deep learning approach for multi-classification of breast cancer histopathology images—A comparative insight. Journal of Digital Imaging. 2020;**33**(3):632-654

[32] Adla D, Reddy GVR, Nayak P, Karuna G. Deep learning-based computer aided diagnosis model for skin cancer detection and classification. Distributed and Parallel Databases. 2022;**40**(4):717-736

[33] Mijwil MM. Skin cancer disease images classification using deep learning solutions. Multimedia Tools and Applications. 2021;**80**(17):26255-26271

[34] Sharma N, Sharma KP, Mangla M, Rani R. Breast cancer classification using snapshot ensemble deep learning model and t-distributed stochastic neighbor embedding. Multimedia Tools and Applications. 2023;**82**(3):4011-4029

[35] Yaqoob A, Kumar N, Rabia V, Aziz M. Optimizing gene selection and cancer classification with hybrid sine cosine and cuckoo search algorithm. Journal of Medical Systems. 2024;**48**:1-18

[36] Wenham CYJ, Grainger AJ, Conaghan PG. The role of imaging modalities in the diagnosis, differential diagnosis and clinical assessment of peripheral joint osteoarthritis. Osteoarthritis and Cartilage. 2014;**22**(10):1692-1702. DOI: 10.1016/j.joca.2014.06.005

[37] Chato L, Latifi S. Machine learning and deep learning techniques to predict overall survival of brain tumor patients using MRI images. Proceedings—2017 IEEE 17th International Conference on Bioinformatics and Bioengineering, BIBE 2017. 2017;**2018-January**(October 2017):9-14

[38] Yaqoob A, Verma NK, Aziz RM. Metaheuristic algorithms and their applications in different fields: A comprehensive review. In: Metaheuristics for Machine Learning: Algorithms and Applications. 2024. pp. 1-35

[39] Raheem AKA, Dhannoon BN. Predication and classification of cancer using sequence alignment and back propagation algorithms in Brca1 and Brca2 genes. International Journal of Pharmaceutical Sciences and Research. 2019;**11**(1):468-475

[40] Punitha S, Amuthan A, Joseph KS. Enhanced monarchy butterfly optimization technique for effective breast cancer diagnosis. Journal of Medical Systems. 2019;**43**(7):206. DOI: 10.1007/s10916-019-1348-8

[41] Umamaheswari TS, Sumathi P. RETRACTED ARTICLE: Enhanced firefly algorithm (EFA) based gene selection and adaptive neuro neutrosophic inference system (ANNIS) prediction model for detection of circulating tumor cells (CTCs) in breast cancer analysis. Cluster Computing. 2019;**22**(6):14035-14047. DOI: 10.1007/s10586-018-2183-2

[42] Romo-Bucheli D, Janowczyk A, Gilmore H, Romero E, Madabhushi A. A deep learning based strategy for identifying and associating mitotic activity with gene expression derived risk categories in estrogen receptor positive breast cancers. Cytometry Part A. 2017;**91**(6):566-573

[43] Chen H, Gao M, Zhang Y, Liang W, Zou X. Attention-based multi-NMF

deep neural network with multimodality data for breast cancer prognosis model. BioMed Research International. 2019;**2019**:1-11

[44] Chen R, Yang L, Goodison S, Sun Y. Deep-learning approach to identifying cancer subtypes using high-dimensional genomic data. Bioinformatics. 2020;**36**(5):1476-1483

[45] Mostavi M, Chiu YC, Huang Y, Chen Y. Convolutional neural network models for cancer type prediction based on gene expression. BMC Medical Genomics. 2020;**13**(Suppl 5):1-13. DOI: 10.1186/s12920-020-0677-2

[46] Liu Q, Hu P. Association analysis of deep genomic features extracted by denoising autoencoders in breast cancer. Cancers (Basel). 2019;**11**(4):4-11

[47] Jiang P, Huang S, Fu Z, Sun Z, Lakowski TM, Hu P. Deep graph embedding for prioritizing synergistic anticancer drug combinations. Computer Structure Biotechnology Journal. 2020;**18**:427-438. DOI: 10.1016/j.csbj.2020.02.006

[48] Danaee P, Ghaeini R, Hendrix DA. A deep learning approach for cancer detection and relevant gene identification. In: Biocomputing. 2017. pp. 219-229 Available from: https://www.worldscientific.com/doi/abs/10.1142/9789813207813_0022

[49] Shimizu H, Nakayama KI. A 23 gene–based molecular prognostic score precisely predicts overall survival of breast cancer patients. eBioMedicine. 2019;**46**:150-159. DOI: 10.1016/j.ebiom.2019.07.046

[50] Simidjievski N, Bodnar C, Tariq I, Scherer P, Andres Terre H, Shams Z, et al. Variational autoencoders for cancer data integration: Design principles and computational practice. Frontiers in Genetics. 2019;**10**(December):1-14

[51] Cruz-Roa A, Gilmore H, Basavanhally A, Feldman M, Ganesan S, Shih N, et al. High-throughput adaptive sampling for whole-slide histopathology image analysis (HASHI) via convolutional neural networks: Application to invasive breast cancer detection. PLoS One. 2018;**13**(5):1-23

[52] Journal I, Computing I. Based on association rules and Pca for detection. The International Journal of Innovative Research in Computer. 2013;**9**(2): 727-739

[53] Toğaçar M, Ergen B, Cömert Z. Application of breast cancer diagnosis based on a combination of convolutional neural networks, ridge regression and linear discriminant analysis using invasive breast cancer images processed with autoencoders. Medical Hypotheses. 2019;**2020**(135):0-3

[54] Tripathy RK, Mahanta S, Paul S. Artificial intelligence-based classification of breast cancer using cellular images. RSC Advances. 2014;**4**(18):9349-9355

[55] Lightweight_Convolutional_Neural_Network_for_Breast_Cancer_Classification_Using_RNA-Seq_Gene_Expression_Data.pdf.crdownload

[56] El-Nabawy A, El-Bendary N, Belal NA. A feature-fusion framework of clinical, genomics, and histopathological data for METABRIC breast cancer subtype classification. Applied Soft Computing Journal. 2020;**91**:106238. DOI: 10.1016/j.asoc.2020.106238

[57] Karakış R, Tez M, Kılıç YA, Kuru Y, Güler İ. A genetic algorithm model based on artificial neural network for prediction of the axillary lymph node status in breast cancer. Engineering

Applications of Artificial Intelligence. 2013;**26**(3):945-950. Available from: https://www.sciencedirect.com/science/article/pii/S0952197612002825

[58] Rawat RR, Ruderman D, Macklin P, Rimm DL, Agus DB. Correlating nuclear morphometric patterns with estrogen receptor status in breast cancer pathologic specimens. NPJ Breast Cancer. 2018;**4**(1):1-7. DOI: 10.1038/s41523-018-0084-4

[59] Ehteshami Bejnordi B, Mullooly M, Pfeiffer RM, Fan S, Vacek PM, Weaver DL, et al. Using deep convolutional neural networks to identify and classify tumor-associated stroma in diagnostic breast biopsies. Modern Pathology. 2018;**31**(10):1502-1512. DOI: 10.1038/s41379-018-0073-z

[60] Mert A, Kılıç N, Akan A. An improved hybrid feature reduction for increased breast cancer diagnostic performance. Biomedical Engineering Letters. 2014;**4**(3):285-291. DOI: 10.1007/s13534-014-0148-9

[61] Ronoud S, Asadi S. An evolutionary deep belief network extreme learning-based for breast cancer diagnosis. Soft Computing. 2019;**23**(24):13139-13159. DOI: 10.1007/s00500-019-03856-0

[62] Fang Y, Zhao J, Hu L, Ying X, Pan Y, Wang X. Image classification toward breast cancer using deeply-learned quality features. Journal of Visual Communication and Image Representation. 2019;**64**:102609. DOI: 10.1016/j.jvcir.2019.102609

[63] Priya G, Radhika A. An effective machine learning approach for disease predictive modelling in medical application. International Journal of Scientific and Technology Research. 2020;**9**(4):2819-2824. Available from: https://www.scopus.com/inward/record.uri?eid=2-s2.0-85083466649&partnerID=40&md5=96a71dfe7cb2fdcd0b19b49f7c35a7e5

[64] Chen YC, Zhang Z, Yoon E. Early prediction of single-cell derived sphere formation rate using convolutional neural network image analysis. Analytical Chemistry. 2020;**92**(11):7717-7724

[65] Ha R, Mutasa S, Karcich J, Gupta N, Pascual Van Sant E, Nemer J, et al. Predicting breast cancer molecular subtype with MRI dataset utilizing convolutional neural network algorithm. Journal of Digital Imaging. 2019;**32**(2):276-282. DOI: 10.1007/s10278-019-00179-2

[66] Ha R, Chin C, Karcich J, Liu MZ, Chang P, Mutasa S, et al. Prior to initiation of chemotherapy, can we predict breast tumor response? Deep learning convolutional neural networks approach using a breast MRI tumor dataset. Journal of Digital Imaging. 2019;**32**(5):693-701. DOI: 10.1007/s10278-018-0144-1

[67] Lim J, Bang S, Kim J, Park C, Cho J, Kim S. Integrative deep learning for identifying differentially expressed (DE) biomarkers. Computational and Mathematical Methods in Medicine. 2019;**2019**:10-20

[68] Elbashir MK, Ezz M, Mohammed M, Saloum SS. Lightweight convolutional neural network for breast cancer classification using RNA-Seq gene expression data. IEEE Access. 2019;**7**:185338-185348

[69] Turkki R, Byckhov D, Lundin M, Isola J, Nordling S, Kovanen PE, et al. Breast cancer outcome prediction with tumour tissue images and machine learning. Breast Cancer Research and Treatment. 2019;**177**(1):41-52. DOI: 10.1007/s10549-019-05281-1

[70] Luo J, Ning Z, Zhang S, Feng Q, Zhang Y. Bag of deep features for preoperative prediction of sentinel lymph node metastasis in breast cancer. Physics in Medicine and Biology. 2018;**63**(24):245014. DOI: 10.1088/1361-6560/aaf241

[71] Kumar A, Singh SK, Saxena S, Lakshmanan K, Sangaiah AK, Chauhan H, et al. Deep feature learning for histopathological image classification of canine mammary tumors and human breast cancer. Information Sciences. 2020;**508**:405-421. Available from: https://www.sciencedirect.com/science/article/pii/S0020025519308229

[72] Lancashire LJ, Powe DG, Reis-Filho JS, Rakha E, Lemetre C, Weigelt B, et al. A validated gene expression profile for detecting clinical outcome in breast cancer using artificial neural networks. Breast Cancer Research and Treatment. 2010;**120**(1):83-93. DOI: 10.1007/s10549-009-0378-1

[73] Jin L, Huang Z, Chen L, Liu M, Li Y, Chou Y, et al. Modified single-output Chebyshev-polynomial feedforward neural network aided with subset method for classification of breast cancer. Neurocomputing. 2019;**350**:128-135. Available from: https://www.sciencedirect.com/science/article/pii/S0925231219303868

[74] Sur C. GSIAR: Gene-subcategory interaction-based improved deep representation learning for breast cancer subcategorical analysis using gene expression, applicable for precision medicine. Medical and Biological Engineering and Computing. 2019;**57**(11):2483-2515. DOI: 10.1007/s11517-019-02038-2

[75] Rafique R, Islam SMR, Kazi JU. Machine learning in the prediction of cancer therapy. Computational and Structural Biotechnology Journal. 2021;**19**:4003-4017. DOI: 10.1016/j.csbj.2021.07.003

[76] Dutta A, Harshith J, Ramamoorthy A, Raj ASA, Balamurugan M, Vinodhini D. Prognosis of breast cancer using machine learning classifiers. Computational Intelligence and Modelling Techniques for Disease Detection in Mammogram Images. 2023;**59**:129-149

[77] Harrison CJ, Sidey-Gibbons CJ. Machine learning in medicine: A practical introduction to natural language processing. BMC Medical Research Methodology. 2021;**21**(1):1-18

[78] Khalid A, Mehmood A, Alabrah A, Alkhamees BF, Amin F, AlSalman H, et al. Breast cancer detection and prevention using machine learning. Diagnostics. 2023;**13**(19):1-21

[79] Balaji S, Arunprasath T, Rajasekaran MP, Vishnuvarthanan G, Sindhuja K. Computer-aided diagnostic system for breast cancer detection based on optimized segmentation scheme and supervised algorithm. Automatika. 2023;**64**(4):1244-1254. DOI: 10.1080/00051144.2023.2244307

Chapter 3

# Clustered Federated Learning: A Review

*Majid Morafah and Mahdi Morafah*

## Abstract

Clustered Federated Learning (CFL) has emerged as a powerful extension of traditional federated learning to address the challenges posed by heterogeneous, non-IID data across distributed clients. This chapter provides a comprehensive review of the state-of-the-art CFL methods, categorizing them into model-based, feature-based, and hybrid approaches. Model-based clustering leverages client model updates to form clusters, while feature-based methods utilize client data characteristics, and hybrid approaches integrate both aspects to achieve robust clustering. The chapter also discusses the evaluation metrics and benchmarks used to assess CFL performance, such as accuracy, personalization, and cluster quality, along with case studies demonstrating CFL's applicability in diverse domains like healthcare, IoT, and autonomous systems. We identify key challenges in CFL, including scalability, dynamic clustering, and privacy preservation, and propose future research directions to further enhance the effectiveness and scalability of CFL frameworks. Overall, this chapter aims to provide a deep understanding of CFL, highlighting its potential to improve federated learning outcomes in complex, real-world scenarios with non-IID data.

**Keywords:** clustered FL, personalized FL, data heterogeneity, hierarchical clustering, feature-based clustering, model-based clustering

## 1. Introduction

Federated Learning (FL) has emerged as a promising paradigm for training machine learning models across decentralized data sources while preserving data privacy and reducing communication costs. This framework enables collaborative learning among a network of clients, such as mobile devices or organizations, without the need to centralize sensitive data. Despite its potential, standard FL faces significant challenges when dealing with heterogeneous, non-IID (non-independent and identically distributed) data across clients. Non-IID data distributions can lead to performance degradation of the global model, slower convergence rates, and unfair outcomes across different clients. These issues arise because the global model is unable to adequately capture the diverse characteristics of the client data, resulting in a model that may perform well on average but poorly for certain subgroups of clients.

To address the limitations of standard FL in the presence of non-IID data, Clustered Federated Learning (CFL) has been proposed as an advanced framework that partitions clients into clusters based on the similarity of their data distributions or model updates. Each cluster is then trained independently, allowing for the development of specialized models that are better suited to the unique data characteristics of each group. This approach not only improves the overall performance and personalization of the models but also enhances the fairness and efficiency of the learning process by reducing the negative impact of data heterogeneity. CFL represents a significant step forward in federated learning, providing a more flexible and scalable solution to the challenges posed by diverse data distributions.

This chapter provides a comprehensive overview of the various CFL methodologies, focusing on their underlying principles, strengths, and limitations. We begin by exploring model-based clustering approaches that leverage model updates to form clusters, followed by feature-based and hybrid methods that integrate data features and model behaviors. We also examine the evaluation metrics and benchmarks used to assess CFL performance, highlighting key metrics such as accuracy, personalization, and cluster quality. Additionally, we discuss real-world applications of CFL in domains such as healthcare, smart devices, and autonomous systems, demonstrating its practical utility in addressing complex federated learning scenarios.

In summary, this chapter aims to offer a detailed review of the current state-of-the-art in clustered federated learning, providing insights into its potential to overcome the challenges of non-IID data in decentralized environments. The chapter is structured as follows: Section 2 covers the background and preliminaries of federated learning and data heterogeneity. Section 3 delves into the background for clustered federated learning, problem formulation and key challenges. Section 4 discusses the existing approaches to clustered federated learning: model-based clustering approaches, feature-based clustering methods and hybrid approaches. Section 5 reviews evaluation metrics and benchmarks. Section 6 discusses the challenges and open problems in CFL, and Section 7 concludes the chapter with final remarks and future research directions.

## 2. Background and preliminaries

### 2.1 Federated learning overview

Federated Learning (FL) is a distributed machine learning paradigm designed to enable collaborative model training across a network of clients, such as mobile devices or organizations, while keeping the data localized. This approach addresses privacy concerns and reduces communication overhead by sharing only model updates instead of raw data [1].

#### *2.1.1 Basic concepts and notations*

Consider a central server and a set of clients denoted as $\mathcal{S}$ participating in the federated learning process. Each client $i \in \mathcal{S}$ holds a local model $f_i(\mathbf{x}; \boldsymbol{\theta}_i)$, which is a neural network with $L$ layers and parameters $\boldsymbol{\theta}_i = \left(\mathbf{W}_i^1, \ldots, \mathbf{W}_i^L\right)$, where $\mathbf{W}_i^l$ represents the weights of the $l$-th layer. The training and test datasets of client $i$ are represented by $\mathcal{D}_i^{\text{train}}$ and $\mathcal{D}_i^{\text{test}}$, respectively.

At the beginning of each communication round $t$, a subset of clients $\mathcal{S}_t \subseteq \mathcal{S}$ is randomly selected with a sampling rate $C \in (0, 1]$ from a total of $N$ available clients. The selected clients receive the current global model parameters from the server and perform local training on their respective datasets for $E$ epochs, using a batch size of $B$ and a learning rate of $\eta$. At the end of round $t$, the clients in $\mathcal{S}_t$ send their updated parameters back to the server. The server then aggregates these updates to produce a new global model.

This process is repeated for a total of $T$ communication rounds. The detailed procedure is outlined in Algorithm 1.

---

Algorithm 1. Federated learning.

---

**Require:** Number of clients ($N$), sampling rate ($C \in (0, 1]$), number of communication rounds ($T$), local dataset of client $i$ ($\mathcal{D}_i^{\text{train}}$), local epochs ($E$), local batch size ($B$), learning rate ($\eta$).
*/* Server Executes */.*

Initialize the global model with parameters $\boldsymbol{\theta}_g^0$
**for** each round $t = 0, 1, \ldots, T-1$ **do**
  $m \leftarrow \max(\lfloor C \cdot N \rfloor, 1)$
  $\mathcal{S}_t \leftarrow$ randomlyselect$m$clientsfrom$\mathcal{S}$ ▷ Set of $m$ selected clients
  **for** each client $i \in \mathcal{S}_t$ **in parallel do**
    $\boldsymbol{\theta}_i^{t+1} \leftarrow \texttt{ClientUpdate}\left(i; \boldsymbol{\theta}_g^t\right)$
  **end for**
  $\boldsymbol{\theta}_g^{t+1} = \texttt{ModelFusion}\left(\{\boldsymbol{\theta}_i^{t+1}\}_{i \in \mathcal{S}_t}\right)$ ▷ FedAvg [1]: $\boldsymbol{\theta}_g^{t+1} = \sum_{i \in \mathcal{S}_t} \frac{|\mathcal{D}_i^{\text{train}}|}{\sum_{j \in \mathcal{S}_t} |\mathcal{D}_j^{\text{train}}|} \boldsymbol{\theta}_i^{t+1}$
**end for**
**function** $\texttt{ClientUpdate}\left(i, \boldsymbol{\theta}_g^t\right)$
  $\boldsymbol{\theta}_i^t \leftarrow \boldsymbol{\theta}_g^t$
  $\mathcal{B} \leftarrow$ randomly partition $\mathcal{D}_i^{\text{train}}$ into batches of size $B$
  **for** each local epoch $e \in \{1, \ldots, E\}$ **do**
    **for** each batch $\mathbf{b} \in \mathcal{B}$ **do**
  $\boldsymbol{\theta}_i^t \leftarrow \boldsymbol{\theta}_i^t - \eta \nabla_{\boldsymbol{\theta}_i^t} \ell\left(f_i(\mathrm{x}; \boldsymbol{\theta}_i^t), y\right)$
    **end for**
  **end for**
  **return** $\boldsymbol{\theta}_i^{t+1} \leftarrow \boldsymbol{\theta}_i^t$
**end function**

---

### *2.1.2 Global vs. personalized federated learning*

In the federated learning literature, two main paradigms have emerged: Global Federated Learning (gFL) and Personalized Federated Learning (pFL).

Global Federated Learning (gFL): The goal is to train a shared global model $\boldsymbol{\theta}_g$ on the server that generalizes well across all clients. This objective can be formalized as follows:

$$\hat{\boldsymbol{\theta}}_g = \arg\min_{\boldsymbol{\theta}_g} \sum_{i=1}^{N} \mathbb{E}_{(\mathrm{x},y) \sim \mathcal{D}_i^{\text{train}}} \left[\ell\left(f_i(\mathrm{x}; \boldsymbol{\theta}_g), y\right)\right], \tag{1}$$

where $\ell(\cdot)$ denotes the loss function, and $(\mathtt{x}, y)$ are data samples drawn from the training dataset $\mathcal{D}_i^{\text{train}}$ of client $i$. FedAvg [1] is a pioneering method proposed to address this problem, using parameter averaging on the server for model aggregation. The evaluation metric for gFL is typically the average performance of global model on the entire test data at the server over the last $\lceil C \cdot N \rceil$ communication rounds.

Personalized Federated Learning (pFL): In contrast, pFL focuses on training individualized models $\boldsymbol{\theta}_i$ for each client, aiming to better fit the unique data distribution of each client. The problem is formulated as follows:

$$\left\{\hat{\boldsymbol{\theta}}_1, \ldots, \hat{\boldsymbol{\theta}}_N\right\} = \arg\min_{\{\boldsymbol{\theta}_1, \ldots, \boldsymbol{\theta}_N\}} \sum_{i=1}^{N} \mathbb{E}_{(\mathtt{x}, y) \sim \mathcal{D}_i^{\text{train}}} \left[\ell\left(f_i(\mathtt{x}; \boldsymbol{\theta}_i), y\right)\right], \tag{2}$$

where each client $i$ optimizes its own model parameters $\boldsymbol{\theta}_i$. One of the simplest approaches to tackle this problem is FedAvg followed by Fine-Tuning (FT) (FedAvg +FT), where each client fine-tunes the global model obtained through FedAvg using its local data. The evaluation metric for pFL is typically the average of final performance of all the clients on their entire local test data.

## 2.2 Statistical heterogeneity in federated learning

Let $\mathcal{P}_i(\mathtt{x}, y)$ denote the local data distribution of client $i$. Clients are said to exhibit data heterogeneity or statistical heterogeneity, or non-IID data distribution, if their data distributions differ significantly, i.e., $\mathcal{P}_i(\mathtt{x}, y) \neq \mathcal{P}_j(\mathtt{x}, y)$ for any two clients $i$ and $j$. One of the most prevalent manifestations of this heterogeneity in federated learning is *label distribution skew*, where clients have varying distributions of class labels (i.e., $\mathcal{P}_i(y) \neq \mathcal{P}_j(y)$) [1].

Two commonly used mechanisms to generate label distribution skew in federated learning are as follows [2]:

- *Label Skew (p)* [3]: In this mechanism, each client receives a subset comprising $p$% of the total classes in the dataset, selected at random. The data points for each class are uniformly distributed among the clients that possess that class in their local datasets.

- *Label Dirichlet Skew ($\alpha$)* [4]: Each client draws a random vector of length equal to the number of classes in the dataset from a Dirichlet distribution parameterized by $\alpha$. The data points of each class are then allocated to clients according to the proportions specified by their respective Dirichlet vectors.

## 2.3 Challenges in federated learning with non-IID data

Training federated models with non-IID data presents a set of unique challenges that can significantly impact the effectiveness and efficiency of the learning process. Unlike traditional centralized learning, federated learning must contend with varying data distributions across a potentially large and diverse set of clients, which complicates the aggregation and optimization of models.

[1] Other mechanisms to induce statistical heterogeneity exist but are less commonly used in the federated learning community.

*DOI: http://dx.doi.org/10.5772/intechopen.1008431*

1. Model divergence: In federated learning, each client trains its local model on its own dataset, which can vary significantly from those of other clients. This variation can cause local models to diverge in their learned representations and parameter updates, especially when the local data distributions $\mathcal{P}_i(\mathrm{x}, y)$ are vastly different. For instance, consider a scenario where one client has data predominantly from class A while another has data mostly from class B. The updates from these clients will likely push the global model in different directions during aggregation, resulting in a global model that fails to generalize well across the entire client population. This divergence is exacerbated when the number of clients is large and the data distributions are highly skewed, leading to severe performance degradation when aggregating local models into a single global model [3, 4].

2. Slow convergence: Non-IID data distributions also impact the convergence speed of federated learning algorithms. In ideal IID scenarios, local updates are expected to be aligned, contributing constructively to the global model. However, in non-IID settings, the local updates can conflict, causing oscillations and slower progress towards the global optimum. As a result, federated learning algorithms often require more communication rounds to converge to an acceptable solution compared to their IID counterparts. This slow convergence can significantly increase the training time and communication cost, especially in resource-constrained environments where bandwidth and client participation are limited [5].

3. Imbalanced contributions: Clients in federated learning may have varying amounts of data and computational resources. In non-IID settings, clients with larger or more representative datasets can disproportionately influence the global model. For example, a client with a large dataset that covers a significant portion of the data distribution will have a more substantial impact on the aggregated model than a client with a small dataset. This imbalance can lead to a situation where the global model is biased towards the data distribution of the more influential clients, resulting in poor performance on underrepresented data distributions. Additionally, clients with limited data or outlier distributions may have little to no influence on the global model, exacerbating the problem of model fairness and inclusiveness.

4. Fairness and personalization: Federated learning aims to learn a single global model that performs well across all clients. However, in the presence of non-IID data, achieving fairness in model performance becomes challenging. Some clients may have data that is drastically different from the overall population, leading to suboptimal performance of the global model on these clients' data. This lack of fairness is particularly problematic in applications such as healthcare or finance, where it is crucial for the model to perform reliably across all participants. Furthermore, the one-size-fits-all approach of the global model may not be suitable for all clients, necessitating the need for personalized models that can cater to the specific needs and data distributions of individual clients [6].

5. Communication overhead: In non-IID settings, the need for more frequent model updates and longer training periods to reach convergence can lead to increased communication costs. Clients with highly diverse data distributions may need to

communicate their model updates more often to ensure that the global model reflects the true underlying distributions. This increased communication can be a bottleneck in federated learning, especially when operating over limited bandwidth networks or when dealing with a large number of clients [7].

## 2.4 Motivation for clustering in federated learning

Given the significant challenges posed by non-IID data in federated learning, clustering clients into groups with similar data distributions has emerged as a promising approach to enhance both model performance and personalization. Clustered Federated Learning (CFL) aims to create sub-groups of clients that share similar characteristics, allowing for the training of separate models tailored to each cluster. The key motivations for clustered federated learning are as follows:

1. Improved model accuracy: In standard federated learning, the global model is trained using data from all clients, potentially diluting the model's ability to perform well on specific subpopulations. By clustering clients based on the similarity of their data distributions, CFL enables the training of distinct models for each cluster, which are better suited to the specific characteristics of the clients in that cluster. This targeted model training can lead to significant improvements in overall accuracy and performance, as the models are not constrained to fit a single distribution that may not be representative of all clients [8]. For instance, in a healthcare application, clustering patients with similar health conditions can result in models that provide more accurate predictions for each patient group.

2. Enhanced personalization: One of the primary goals of CFL is to balance the need for a global model with the demand for personalized solutions. By creating clusters of clients with similar data distributions, CFL allows each cluster model to be personalized to a specific subset of clients. This approach not only improves the relevance and applicability of the model for individual clients but also addresses the fairness issue inherent in traditional federated learning. Clients within a cluster benefit from a model that is more closely aligned with their unique data distribution, leading to better individual performance and user satisfaction [9].

3. Reduced model divergence: Clustering can also mitigate the issue of model divergence by reducing the variability in local updates within each cluster. Since clients in the same cluster share similar data distributions, their local updates are more likely to be aligned, leading to more coherent and stable aggregated models. This reduction in update variability can accelerate convergence and improve the robustness of the training process, making CFL more efficient than traditional federated learning in non-IID settings [10]. Moreover, the use of separate models for each cluster reduces the risk of catastrophic forgetting, where the global model forgets information about rare client distributions due to the overwhelming influence of the majority.

4. Scalability and resource optimization: CFL also offers scalability benefits by reducing the overall communication and computational load. Instead of aggregating model updates from all clients at every round, the server can manage

smaller clusters, each with its own model aggregation and update process. This decentralized approach to model training can significantly lower the communication overhead and make the federated learning process more scalable. Additionally, by focusing computational resources on clusters rather than individual clients, CFL can more effectively utilize available resources, leading to faster and more efficient model training [8].

5. Improved privacy preservation: Clustering can also enhance privacy preservation in federated learning. By grouping clients with similar data distributions, the clustering mechanism can mask the specific attributes of individual client data, making it more difficult to infer sensitive information about a particular client from the cluster-level model updates. Moreover, CFL can be combined with techniques such as differential privacy or secure multiparty computation to provide additional layers of privacy protection, further reducing the risk of data leakage [10].

6. Flexibility in model training: CFL provides flexibility in model training by allowing different training strategies for different clusters. For example, clusters with more homogeneous data can use simpler models or fewer communication rounds, while more heterogeneous clusters may benefit from more complex models or additional training. This adaptability makes CFL a versatile approach that can be customized to the specific needs and constraints of each federated learning scenario.

Clustered Federated Learning thus represents a powerful extension of traditional federated learning, addressing the inherent challenges of non-IID data and enabling more accurate, personalized, and efficient model training across diverse client populations.

## 3. Clustered federated learning

In this section, we delve into the concept of Clustered Federated Learning (CFL), a paradigm designed to address the challenges posed by statistical heterogeneity in federated learning environments.

### 3.1 Background and motivation

Traditional federated learning (FL) aims to collaboratively train a single global model across a network of clients, each holding decentralized and often diverse datasets. The underlying assumption is that the aggregated updates from all clients will converge to a model that generalizes well across the entire client population. However, in practice, this assumption is frequently violated due to the presence of non-IID (non-identically distributed) data among clients. Specifically, clients may have significantly different data distributions $\mathcal{P}_i(\mathrm{x}, y)$, which can lead to suboptimal global model performance [3, 8].

This statistical heterogeneity results in a global model that may perform well on average but fails to capture the unique characteristics of individual client data distributions. Consequently, the global model could perform poorly for a subset of clients, diminishing the overall efficacy of federated learning [5]. This limitation is particularly pronounced in applications where client data is inherently diverse, such as in personalized healthcare, where patients exhibit different medical conditions, or in smart devices, where usage patterns vary greatly among users.

Clustered Federated Learning (CFL) seeks to overcome this limitation by leveraging the intrinsic similarities among subsets of clients. The core idea behind CFL is to partition the set of clients into clusters, each representing a group of clients with similar data distributions. Instead of training a single global model, CFL trains a separate model for each cluster, effectively allowing for personalized model training at the group level [8, 9]. This approach aims to achieve a balance between the centralized global model of traditional FL and the highly personalized models of individualized federated learning, offering a middle ground that enhances model performance and personalization for heterogeneous client populations.

In healthcare, CFL can outperform traditional federated learning by clustering hospitals with similar patient demographics or disease profiles to train more specialized models. For example, hospitals serving distinct populations benefit from cluster-specific models tailored to their data, leading to more accurate disease predictions than a single global model would provide. Similarly, in IoT applications like smart home energy management, CFL clusters devices by usage patterns, enabling localized energy prediction models that respond effectively to regional conditions. By capturing these local differences, CFL improves accuracy and personalization across diverse environments.

### 3.2 Approaches to clustered federated learning

Several methodologies have been proposed to implement CFL, focusing on different strategies for clustering clients based on their data or model characteristics:

Model-based Clustering Model-based clustering methods group clients based on the similarity of their local model updates. Algorithms such as `IFCA` (Iterative Federated Clustering Algorithm) [10] cluster clients by comparing the gradients or parameter updates sent to the server. The server iteratively assigns clients to clusters and trains a distinct model for each cluster, using feedback from the clustering step to refine the client assignments. This approach is advantageous in scenarios where client-specific model updates reflect the underlying data distribution well, enabling effective partitioning even when client-side data features are unavailable or sensitive.

Feature-based Clustering Feature-based clustering, as seen in `Clustered FL` [8], relies on client-side features, such as statistical properties of the local data, to group clients. For instance, clustering might be performed based on the distribution of labels, the mean and variance of features, or other statistical summaries that describe the data. This method directly leverages information about the data distributions, making it particularly useful when client data characteristics can be quantified and shared without compromising privacy. Feature-based clustering can yield more meaningful clusters in contexts where model updates alone do not fully capture the data distribution differences among clients.

Hybrid Clustering Approaches Hybrid approaches combine model-based and feature-based clustering to utilize both model updates and client-side data characteristics. These methods seek to enhance clustering accuracy and robustness by leveraging multiple sources of information. For example, initial clustering might be performed based on model updates, followed by refinement using feature-based metrics. Such approaches can provide a more comprehensive understanding of client similarities, leading to more effective clustered models.

**Figure 1** shows the overview of clustered FL procedure for different approaches.

### 3.3 Problem formulation

Formally, let $\mathcal{S}$ denote the set of all participating clients in the federated learning process. The goal of Clustered Federated Learning is to partition this set into $K$ disjoint clusters $\{\mathcal{C}_1, \mathcal{C}_2, \dots, \mathcal{C}_K\}$, where each cluster $\mathcal{C}_k$ consists of clients with similar data distributions, and the union of all clusters covers the entire client set, i.e., $\cup_{k=1}^{K}\mathcal{C}_k = \mathcal{S}$ and $\mathcal{C}_i \cap \mathcal{C}_j = \varnothing$ for $i \neq j$.

For each cluster $\mathcal{C}_k$, the objective is to train a local model $\boldsymbol{\theta}_k$ that minimizes the average loss over the clients within that cluster. This can be mathematically formulated as:

$$\hat{\boldsymbol{\theta}}_k = \arg\min_{\boldsymbol{\theta}_k} \sum_{i \in \mathcal{C}_k} \mathbb{E}_{(\mathrm{x},y)\sim\mathcal{D}_i^{\text{train}}}\left[\ell\left(f_i(\mathrm{x};\boldsymbol{\theta}_k),y\right)\right], \quad \forall k = 1, 2, \dots, K. \tag{3}$$

The ultimate goal is to identify an optimal partitioning $\{\mathcal{C}_1, \mathcal{C}_2, \dots, \mathcal{C}_K\}$ and corresponding cluster-specific models $\{\boldsymbol{\theta}_1, \boldsymbol{\theta}_2, \dots, \boldsymbol{\theta}_K\}$ that collectively minimize the overall loss across all clusters:

$$\min_{\{\mathcal{C}_k\}_{k=1}^{K},\,\{\boldsymbol{\theta}_k\}_{k=1}^{K}} \sum_{k=1}^{K} \sum_{i \in \mathcal{C}_k} \mathbb{E}_{(\mathrm{x},y)\sim\mathcal{D}_i^{\text{train}}}\left[\ell\left(f_i(\mathrm{x};\boldsymbol{\theta}_k),y\right)\right]. \tag{4}$$

This formulation effectively captures the trade-off between intra-cluster model performance and inter-cluster diversity, providing a framework that accommodates the heterogeneous nature of client data while enhancing the overall model performance.

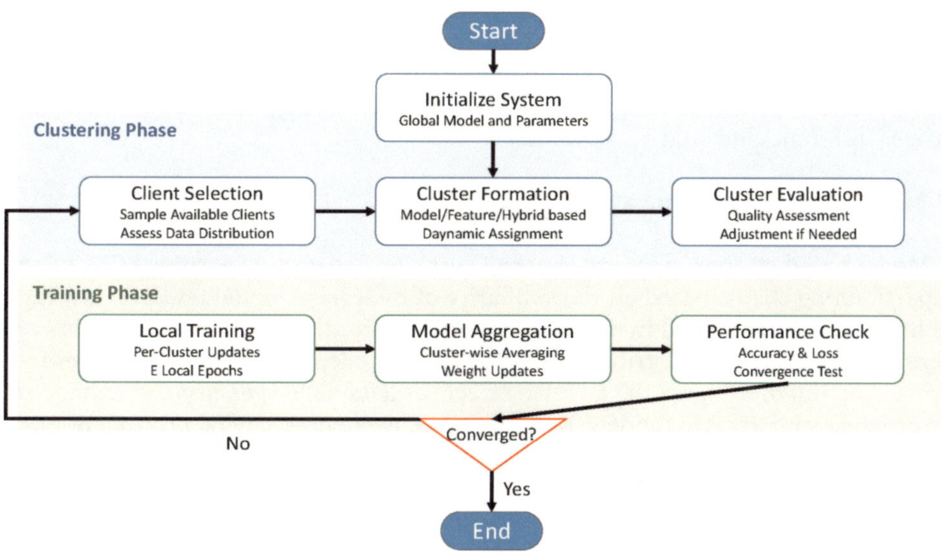


**Figure 1.**
*Overview of clustered federated learning procedure.*

### 3.4 Key challenges and considerations

While Clustered Federated Learning provides a promising approach to address data heterogeneity, several challenges must be addressed to ensure its efficacy:

- Cluster Initialization and Client Assignment Determining the initial clusters and assigning clients accurately is a critical step. Poor initialization can lead to suboptimal clusters and models, reducing the benefits of CFL. Iterative refinement and dynamic clustering strategies are often employed to mitigate this issue.

- Scalability and Communication Efficiency As the number of clients and clusters increases, so does the communication overhead and computational burden. Efficient algorithms for cluster management and model aggregation are necessary to maintain scalability.

- Privacy and Security Considerations Ensuring the privacy of client data during the clustering process is paramount. Methods that minimize information leakage, such as differential privacy or secure multi-party computation, are essential to maintain client trust and data integrity.

Clustered Federated Learning represents a significant advancement in federated learning, addressing the limitations of traditional methods and paving the way for more robust and personalized models in heterogeneous environments.

## 4. Approaches to clustered federated learning

Clustered Federated Learning (CFL) has emerged as a promising extension of traditional federated learning, aiming to tackle the challenges posed by heterogeneous and non-IID client data distributions. CFL partitions clients into clusters based on various criteria and trains separate models for each cluster, thus enhancing both model accuracy and personalization. This section delves into the various state-of-the-art approaches to CFL, starting with model-based clustering methods. **Table 1** summarizes different clustered FL approaches.

### 4.1 Model-based clustering approaches

Model-based clustering approaches in Clustered Federated Learning (CFL) focus on partitioning clients based on the similarity of their local model updates, leveraging the information embedded in model parameters or gradients to identify clusters of clients with similar data distributions. By clustering clients in this manner, these approaches aim to mitigate the adverse effects of data heterogeneity and enhance the performance of federated models. In this section, we review several prominent model-based clustering methods, discussing their unique characteristics and comparative advantages.

The Iterative Federated Clustering Algorithm (IFCA) [10] is a foundational method that dynamically partitions clients into clusters by minimizing the loss of multiple cluster models on local datasets. Each client evaluates all cluster models and selects the one yielding the lowest loss, ensuring that clients with similar data

| Approach | Description | Notable methods | Comparison/Advantages |
|---|---|---|---|
| Model-based clustering | Partitions clients by similarity in local model updates, often using gradient or parameter comparisons to group clients. | *IFCA*: Iteratively assigns clients to clusters based on lowest loss evaluation. *FedCluster*: Clusters clients by cosine similarity of updates with metadata use. | Effective in scenarios with clear client-model update patterns, requires predefined cluster number, dynamically re-clusters for optimal cluster formation. |
| Feature-based clustering | Clusters clients based on statistical data features, including label distributions or feature summaries, independent of model updates. | *FedGroup*: Adapts clusters dynamically. *PACFL*: Uses principal angles to reduce communication complexity. | Ideal for applications with distinct, quantifiable data features; provides privacy-friendly clustering with lower dependency on model data. |
| Hybrid clustering | Combines both model-based and feature-based approaches to refine clusters by considering data and model characteristics. | *FedSoft*: Soft clustering allowing clients in multiple clusters. *Fed-CAM*: Combines global and cluster models to avoid collapse. | Balances client data and model characteristics, suitable for complex heterogeneity, allows dynamic client-cluster re-assignments for scalable, adaptive systems. |

**Table 1.**
*Summary of Clustered Federated Learning Approaches.*

distributions are grouped together. IFCA then updates cluster models based on aggregated local updates, iteratively refining both the model parameters and client assignments. While effective in improving convergence on non-IID data, IFCA requires a predefined number of clusters, which can be a limitation when the optimal number of clusters is unknown.

Building on this concept, FedCluster [8] introduces a more flexible framework by clustering clients based on the cosine similarity of their model updates and incorporating client metadata, such as data quantity and computational resources. This additional information enables FedCluster to form balanced clusters, dynamically re-clustering clients to adapt to changes in data distribution or client availability. The dynamic re-clustering ensures that the models remain well-aligned with the evolving data distributions, maintaining optimal cluster structures throughout the training process.

To address the limitations of static cluster definitions, Adaptive Clustering methods [9] have been proposed to dynamically adjust the number of clusters based on observed data heterogeneity and model performance. These methods eliminate the need to predefine the number of clusters, allowing for a flexible adaptation to varying levels of client heterogeneity. By continuously monitoring cluster quality, they can merge or split clusters as needed, ensuring optimal clustering even as client data distributions change.

Multi-Task Learning (MTL)-based approaches [11] extend the CFL framework by training a global model with shared parameters and additional task-specific components for each cluster. This structure captures both global generalization and local specialization, making it particularly effective for applications where clusters share some common characteristics but also have distinct nuances, such as in multi-region healthcare applications.

Hierarchical Clustering methods [12] take a two-level approach, first grouping clients into smaller clusters based on local model updates and then aggregating these clusters into larger groups based on similarities in their aggregated updates. This hierarchical structure reduces computational and communication overhead and allows for more granular clustering, effectively capturing subtle differences in client data distributions.

Another extension, Federated Model Agnostic Meta-Learning (FL-MAML) with clustering [13], combines meta-learning with CFL by training a global meta-model that serves as an effective initialization for cluster-specific models. This significantly reduces training time and improves convergence, making it suitable for settings with limited computational resources or where rapid adaptation to new data is required.

In scenarios involving adversarial clients, Byzantine Robust CFL [14] leverages the clustering mechanism to detect and isolate Byzantine clients based on the cosine similarity of their model updates. This method dynamically partitions clients into benign and adversarial clusters, ensuring that the main training process remains robust and stable even in the presence of malicious behavior.

These model-based clustering approaches demonstrate the breadth of strategies available to tackle non-IID data challenges in federated learning. By effectively partitioning clients into meaningful clusters and training specialized models, they enhance model performance and personalization in CFL, paving the way for more advanced and adaptive federated learning frameworks.

### 4.2 Feature-based clustering approaches

Feature-based clustering approaches in Clustered Federated Learning (CFL) leverage the characteristics of client data, such as statistical properties, feature distributions, and label distributions, to form clusters that are more representative of client heterogeneity. Unlike model-based clustering, which relies solely on model updates, these methods incorporate explicit information about the client data to create meaningful clusters, particularly beneficial in scenarios where model updates do not fully capture the underlying data heterogeneity.

Hsu et al. [15] proposed one of the foundational methods in this category, clustering clients based on the Dirichlet distribution of their label proportions. Each client is represented by a vector indicating the proportion of each label in its dataset, and clustering is performed using traditional algorithms like K-means, effectively capturing label distribution skew among clients. Similarly, Sattler et al. [8] extended this concept by using statistical summaries such as mean and variance of features to represent clients in a lower-dimensional space, preserving privacy while enhancing cluster homogeneity.

Building on these approaches, Duan et al. [16] introduced FedGroup, which dynamically adapts client assignments to clusters based on evolving feature statistics, making it particularly suitable for non-stationary environments. Li et al. [17] advanced feature-based clustering by integrating meta-learning characteristics, clustering clients based on learning behaviors such as convergence speed.

Further innovation was presented by Vahidian et al. [18] where they proposed PACFL, which clusters clients using principal angles between data subspaces derived from truncated Singular Value Decomposition (SVD), significantly reducing communication overhead and computational complexity.

These feature-based clustering methods illustrate the diverse strategies employed to leverage client data characteristics for effective clustered federated learning, enhancing model performance and robustness in handling non-IID data. As the field progresses, integrating more sophisticated data-driven techniques will be crucial for further improving the scalability and adaptability of CFL systems.

### 4.3 Hybrid approaches

Hybrid approaches in Clustered Federated Learning (CFL) seek to leverage both model-based and feature-based clustering techniques to better capture the complexities of client data distributions, ultimately enhancing model performance and personalization. By integrating information from both local model updates and client-specific data characteristics, these methods aim to create more cohesive and representative clusters. In this section, we review several state-of-the-art hybrid approaches and their unique strategies for addressing the challenges posed by non-IID data in federated learning.

Briggs et al. [12] introduced a hierarchical clustering approach that integrates both client data features and model updates. This two-level clustering process first groups clients into small clusters based on feature distributions, such as statistical data summaries, and then refines these clusters using model update similarities. This approach effectively reduces computational and communication overhead in large-scale federated learning scenarios. Similarly, Long et al. [19] proposed Multi-Center Federated Learning (MCFL), which employs Gaussian Mixture Models (GMMs) to establish multiple cluster centers that represent both data and model characteristics. Unlike hierarchical clustering, MCFL allows clients to dynamically switch clusters based on the similarity of their model updates, thus capturing shifts in data distributions over time and preventing rigid cluster boundaries.

FedSoft [20] extends traditional CFL by allowing clients to belong to multiple clusters simultaneously. This soft clustering mechanism integrates multiple source distributions into a single optimization objective, reducing client workload and enabling efficient training. FLIS [21] takes a different approach by dynamically clustering clients based on inference similarities, using an auxiliary dataset to evaluate local models without accessing private data. This method effectively accommodates unseen clients and varying non-IID settings through hierarchical clustering.

Clustered Additive Modeling (CAM) [22] introduces an additive framework that combines a global model with cluster-specific models to address clustering collapse and enhance generalization. This approach, implemented through the Fed-CAM algorithm, alternates between client clustering and joint optimization of global and cluster models. On the other hand, a communication-aware approach proposed by Shlezinger et al. [23] clusters clients based on data distributions while respecting communication constraints, balancing cluster-specific accuracy with global model generalization.

Flexible methods like FLSC [24] and the Dynamic GAN-based Clustering [25] further extend hybrid CFL by allowing overlapping clusters and adapting clusters dynamically over time, respectively. FlexCFL [26] addresses client-level data shifts with a novel clustering method using Euclidean Distance of Decomposed Cosine similarity (EDC) and dynamic client migration. AutoCFL [27] tackles non-IID and imbalanced data by adjusting local training epochs and employing adaptive clustering based on weighted voting.

In summary, these hybrid approaches demonstrate the versatility and potential of combining model-based and feature-based clustering techniques. By leveraging the strengths of both, they provide a comprehensive framework for managing the complex heterogeneity in client populations, enhancing model performance, personalization, and scalability in CFL systems.

## 5. Evaluation metrics and benchmarks

Evaluating the performance of Clustered Federated Learning (CFL) is essential for understanding the effectiveness of various methodologies. This section discusses common metrics used to assess CFL performance, benchmark datasets and protocols, and highlights real-world applications.

### 5.1 Common metrics for evaluating CFL performance

Evaluating Clustered Federated Learning (CFL) involves a range of metrics that capture model accuracy, personalization, fairness, and clustering quality. Accuracy, a fundamental metric, measures the average performance of cluster-specific models across all clients and serves as an indicator of how well the models generalize to diverse client data. Personalization metrics, such as local accuracy, assess the effectiveness of cluster models on individual client data, quantifying the benefit of CFL over a baseline global model in terms of personalized performance improvements. Fairness is another critical aspect, gauged by the uniformity of model performance across clients. Metrics like the standard deviation of client accuracies and the worst-case accuracy are used to ensure that no client is disproportionately disadvantaged. Beyond these, clustering quality is evaluated using cluster purity and cohesion measures. Cluster purity, often assessed with Normalized Mutual Information (NMI), reflects how effectively the clusters group clients with similar data distributions, while cluster cohesion, measured by intra-cluster distance, indicates the compactness of clusters and the similarity of clients within each cluster. Together, these metrics provide a comprehensive framework for assessing the performance and robustness of CFL methods in diverse and heterogeneous federated learning environments.

### 5.2 Benchmark datasets and experimental protocols

Benchmark datasets and standardized protocols are crucial for evaluating CFL methods under controlled conditions. Traditional federated learning benchmarks such as FATE [28], PaddleFL [29], TensorFlow Federated (TFF) [30], and FedLearner [31] primarily support global FL algorithms like FedAvg, but they lack features tailored to clustered or personalized federated learning. To address these limitations, advanced benchmarks like FLOWER [32], FedML [33], FLUTE [34], and NIID-Bench [17] have been introduced, providing more comprehensive support for a broader range of FL algorithms, enabling rigorous evaluation and comparison of different methods. However, these platforms still primarily focus on global FL scenarios. For evaluating clustered and personalized federated learning approaches, more specialized benchmarks are needed. Recently developed benchmarks such as pFL-Bench [35] and Motley [36] aim to fill this gap by focusing on personalized FL, yet they remain limited in their support for CFL-specific requirements, such as clustering strategies and handling dynamic client participation. In contrast, FedZoo-Bench [2] offers a more comprehensive evaluation framework, supporting both global and personalized FL methods, and includes implementation of 22 state-of-the-art methods, allowing for detailed assessment of generalization capabilities and the impact of various experimental variables. These benchmarks are essential for advancing CFL research by providing standardized evaluation protocols and facilitating the comparison of different methodologies under consistent conditions.

### 5.3 Case studies and real-world applications

Clustered Federated Learning (CFL) has shown significant potential in a variety of real-world scenarios, demonstrating its ability to address heterogeneous data distributions across diverse domains. In healthcare, CFL is employed to train models across hospitals with varying patient demographics and medical practices, leading to improved personalized disease prediction and diagnosis [37]. For smart devices and IoT, CFL facilitates the training of models for devices with different usage patterns and hardware specifications, enhancing tasks such as user activity recognition and personalized recommendations [38]. In the context of autonomous vehicles, CFL enables the clustering of vehicles based on driving environments or sensor types, allowing for the development of specialized models tailored to specific driving conditions, which enhances the reliability and safety of autonomous systems [39]. Similarly, in industrial IoT applications, CFL clusters devices based on production line characteristics, optimizing predictive maintenance and quality control models [38]. These applications underscore the versatility and impact of CFL in effectively managing non-IID data distributions, and as research in this area progresses, its adoption in even more diverse fields is expected, highlighting its transformative potential in federated learning.

## 6. Challenges and open problems in clustered federated learning

Clustered Federated Learning (CFL) has emerged as a promising solution to address the challenges of non-IID data in federated learning environments. While CFL offers significant improvements in terms of model performance and personalization, it also introduces a new set of challenges and open problems that must be addressed to fully realize its potential. In this section, we explore these challenges, focusing on scalability, cluster initialization, communication efficiency, privacy preservation, and dynamic client participation.

### 6.1 Scalability and computational overhead

One of the most pressing challenges in CFL is scalability. As the number of clients participating in federated learning increases, the complexity of managing clusters and models for each cluster grows significantly. This scalability issue manifests in several ways:

1. Large-scale client management: In a federated learning system with thousands or even millions of clients, managing the formation and maintenance of clusters becomes a non-trivial task. The process of clustering clients based on model updates or data features requires significant computational resources and can lead to increased latency in the learning process. Furthermore, as the number of clusters grows, the server must maintain separate models for each cluster, increasing the memory and computational requirements on the server-side

[18, 40]. Hybrid and hierarchical clustering approaches, while offering a scalable solution, still face challenges in efficiently managing client clusters at scale.

2. Computational overhead of clustering: The computational cost of clustering algorithms, particularly in feature-based and hybrid methods, can be substantial. Algorithms such as K-means or hierarchical clustering have a computational complexity that scales poorly with the number of clients and the dimensionality of the feature space. This overhead is exacerbated in dynamic environments where frequent re-clustering is required to adapt to changes in client data distributions [16]. Techniques such as approximate clustering, dimensionality reduction, or decentralized clustering algorithms may help mitigate this overhead, but their effectiveness in large-scale federated settings remains an open question.

3. Model training and aggregation: As the number of clusters increases, the server must aggregate model updates from multiple clusters and maintain distinct models for each one. This can lead to significant computational overhead, especially when the clusters are large and the models are complex. The challenge is further compounded by the need to synchronize model updates across clusters, which can introduce delays and bottlenecks in the training process. Efficient model aggregation techniques that can scale with the number of clusters and clients are needed to address this issue [41].

### 6.2 Cluster initialization and update strategies

The process of initializing and updating clusters is crucial to the success of CFL but presents several challenges that can affect model performance and convergence.

1. Optimal number of clusters: Determining the optimal number of clusters is a fundamental challenge in CFL. An incorrect choice of the number of clusters can lead to suboptimal model performance, either by overfitting to small clusters or by failing to capture the heterogeneity of large, diverse clusters [10]. Methods that dynamically adjust the number of clusters based on the observed data distributions and model performance have been proposed, but they require robust mechanisms to detect when and how to split or merge clusters effectively.

2. Cluster initialization: The initial formation of clusters can have a lasting impact on the overall learning process. Poorly initialized clusters can lead to slow convergence and reduced model performance. Common initialization techniques, such as random initialization or clustering based on a small subset of clients, may not capture the true underlying data distributions, leading to suboptimal cluster formation. More sophisticated initialization strategies that incorporate prior knowledge or that use meta-learning techniques to bootstrap the clustering process may be necessary to improve the initial cluster quality [13].

3. Cluster re-assignment and update: Dynamic environments, where client data distributions change over time, necessitate mechanisms for updating clusters and re-assigning clients. However, frequent re-clustering can disrupt the training process and increase communication costs. Balancing the need for dynamic

adaptation with the stability of cluster assignments is a complex challenge. Techniques such as incremental clustering, where only a subset of clients are re-clustered at each round, or methods that use historical data to guide re-clustering, can help mitigate these issues but require careful design and tuning [18].

### 6.3 Communication efficiency and convergence issues

Communication efficiency and convergence are critical concerns in federated learning, and CFL introduces additional complexities that must be addressed.

1. Increased communication overhead: The clustering process in CFL often requires additional communication between clients and the server to share data features or model updates necessary for clustering. Feature-based methods, in particular, can incur significant communication costs if the feature space is large or if frequent re-clustering is needed [21]. Strategies to reduce this overhead, such as using compressed representations of client features or sharing only the most relevant data, are essential to maintain the scalability of CFL in bandwidth-constrained environments.

2. Slow convergence: The introduction of clusters can lead to slower convergence rates, especially if the clusters are not well-formed or if clients frequently switch between clusters. This issue is particularly pronounced in hybrid methods that rely on both model updates and feature-based clustering, as the need to reconcile different sources of information can introduce inconsistencies in the training process [36]. Adaptive learning rates, cluster-specific convergence criteria, and techniques that allow for asynchronous model updates may help address these convergence issues, but they require careful implementation to avoid destabilizing the learning process.

3. Cross-cluster model consistency: Ensuring consistency across cluster models is another challenge in CFL. Clients that share similar data distributions but belong to different clusters may receive inconsistent model updates, leading to potential performance degradation. Techniques such as knowledge distillation between clusters or the use of a global model as a regularizer can help maintain cross-cluster consistency, but they also introduce additional communication and computational costs [21, 36].

### 6.4 Privacy preservation in clustered settings

Privacy preservation is a cornerstone of federated learning, and CFL introduces new challenges in maintaining client privacy.

1. Privacy risks in feature-based clustering: Feature-based clustering methods often require clients to share statistical summaries or feature vectors with the server. Even though raw data is not shared, these summaries can still reveal sensitive information about the client's data distribution. Techniques such as differential privacy or secure multiparty computation can help mitigate these risks, but they also introduce additional complexity and computational overhead [15].

Designing privacy-preserving clustering algorithms that provide strong guarantees without compromising clustering accuracy remains an open problem.

2. Inference attacks in clustered settings: In clustered federated learning, the clustering information itself can be exploited by an adversary to infer properties about a client's data. For example, knowing which cluster a client belongs to can provide clues about the client's data distribution. This risk is exacerbated in dynamic environments where clients frequently switch clusters, potentially revealing information about changes in their data over time. Robust privacy-preserving techniques that obscure cluster membership and protect against inference attacks are needed to secure CFL systems [8].

3. Privacy-preserving model aggregation: In CFL, the server aggregates model updates from multiple clusters. If the server is compromised, the updates from a single cluster can be used to infer information about all the clients within that cluster. Privacy-preserving aggregation techniques, such as secure aggregation or the use of noise to obfuscate individual contributions, are essential to protect client data. However, these techniques must be carefully designed to ensure that they do not degrade the performance or stability of the learning process [42].

### 6.5 Handling dynamic client participation

Federated learning systems often operate in environments where client participation is dynamic, with clients joining and leaving the system over time. CFL must be robust to these changes to ensure stable and effective model training.

1. Client arrival and departure: The arrival of new clients with previously unseen data distributions can disrupt existing clusters and degrade model performance. Similarly, the departure of clients can leave clusters underrepresented, reducing their effectiveness. CFL systems must be able to dynamically adjust to these changes, either by incorporating new clients into existing clusters or by forming new clusters as needed [10]. Techniques such as incremental clustering, where clusters are updated incrementally as new clients arrive, can help maintain the stability of the learning process but require careful management to avoid excessive re-clustering.

2. Variability in client participation: In federated learning, clients may not always be available to participate in every round of training. This variability can lead to inconsistencies in model updates and affect the stability of clusters. CFL systems must be designed to handle this variability, either by using techniques such as client selection, where only a subset of the most reliable clients are selected for training, or by incorporating mechanisms that allow clients to contribute asynchronously to the learning process [43]. Ensuring that the clusters remain representative and effective despite variability in client participation is a key challenge.

3. Long-tail client distributions: In many federated learning scenarios, a small number of clients may have a disproportionately large amount of data or may exhibit unique data distributions that are not well-represented in the larger population. These" long-tail" clients can be challenging to accommodate within a

standard clustering framework, as they may not fit well into any existing cluster. CFL methods must be able to identify and appropriately handle these clients, either by creating specialized clusters for them or by using techniques such as personalized models or transfer learning to ensure that their contributions are adequately captured.

In conclusion, while CFL offers significant advantages in handling non-IID data and improving model performance, it also presents a range of challenges that must be addressed to fully realize its potential. Addressing these challenges will require advances in clustering algorithms, communication protocols, privacy-preserving techniques, and adaptive learning strategies. As research in this area continues to evolve, we can expect new methods and frameworks that will further enhance the robustness, scalability, and effectiveness of clustered federated learning.

## 7. Conclusion

This chapter has explored the landscape of Clustered Federated Learning (CFL), highlighting its ability to effectively address the challenges posed by non-IID data through various model-based, feature-based, and hybrid clustering approaches. Key concepts such as model accuracy, personalization, fairness, and clustering quality have been discussed, along with the evaluation metrics and benchmarks that facilitate rigorous comparison of CFL methods. Despite significant advancements, several open challenges remain, including scalability, efficient cluster management, and privacy preservation, which present opportunities for future research to further refine and expand CFL methodologies. As CFL continues to evolve, its potential to enhance federated learning in diverse real-world applications is substantial, offering more personalized and robust solutions for decentralized machine learning in complex environments.

## Author details

Majid Morafah[1] and Mahdi Morafah[2]*

1 Arizona State University, Arizona, USA

2 University of California, San Diego, USA

*Address all correspondence to: mmorafah@ucsd.edu

## References

[1] McMahan B, Moore E, Ramage D, Hampson S, Arcas BAY. Communication-efficient learning of deep networks from decentralized data. In: Artificial Intelligence and Statistics. Fort Lauderdale, FL, USA: PMLR; 2017. pp. 1273-1282

[2] Morafah M, Wang W, Lin B. A practical recipe for federated learning under statistical heterogeneity experimental design. In: IEEE Transactions on Artificial Intelligence. 2023

[3] Zhao Y, Li M, Lai L, Suda N, Civin D, Chandra V. Federated learning with non-iid data. arXiv preprint arXiv: 1806.00582. 2018

[4] Karimireddy SP, Kale S, Mohri M, Reddi S, Stich S, Suresh AT. Scaffold: Stochastic controlled averaging for federated learning. In: International Conference on Machine Learning. Virtual, Vienna: PMLR; 2020. pp. 5132-5143

[5] Li T, Sahu AK, Talwalkar A, Smith V. Federated learning: Challenges, methods, and future directions. IEEE Signal Processing Magazine. 2020;**37**(3): 50-60

[6] Li T, Sanjabi M, Beirami A, Smith V. Fair resource allocation in federated learning. arXiv preprint arXiv: 1905.10497. 2019

[7] Kairouz P, McMahan HB, Avent B, Bellet A, Bennis M, Bhagoji AN, et al. Advances and open problems in federated learning. Foundations and Trends® in Machine Learning. 2021;**14** (1–2):1-210

[8] Sattler F, Müller K-R, Samek W. Clustered federated learning: Model-agnostic distributed multitask optimization under privacy constraints. IEEE Transactions on Neural Networks and Learning Systems. 2020;**32**(8):3710-3722

[9] Mansour Y, Mohri M, Ro J, Suresh AT. Three approaches for personalization with applications to federated learning. arXiv preprint arXiv: 2002.10619. 2020

[10] Ghosh A, Chung J, Yin D, Ramchandran K. An efficient framework for clustered federated learning. Advances in Neural Information Processing Systems. 2020;**33**:19 586-19 597

[11] Marfoq O, Neglia G, Bellet A, Kameni L, Vidal R. Federated multi-task learning under a mixture of distributions. Advances in Neural Information Processing Systems. 2021; **34**:15 434-15 447

[12] Briggs C, Fan Z, Andras P. Federated learning with hierarchical clustering of local updates to improve training on non-iid data. In: 2020 International Joint Conference on Neural Networks (IJCNN). Glasgow, UK: IEEE; 2020. pp. 1-9

[13] Fallah A, Mokhtari A, Ozdaglar A. Personalized federated learning: A meta-learning approach. arXiv preprint arXiv: 2002.07948. 2020

[14] Sattler F, Müller K-R, Wiegand T, Samek W. On the byzantine robustness of clustered federated learning. In: ICASSP 2020–2020 IEEE International Conference on Acoustics, Speech and Signal Processing (ICASSP). Virtual Barcelona: IEEE; 2020. pp. 8861-8865

[15] Hsu TMH, Qi H, Brown M. Measuring the effects of non-identical data distribution for federated visual

classification. arXiv preprint arXiv: 1909.06335. 2019

[16] Duan M, Liu D, Ji X, Liu R, Liang L, Chen X, et al. Fedgroup: Efficient federated learning via decomposed similarity-based clustering. In: 2021 IEEE Intl Conf on Parallel & Distributed Processing with Applications, Big Data & Cloud Computing, Sustainable Computing & Communications, Social Computing & Networking (ISPA/BDCloud/SocialCom/SustainCom). New York, USA: IEEE; 2021. pp. 228-237

[17] Li Q, Diao Y, Chen Q, He B. Federated learning on non-iid data silos: An experimental study. arXiv preprint arXiv:2102.02079. 2021

[18] Vahidian S, Morafah M, Wang W, Kungurtsev V, Chen C, Shah M, et al. Efficient distribution similarity identification in clustered federated learning via principal angles between client data subspaces. In: Proceedings of the AAAI Conference on Artificial Intelligence. Vol. 37, no. 8. Vancouver, Canada: 2023. pp. 10 043–10 052

[19] Long G, Xie M, Shen T, Zhou T, Wang X, Jiang J. Multi-center federated learning: Clients clustering for better personalization. World Wide Web. 2023; **26**(1):481-500

[20] Ruan Y, Joe-Wong C. Fedsoft: Soft clustered federated learning with proximal local updating. Proceedings of the AAAI Conference on Artificial Intelligence. 2022;**36**(7):8124-8131

[21] Morafah M, Vahidian S, Wang W, Lin B. Flis: Clustered federated learning via inference similarity for non-iid data distribution. IEEE Open Journal of the Computer Society. 2023;**4**:109-120

[22] Ma J, Zhou T, Long G, Jiang J, Zhang C. Structured federated learning through clustered additive modeling. Advances in Neural Information Processing Systems. 2023;**36**:43 097-43 107

[23] Shlezinger N, Rini S, Eldar YC. The communication-aware clustered federated learning problem. In: 2020 IEEE International Symposium on Information Theory (ISIT). Los Angeles, CA, USA: IEEE; 2020. pp. 2610-2615

[24] Li C, Li G, Varshney PK. Federated learning with soft clustering. IEEE Internet of Things Journal. 2021;**9**(10): 7773-7782

[25] Kim Y, Al Hakim E, Haraldson J, Eriksson H, da Silva JMB, Fischione C. Dynamic clustering in federated learning. In: ICC 2021-IEEE International Conference on Communications. Virtual: IEEE; 2021. pp. 1-6

[26] Duan M, Liu D, Ji X, Wu Y, Liang L, Chen X, et al. Flexible clustered federated learning for client-level data distribution shift. IEEE Transactions on Parallel and Distributed Systems. 2021; **33**(11):2661-2674

[27] Gong B, Xing T, Liu Z, Xi W, Chen X. Adaptive Client Clustering for Efficient Federated Learning Over Non-IID and Imbalanced Data. In: IEEE Transactions on Big Data. Dec. 2024;**10** (6):1051-1065. DOI: 10.1109/TBDATA.2022.3167994

[28] Liu Y, Fan T, Chen T, Xu Q, Yang Q. Fate: An industrial grade platform for collaborative learning with data protection. Journal of Machine Learning Research. 2021;**22**(226):1-6

[29] Paddlefl. Available from: https://github.com/PaddlePaddle/PaddleFL [Accessed: January 10, 2023]

[30] Tff. Available from:https://github.com/tensorflow/federated [Accessed: January 10, 2023]

[31] Fedlearner. Available from:https://github.com/bytedance/fedlearner [Accessed: January 10, 2023]

[32] Beutel DJ, Topal T, Mathur A, Qiu X, Parcollet T, de Gusmão PP, et al. Flower: A Friendly Federated Learning Research Framework, arXiv preprint arXiv: 2007.14390, 2020

[33] He C, Li S, So J, Zeng X, Zhang M, Wang H, et al. Fedml: A research library and benchmark for federated machine learning. arXiv preprint arXiv: 2007.13518. 2020

[34] Dimitriadis D, Garcia MH, Diaz DM, Manoel A, Sim R. Flute: A scalable, extensible framework for high-performance federated learning simulations. arXiv preprint arXiv: 2203.13789. 2022

[35] Chen D, Gao D, Kuang W, Li Y, Ding B. pfl-Bench: A comprehensive benchmark for personalized federated learning. arXiv preprint arXiv: 2206.03655. 2022

[36] Wu S, Li T, Charles Z, Xiao Y, Liu Z, Xu Z, Smith V. Motley: Benchmarking heterogeneity and personalization in federated learning. arXiv preprint arXiv: 2206.09262. 2022

[37] Qayyum A, Ahmad K, Ahsan MA, Al-Fuqaha A, Qadir J. Collaborative federated learning for healthcare: Multi-modal covid-19 diagnosis at the edge. IEEE Open Journal of the Computer Society. 2022;**3**:172-184

[38] Nguyen DC, Ding M, Pathirana PN, Seneviratne A, Li J, Poor HV. Federated learning for internet of things: A comprehensive survey. IEEE Communications Surveys & Tutorials. 2021;**23**(3):1622-1658

[39] Chellapandi VP, Yuan L, Brinton CG, Żak SH, Wang Z. Federated Learning for Connected and Automated Vehicles: A Survey of Existing Approaches and Challenges. In: IEEE Transactions on Intelligent Vehicles. Jan. 2024;**9**(1)119-137. DOI: 10.1109/TIV.2023.3332675

[40] Yu L, Albelaihi R, Sun X, Ansari N, Devetsikiotis M. Jointly optimizing client selection and resource management in wireless federated learning for internet of things. IEEE Internet of Things Journal. 2021;**9**(6):4385-4395

[41] Liu L, Zhang J, Song S, Letaief KB. Client-edge-cloud hierarchical federated learning. In: ICC 2020–2020 IEEE International Conference on Communications (ICC). Virtual: IEEE; 2020. pp. 1-6

[42] Liu Z, Guo J, Yang W, Fan J, Lam K-Y, Zhao J. Privacy-Preserving Aggregation in Federated Learning: A Survey. In: IEEE Transactions on Big Data. DOI: 10.1109/TBDATA.2022.3190835

[43] Yu X, Cherkasova L, Vardhan H, Zhao Q, Ekaireb E, Zhang X, et al. Async-hfl: Efficient and robust asynchronous federated learning in hierarchical iot networks. In: Proceedings of the 8th ACM/IEEE Conference on Internet of Things Design and Implementation. New York, NY, United States: 2023. pp. 236-248

Chapter 4

# Application of Artificial Intelligence-Driven Federated Learning Based on Machine Learning and Deep Learning in Medicine

*Luwei Li*

## Abstract

Currently, artificial intelligence (AI) technology is developing rapidly. Machine learning and deep learning are algorithms in the field of AI, and their combined use in federated learning is becoming increasingly common in medical research. The emergence of federated learning technology aims to train machine learning and deep learning algorithms across multiple distributed devices or servers. Federated learning has greatly promoted the development of AI in the medical field. The core of this approach is to construct complex and accurate models by automatically learning and extracting useful features from large amounts of data from multiple data sources, thereby building models with both high accuracy and precision. The widespread adoption of federated learning is bound to lead to breakthrough advances in areas such as precision medicine, clinical decision support, new drug development, medical image recognition, medical language processing, and medical speech recognition. This chapter draws on the author's experience in big data medical modeling and validation from multiple data sources to introduce algorithms and operational modes in the field of federated learning, offering a glimpse into the promising future of the intelligent world.

**Keywords:** federated learning, machine learning, deep learning, medicine, artificial intelligence

## 1. Introduction

Artificial Intelligence (AI) [1] is a general term referring to the use of computers to simulate intelligent behavior with minimal human intervention, among which federated learning is one of the most advanced paradigms under AI models. Federated Learning [2] is a machine learning framework that effectively helps multiple institutions use data and build machine learning models while meeting user privacy protection, data security, and government regulations. Federated learning is defined as a special method for training machine learning and deep learning algorithms, which

 IntechOpen

means data remains private, applicable, and scalable. Specifically, federated learning technology aims to train machine learning and deep learning algorithms across multiple distributed devices or servers, each possessing its own local and private data. Federated learning is an increasingly prominent topic that can be associated with data privacy, distributed systems, machine learning, and deep learning. It represents a trend in the application of current AI algorithms. As AI algorithms mature, the joint application of related algorithms becomes tighter, and machine learning algorithms [3] and deep learning algorithms [4] fall within the scope of AI algorithms, indicating that their combined use is significant for scientific research into intrinsic patterns. However, due to constraints imposed by laws and regulations, policy supervision, commercial secrets, and personal privacy, multiple data sources cannot directly exchange data, resulting in "data islands" [5], which restrict the further enhancement of AI big data models such as machine learning and deep learning. The birth of federated learning addresses this issue. In the field of medical research, the application of machine learning combined with deep learning and the analysis of data sets from different sources through federated learning has broad application prospects. The author provides an overview of experiences gained from federated learning algorithm modeling and validation in the medical field to offer reference for scientists engaged in medical research and engineers and programmers working in medical engineering.

Firstly, machine learning and deep learning are the cornerstones of federated learning, while the goal of federated learning is to achieve reliable results through big data modeling and validation from multiple data sources. With the acceleration of the digitalization process today, a vast amount of data has been generated. Machine learning and deep learning technologies can automatically mine the treasures embedded in the data. Machine learning models trained on large amounts of data are now applied in various scenarios such as edge computing, healthcare, autonomous driving, intelligent transportation, financial services, and industrial automation, profoundly changing our world. Consequently, the federated learning model has emerged.

This collaborative approach contrasts sharply with traditional machine learning or deep learning techniques, which are essentially centralized and rely on collecting all data samples into a single dataset before use. Federated Learning [6], on the other hand, is not confined to a particular dataset. It is designed to perform data mining across multiple data sources and is not restricted to a specific algorithm. Instead, it selects algorithms based on their performance to optimize the model to the greatest extent. Therefore, federated learning provides a broader paradigm for implementing machine learning or deep learning algorithm solutions and offers greater flexibility in managing data. Federated learning is not limited to specific algorithms; it can be utilized in various situations. It mainly adjusts the implementation methods of these algorithms' training processes and can be considered for both offline and online learning. Thus, this paper will separately discuss the collaborative mode of multiple algorithms in federated learning and the cooperative mode of multiple data sources.

## 2. Federated learning mode with multiple algorithm collaboration

In the construction of clinical prediction and diagnostic models, multiple machine learning and deep learning algorithms can be used simultaneously in federated learning. Machine learning [7] is a subset of artificial intelligence (AI) and is one approach to achieving AI, but it is not the only one. It is a discipline focused on how computers can simulate or implement human learning behavior to acquire new knowledge or skills and reorganize existing knowledge structures to continuously improve their performance. Deep learning [8, 9] is a subset of machine learning, inspired by the human brain, and consists of artificial neural networks that mimic similar structures in the human brain. In deep learning, learning occurs through a deep, multi-layered "network" of interconnected "neurons." The term "deep" typically refers to the number of hidden layers in the neural network.

Traditional machine learning algorithms [10] include logistic regression, decision trees, random forests, support vector machines, Bayesian learning, and other supervised and unsupervised learning algorithms, as well as reinforcement learning. Deep learning [11, 12] encompasses techniques such as convolutional neural networks (CNN), recurrent neural networks (RNN), long short-term memory (LSTM), generative adversarial networks (GAN), residual networks (ResNet), diffusion models, transformers, autoencoders, deep neural networks (DNN), Word2Vec, graph neural networks (GNN), deep Q-networks (DQN), generative pre-trained transformers (GPT), and capsule networks (CapsNet).

In previous work, the author has used various artificial intelligence algorithms in combination with large clinical datasets for modeling and validation of chronic diseases such as diabetes, hypertension, hyperlipidemia, and hyperuricemia. The datasets collected include those from a medical university hospital's examination population, covering data from the same month across two years, amounting to 10,000 to 20,000 cases. The indicators include common clinical laboratory tests, imaging examination indicators, and some calculated indicators. Both traditional machine learning algorithms and deep learning algorithms were used for modeling and validation. The machine learning algorithms included logistic regression and nomograms, decision trees, random forests, and support vector machines. The deep learning algorithms included backpropagation (BP) neural networks and radial basis function (RBF) neural networks.

Medical data generally consists of basic research data and clinical research data, and different sample data require different processing methods. Clinical research data includes conventional anthropometric indicators such as height, weight, age, and sex, as well as liver and kidney function indicators such as alanine transaminase, aspartate transaminase, creatinine, urea nitrogen, and uric acid. Blood lipid indicators such as triglycerides and cholesterol, and blood indicators such as white blood cells, hemoglobin, and platelets are also included. Unlike other fields, some medical indicators may need imputation for further statistical analysis. Imputation analysis is based on the fact that clinical laboratory indicators have critical values. These critical values serve as diagnostic criteria, dividing biochemical indicators into two parts based on a threshold of 0 and 1, potentially leading to results that are more beneficial for guiding clinical diagnosis and treatment.

Certainly, performing extensive statistical preprocessing of clinical data is an exceptionally tedious task, but effective data processing can greatly facilitate subsequent federated learning modeling and validation. It is observed that some clinical data, when not imputed, might yield higher accuracy, specificity, and sensitivity in certain algorithms. However, crucial indicators for guiding clinical diagnosis, such as odds ratios (OR) and relative risks (RR), may produce better results with imputation. Therefore, the decision to impute clinical data for analysis should be based on an overall assessment of the data and the strengths and weaknesses of the algorithms used.

For basic research data, the preprocessing methods differ from those used for clinical data. Basic data generally falls into numerical data and image data categories. Some image data require preprocessing using the instrument's software. Basic research data results are primarily based on enzyme-linked immunosorbent assay

(ELISA) results, Western blot results, flow cytometry results, and fluorescence microscopy images. For pure numerical basic research data, preliminary processing includes excluding blank values, converting data to ratios or absolute values for uniform analysis, and storing data in formats such as blank controls, negative controls, treatment groups, and positive controls.

Image-type basic research data, such as Western blot results and animal morphology images, typically do not require special software preprocessing and can be used directly. In contrast, images from flow cytometry and confocal microscopy, which are output by instruments with built-in software, do require preprocessing. These instruments usually come with proprietary analysis software. Since the output data from these instruments can be difficult for other software to reprocess, researchers must conduct appropriate data analysis on the measurement instruments.

Overall, preprocessing clinical research data tends to require more time and effort compared to basic research data. The detailed discussion on data preprocessing emphasizes its critical role in the effectiveness and performance evaluation of models derived from modeling and validation. Hence, it is important to summarize this content thoroughly.

Moreover, the results obtained from using a single artificial intelligence (AI) algorithm compared to multiple combined algorithms can vary significantly. A single AI algorithm may not be suitable for all medical research data, and the resulting model may not always provide optimal accuracy, specificity, sensitivity, or reliability. In contrast, combining multiple AI algorithms can leverage their respective strengths, validate and corroborate results, and yield more reliable conclusions that are better suited for clinical application.

Furthermore, parameter tuning during the modeling process is crucial. Poorly adjusted parameters can greatly affect the research outcomes. In the author's experience with federated learning modeling for chronic diseases using random forests, support vector machines (SVM), and backpropagation (BP) neural networks, the SVM model had the longest running time, the random forest model required the most complex parameter adjustments, and the BP neural network model achieved the highest accuracy. This suggests that deep learning neural network models may offer superior accuracy, specificity, and sensitivity with relatively shorter running times, potentially making them the preferred choice for clinical data modeling in the future. Conversely, while SVMs provide good accuracy and specificity, their lengthy running times may make them less suitable for large-scale clinical data modeling. Random forests, although they balance accuracy, specificity, sensitivity, and speed between SVMs and neural networks, require numerous parameter adjustments, demanding higher computational and statistical skills from modelers.

The author has also conducted federated learning modeling for chronic diseases using logistic regression, decision trees, and radial basis function (RBF) neural networks. Compared to random forests, SVMs, and BP neural networks, this approach was simpler and did not involve extensive parameter adjustments or lengthy computation times. This modeling can be performed in SPSS without the need for complex code tuning in R or Python, making it relatively straightforward. RBF neural networks demonstrated better accuracy, specificity, and sensitivity compared to logistic regression and decision tree algorithms, highlighting the advantages of deep learning algorithms in clinical research.

However, neural network models are often considered "black boxes, " providing reliable results without detailed insights into the modeling process. In clinical modeling, where specific indicators' detailed analysis is necessary to derive clinical value, logistic regression-based nomograms are particularly useful. Nomograms can visually represent the significance of clinical indicators for disease diagnosis and prognosis. When combined with decision trees for clinical indicator classification and imputation, they complement each other effectively. This combined approach is a highly valuable federated learning algorithm collaboration mode worth promoting.

Validation and evaluation of models built using multiple artificial intelligence (AI) algorithms are equally important. The author recommends using more than one algorithm for validation. Currently, ROC curve analysis is widely used in clinical research to assess a model's accuracy, specificity, and sensitivity. However, ROC curves only evaluate the overall accuracy of the model. AI-based clinical big data models have unique characteristics and also require assessment of discriminative ability and clinical utility.

For this purpose, calibration curves are typically used to evaluate a model's discriminative ability, while decision curve analysis and clinical impact curves are used to assess clinical utility. Comprehensive evaluation algorithms can provide a thorough functional assessment of multi-model medical federated learning approaches, yielding results that are more aligned with clinical use.

Additionally, the author recommends employing various validation methods, such as random split validation, bootstrap resampling, and k-fold cross-validation, to achieve more accurate evaluation results. The use of confusion matrix algorithms is also suggested, with metrics such as accuracy, precision, recall, and F1 score for evaluating the precision of clinical models, rather than relying solely on ROC curves.

## 3. Federated learning mode with multiple data sources

The emergence of federated learning has specific implications. With the rapid advancement of artificial intelligence (AI) technologies, single-source data algorithms are increasingly insufficient. AI models, particularly those involving multi-modal big data, require diverse types of data sources. Moreover, training these models is not conducted on centralized servers but across multiple devices or nodes. Each node trains the model locally and only shares updates to model parameters without sharing the original data [13]. This approach addresses privacy and data security concerns, as data remains on local devices. Federated learning shows potential for applications involving sensitive data, such as smartphones, edge devices, and healthcare, and can achieve higher model personalization.

Model collaboration refers to multiple independent models working together to solve complex problems. These models may be distributed across different environments, such as cloud and edge devices, or across different applications. Model collaboration can facilitate knowledge sharing and integration, thereby enhancing overall model performance [14]. For instance, in the medical field, voice recognition models and natural language processing models can collaborate to improve accuracy in speech-to-text conversion and text understanding [15]. This can significantly save clinical time, optimize doctor-patient interactions, and will be discussed in more detail below.

Currently, leading global medical institutions and some advanced hospitals in China have adopted generative AI models for clinical history consultation and medical record documentation. For example, Shanghai First People's Hospital in Shanghai, China, has pioneered in addressing complex and unfamiliar medical processes for patients and the cumbersome and repetitive nature of medical record writing for doctors. The hospital uses large models and digital humans to provide interactive, companion-based medical services. AI large models assist doctors in generating electronic medical records, greatly reducing the time required for record writing and thus allowing more time for high-quality clinical care.

Specifically, the AI medical assistant uses digital avatars as interactive interfaces, with voice input/output and recognition as the primary interaction methods. It leverages large language models as the core intelligent engine to precisely understand and quickly respond to patient needs, thereby improving the patient experience. The medical record documentation and consultation processes involve fine-tuning a large language model with 10,000 historical records. The development team designed specific prompts to train the model on how to draft medical histories. This mechanism exemplifies the federated learning model's assistance paradigm and represents a promising model for future adoption.

Based on the author's experience with multi-data-source modeling and validation, federated learning across multiple data sources indeed offers significant advantages. With China's large population, each region has its own disease prevalence, which can vary due to geographic, environmental, and climatic factors, as well as the genetic profiles of local populations. For example, the author modeled and validated factors related to systemic lupus erythematosus (SLE) in the United States and China. The results showed that even for the same disease, clinical indicators used in modeling can have different significance during disease progression in different populations.

When considering American populations as representatives of Caucasians and Chinese populations as representatives of Asians, federated learning of these data sources can provide results that are more applicable to a majority of the global population. However, due to geographic constraints and data privacy laws that prohibit transferring data across borders, global medical datasets are not consolidated for AI training [16]. Therefore, collaborative research within countries like China and the US, or between different regions, remains more common. We hope that increasing collaboration among data centers will lead to the establishment of research databases based on national population data.

For example, the National Rheumatology and Immunology Disease Population Database Software, known as "Fengyun Assistant," spearheaded by Peking Union Medical College Hospital in China, aggregates disease data from major hospitals across the country. This dataset aims to cover the population characteristics nationwide, mitigating regional biases and yielding models more applicable to clinical practice. However, this model is not without limitations, as there remains a risk of data privacy breaches when uploading clinical data to such a platform.

The author's research comparing lupus data from Chinese populations with data from public databases in the United States showed that, while environmental, climatic, and genetic factors differ, the fundamental important factors identified were consistent. However, the response to drug treatments varied, highlighting the importance of federated learning in developing treatments and therapies applicable to diverse populations and assessing their effectiveness. Building more reliable mechanisms for disease prevention and monitoring relies heavily on the federated learning model that integrates data from different locations and populations.

Federated learning and model collaboration can be utilized for cross-device and cross-institution medical image analysis, disease diagnosis, and patient monitoring, enhancing healthcare efficiency and precision. Nonetheless, combining public databases with local clinical databases, while beneficial, does not guarantee complete data security. Improving data security and ensuring patient privacy remain critical issues that need to be addressed for the broader adoption of federated learning modeling.

## 4. Prospects and challenges of federated learning in healthcare

Federated learning was introduced as a novel AI paradigm to address the dual challenges of "data protection" and "data silos." However, the issues federated learning needs to address extend beyond these concerns. The concept of federated learning was first proposed by Google in 2016, aiming to shift the focus of artificial intelligence toward algorithms centered around secure and privacy-preserving big data architectures. Currently, numerous companies and research institutions are actively exploring federated learning applications, which may become a solution to emerging AI challenges. Similarly, medical universities and hospitals are also integrating into this exploration trend. Based on my clinical practice and research experience intersecting with artificial intelligence, I will outline the future prospects and challenges of federated learning in healthcare.

Firstly, it is essential to establish a central server at the largest and most research-intensive medical universities or hospitals worldwide, while setting up multiple clients at participating locations [17]. The central server is responsible for coordinating the training process without accessing the clients' medical data. Each client trains the model on local data and sends the parameter updates or gradient information to the central server. The central server then aggregates the updates from all clients, including its own, generates a global model update, and distributes it to all clients. Clients apply these updates to their models for the next round of training. As the algorithm training progresses, the model's effectiveness and performance steadily improve. This represents the optimal federated learning model, allowing multiple participants to collaboratively train a shared machine learning or deep learning model while maintaining data privacy and localization. The core idea of this learning method is that data does not need to leave its original location; instead, model parameters or gradient information are exchanged to train and optimize the model. The resulting model can be shared and analyzed across all participating institutions, minimizing the risk of data leakage and information exposure. Data privacy protection is the primary goal of federated learning, as medical data often contains sensitive information, such as patient identities and health records. Federated learning ensures data privacy and security by processing data and training models locally. Data sharing is also a crucial objective of federated learning, as it allows multiple healthcare institutions to collaborate without disclosing their raw data, instead sharing the results of model training, thereby enhancing model generalization and accuracy.

In the process of modeling and validation, efforts are focused on developing the most effective collaborative model algorithms. However, the distribution of populations varies across regions, leading to diverse data formats. The same algorithm may not always be optimal across different data sources. Even though, based on my experience, deep learning algorithms often exhibit better accuracy, discrimination, and clinical applicability compared to other algorithms, with moderate transport speed and shorter runtime, it is important to emphasize that this is specific to my current research. It may not apply universally to all regions and populations. Therefore, employing a combination of various algorithms, including machine learning and deep learning, for collaborative modeling and validation is essential for achieving better model performance and optimizing the model through continuous training to better align with clinical applications. The enhancement of model performance through federated learning, which integrates data from different medical institutions, is crucial for disease diagnosis, treatment, and prevention.

Future trends in federated learning include [18] enhanced privacy protection, where distributed AI will focus more on advanced encryption and privacy protection technologies to ensure the security of personal data. Broader collaboration [19] is also anticipated, with distributed AI expected to enable model cooperation across multiple vertical domains to address more complex issues. This includes autonomous intelligent systems, where distributed AI will become more self-reliant and intelligent, capable of making independent decisions rather than merely executing centralized models. Additionally, integration with augmented reality (AR) and virtual reality (VR) is expected, aiming to provide a more immersive user experience and higher levels of interaction. Lastly, the growth of edge computing [20] will drive the continued expansion of distributed AI applications on edge devices to achieve lower latency and higher performance.

Despite its advantages, federated learning faces several challenges [21], including Privacy and Security. Privacy breaches during model training and application remain a major obstacle to AI development. Although federated learning is an efficient privacy protection method that trains models locally without accessing raw data, it is still vulnerable to security risks such as poisoning attacks, adversarial attacks, and privacy leaks [22]. Communication efficiency is also a main issue [23], training complex machine learning algorithms, especially deep learning models, requires handling a large number of parameters. For instance, Convolutional Neural Networks (CNNs) may involve millions of parameters, and updating these parameters can be costly. Furthermore, network conditions such as instability and inconsistent upload/download speeds can significantly increase the communication cost of model training. Another major issue in federated learning is the heterogeneity among numerous client devices [24], which includes differences in storage, CPU computing power, and network transmission. These discrepancies can lead to varying computation times and even cause some devices to drop out entirely. Additionally, data heterogeneity [25, 26] poses a challenge in federated learning. Devices often generate and collect data in a non-independent and identically distributed manner. For instance, data heterogeneity can occur when users of different languages input text into a predictive text application on mobile devices. Furthermore, the quantity of data held by different devices across the network is often unevenly distributed. Consequently, many optimization algorithms designed for independent and identically distributed data are not suitable for federated learning.

Overall, federated learning aims to address data protection and data silos by allowing data to be shared and models to be trained while maintaining privacy. Through these methods, federated learning enables data sharing and model training without sharing the raw data, thereby protecting user privacy while advancing artificial intelligence.

Collaboration models also play a crucial role in the modeling process. Sometimes, a single model algorithm may not yield reliable results for complex problems. Instead, multiple independent models working together can provide more credible solutions, making this collaborative approach a reasonable model for future federated learning. Although federated learning faces challenges and obstacles in its future adoption and application, the rapid development of artificial intelligence cannot be halted. The industry transformation and social progress driven by AI will impact more people. All problems represent both challenges and opportunities. As scientists, seizing these opportunities and contributing to advancements will lead to greater achievements and create a brighter future for humanity.

**Author details**

Luwei Li
Guangxi Hospital Division of the First Affiliated Hospital, Sun Yat-sen University, Nanning, Guangxi, China

*Address all correspondence to: llw135318@gmail.com

## References

[1] Hamet P, Tremblay J. Artificial intelligence in medicine. Metabolism. 2017;**69S**:S36-S40

[2] Li H, Cai Z, Wang J, Tang J, Ding W, Lin CT, et al. Fed TP: Federated learning by transformer personalization. IEEE Transactions on Neural Networks and Learning Systems. Oct 2024;**35**(10):13426-13440

[3] Deo RC. Machine learning in medicine. Circulation. 2015;**132**(20):1920-1930

[4] Choi RY, Coyner AS, Kalpathy-Cramer J, Chiang MF, Campbell JP. Introduction to machine learning, neural networks, and deep learning. Translational Vision Science & Technology. 2020;**9**(2):14

[5] Asiimwe R, Lam S, Leung S, Wang S, Wan R, Tinker A, et al. From biobank and data silos into a data commons: Convergence to support translational medicine. Journal of Translational Medicine. 2021;**19**(1):493

[6] Sheller MJ, Edwards B, Reina GA, Martin J, Pati S, Kotrotsou A, et al. Federated learning in medicine: Facilitating multi-institutional collaborations without sharing patient data. Scientific Reports. 2020;**10**(1):12598

[7] Zhou H, Tang J, Zheng H. Machine learning for medical applications. The Scientific World Journal. 2015;**2015**:825267

[8] Wang H, Hu X. Deep learning in bioinformatics and biomedicine. Methods. 2023;**209**:38-39

[9] Wainberg M, Merico D, Delong A, Frey BJ. Deep learning in biomedicine. Nature Biotechnology. 2018;**36**(9):829-838

[10] Jorayeva M, Akbulut A, Catal C, Mishra A. Machine learning-based software defect prediction for Mobile applications: A systematic literature review. Sensors (Basel). 2022;**22**(7):2551

[11] Georgevici AI, Terblanche M. Neural networks and deep learning: A brief introduction. Intensive Care Medicine. 2019;**45**(5):712-714

[12] Data sharing in the age of deep learning. Nature Biotechnology. 2023;**41**(4):433

[13] Patel M, Dayan I, Fishman EK, Flores M, Gilbert FJ, Guindy M, et al. Accelerating artificial intelligence: How federated learning can protect privacy, facilitate collaboration, and improve outcomes. Health Informatics Journal. 2023;**29**(4):14604582231207744

[14] Huang D, Ye X, Sakurai T. Multi-party collaborative drug discovery via federated learning. Computers in Biology and Medicine. 2024;**171**:108181

[15] Li S, Liu P, Nascimento GG, Wang X, Leite FRM, Chakraborty B, et al. Federated and distributed learning applications for electronic health records and structured medical data: A scoping review. Journal of the American Medical Informatics Association. 2023;**30**(12):2041-2049

[16] Nguyen TV, Dakka MA, Diakiw SM, Ver Milyea MD, Perugini M, Hall JMM, et al. A novel decentralized federated learning approach to train on globally distributed, poor quality, and protected private medical data. Scientific Reports. 2022;**12**(1):8888

[17] Chen Y, Lu W, Qin X, Wang J, Xie X. Meta fed: Federated learning among federations with cyclic knowledge distillation for personalized healthcare. IEEE Transactions on Neural Networks and Learning Systems. Nov 2024;**35**(11):16671-16682

[18] Brauneck A, Schmalhorst L, Kazemi Majdabadi MM, Bakhtiari M, Völker U, Baumbach J, et al. Federated machine learning, privacy-enhancing technologies, and data protection Laws in medical research: Scoping review. Journal of Medical Internet Research. 2023;**25**:e41588

[19] Yang B, Yuen PC, Zhang Y, Zeng A. Allosteric feature collaboration for model-heterogeneous federated learning. IEEE Transactions on Neural Networks and Learning Systems. 25 Dec 2023

[20] Abreha HG, Hayajneh M, Serhani MA. Federated learning in edge computing: A systematic survey. Sensors (Basel). 2022;**22**(2):450

[21] Aouedi O, Sacco A, Piamrat K, Marchetto G. Handling privacy-sensitive medical data with federated learning: Challenges and future directions. IEEE Journal of Biomedical and Health Informatics. 2023;**27**(2):790-803

[22] Loftus TJ, Ruppert MM, Shickel B, Ozrazgat-Baslanti T, Balch JA, Efron PA, et al. Federated learning for preserving data privacy in collaborative healthcare research. Digital Health. 2022;**8**:20552076221134455

[23] Chen M, Shlezinger N, Poor HV, Eldar YC, Cui S. Communication-efficient federated learning. Proceedings of the National Academy of Sciences of the United States of America. 2021;**118**(17):e2024789118

[24] Qu L, Zhou Y, Liang PP, Xia Y, Wang F, Adeli E, et al. Rethinking architecture Design for Tackling Data Heterogeneity in federated learning. Proceedings of the IEEE Computer Society Conference on Computer Vision and Pattern Recognition. 2022;**2022**:10051-10061

[25] Rajendran S, Xu Z, Pan W, Ghosh A, Wang F. Data heterogeneity in federated learning with electronic health records: Case studies of risk prediction for acute kidney injury and sepsis diseases in critical care. PLos Digital Health. 2023;**2**(3):e0000117

[26] Yan R, Qu L, Wei Q, Huang SC, Shen L, Rubin DL, et al. Label-efficient self-supervised federated learning for tackling data heterogeneity in medical imaging. IEEE Transactions on Medical Imaging. 2023;**42**(7):1932-1943

Chapter 5

# Federated Learning with Partially Class-Disjoint Data

*Ziqing Fan and Jiangchao Yao*


## Abstract

Essentially, the federation of multiple clients is to acquire more complete information to promote learning a powerful model that recognizes general patterns of wider classes. However, a natural case usually presents in the real-world situation under a large label space, where only a subset of classes of samples are provided by individual clients. We term this practical setting as "federated learning with partially class-disjoint data" (PCDD), to differentiate from the ordinary study without emphasizing this extreme scenario. Generally, this setting is very challenging as different clients own partial classes and the resulting model on the client side cannot well support full-class topology for aggregation. In this chapter, we first show the significant difference of federation in PCDD compared to that in traditional non-IID studies, and then dissect recent advances concerning this challenge, following with discussion about the future trends. We illustrate the challenges using experimental results on benchmark datasets under PCDD conditions, finding that effective solutions to PCDD problems should provide optimal structures for global objective and allow flexible structures for personalized tasks. We make systematical analysis to underscore the significance of PCDD in heterogeneous federated learning and to inspire more explorations in the future.


**Keywords:** federated learning, heterogeneity, partially class-disjoint data, representation learning, neural collapse

## 1. Introduction

Federated learning (FL) has garnered significant attention in response to the growing emphasis on collaborative learning methodologies. Its foundational framework, FedAvg [1], enables clients to retain their private data locally while collectively contributing to the development of a more comprehensive and powerful model. However, the performance of federated learning is substantially constrained by statistical heterogeneity, which arises from the non-IID (non-independent and identically distributed) nature of data across clients [2–4].

The challenge, data heterogeneity among clients, can be roughly divided into label distribution skew, feature distribution skew, and quantity skew [3]. To address the problem, extensive efforts have been made to enhance federated optimization

 IntechOpen

techniques [2, 5–11]. However, most of the recent algorithms in solving label distribution skew have concentrated on heterogeneous scenarios, where each client typically retains a majority of the classes of samples, albeit with variations in covariate shifts, as depicted in **Figure 1(a)**. In practical real-world applications, a common issue arises wherein individual clients are only able to provide a subset of the overall classes of samples, a situation we term partially class-disjoint data (PCDD), as illustrated in **Figure 1(b)**. For instance, due to regional diversity, hospitals in different locations may encounter both shared and distinct thyroid diseases [13]. These hospitals can form a federation to collaboratively develop a comprehensive diagnostic model for thyroid diseases, but contend with the challenges presented by PCDD.

In the context of PCDD, each client possesses only a small subset of the overall categories, with the complete set of classes being collectively distributed across all clients. In the chapter, we analyze the federated optimization under PCDD settings from the views of the layer-peeled model [14–16] that dividing model weights into feature and classifier. This incomplete representation of classes leads to a significant optimization difference of the feature space and classifier angle between the client and the global server. Behind the optimization dilemma, we observe two phenomena named angle collapse for the classifier vectors of locally absent classes and inefficient utilization of feature space for locally present classes. Ideally, as illustrated in **Figure 2a**, the global feature space and corresponding classifier vectors should maintain a well-structured alignment to achieve optimal class separation. However, when training on individual clients with partially class-disjoint data, the angles of the classifier vectors for locally missing classes tend to collapse, as demonstrated in **Figure 2b** and **c**. Recent studies that try to constrain local structure with idea global all-class topology will cause the waste of feature space as shown in **Figure 2d**, which might limit the model capacity for personal task.

We classify recent studies directly or potentially addressing the PCDD problem into two broad categories: generic federated learning (G-FL) and personalized federated learning (P-FL) algorithms, as summarized in **Table 1**. G-FL algorithms [5, 6,

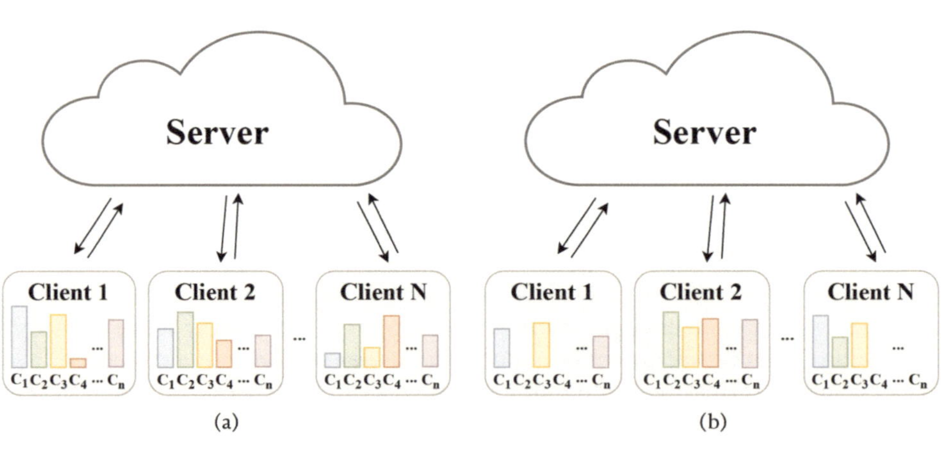


**Figure 1.**
*Federated learning under typical heterogeneous setting and partially class-disjoint data (PCDD) from FedMR [12]. In typical heterogeneous federated learning, each client usually contains most classes of samples but under different covariate shifts as shown in (a). In PCDD settings, each client only has a subset of classes of samples can be provided by individual clients as shown in (b). (a) Typical federated learning. (b) Federated learning under PCDD.*

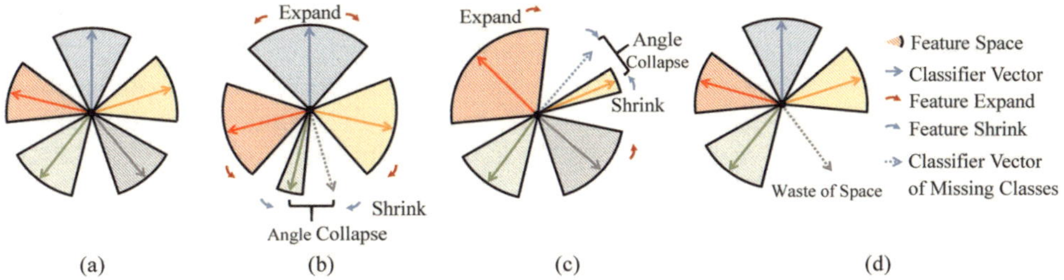


**Figure 2.**
*Illustration of feature spaces and classifier vectors trained on the global dataset, two partially class-disjoint datasets (A and B), and restricted by federated algorithms from FedGELA [11]. (a) is trained on the globally balanced dataset with full classes. (b) and (c) are trained on datasets A and B, respectively, which suffer from different patterns of classifier angle collapse problems. (d) is averaged in the server or constrained by some federated algorithms. (a) Ideal Structure (b) Collapsed Structure A (c) Collapsed Structure B (d) Restricted Structure.*

| Target | Research work | Mitigate angle collapse | Save feature space |
|---|---|---|---|
| G-FL | FedMR [12] | ✓ | — |
| | MOON [5] | ✓ | — |
| | FedProx [6] | ✓ | — |
| | FedGen [10] | ✓ | — |
| | FedAWS [17] | ✓ | — |
| | FedRS [18] | ✓ | — |
| | FedLC [19] | ✓ | — |
| P-FL | FedRep [7] | — | ✓ |
| | FedProto [8] | — | ✓ |
| | FedBABU [9] | — | ✓ |
| | FedBN [20] | — | ✓ |
| | FedPER [21] | — | ✓ |
| G&P-FL | FedRod [22] | — | ✓ |
| | FedGELA [11] | ✓ | ✓ |

**Table 1.**
*Key differences between recent innovations categorized by their targets on personalized federated learning (P-FL) or generic federated learning (G-FL), and whether directly mitigate angle collapse of classifier vectors or save locally wasted feature spaces caused by PCDD.*

10, 12, 17–19] typically adopt a uniform approach to all classes within the federation, primarily constraining local logits, features, or model weights to align with the global model. In contrast, P-FL algorithms [7–9, 20, 21] place less emphasis on classes absent locally, often allowing for greater flexibility in client-specific model structures. Notably, some recent studies incorporate elements of both G-FL and P-FL methodologies. For instance, FedRod [22] seeks to bridge this gap by introducing a two-head framework and employing logit adjustment in the global head to approximate a generic distribution. FedGELA [11] globally fixes the classifier as a simplex equiangular tight frame (ETF) while allowing local adaptation to personal distributions. Additionally, based on our observations, we distinguish these algorithms by their capacity to either mitigate angle collapse for the global task or optimize feature space utilization for the personal task. G-FL algorithms can mitigate angle collapse problem but waste the feature spaces for locally existing classes as shown in **Figure 2d**, while P-FL methods save feature spaces but meet significant collapse and fail in global task as shown in **Figure 2b** and **c**. FedRod cannot address the issue of angle collapse, while FedGELA is the only one that can both mitigate the angle collapse and the waste space problem caused by PCDD.

Finally, we benchmark three widely-used datasets—SVHN [23], CIFAR10, and CIFAR100 [24] in the context of federated learning and re-show the experimental results of FedGELA [11] to compare related algorithms targeting both P-FL and G-FL objectives under PCDD settings. The results indicate that, under PCDD conditions, the overall performance of generic models is constrained, whereas personal distributions are more readily captured, highlighting the significant angle collapse phenomenon. For P-FL methods, performance on global tasks deteriorates, particularly in severe PCDD scenarios, as these methods often share less model structure and neglect global convergence during training. Conversely, while G-FL algorithms show improved performance in generic tasks, their efficacy in personalized tasks is limited due to the constraints imposed on local structures. In conclusion, designing a comprehensive federated algorithm that effectively addresses both P-FL and G-FL objectives under PCDD conditions requires balancing the ideal structure for global tasks with the collapsed structure for personal tasks. Algorithms that are designed to accommodate both P-FL and G-FL considerations tend to perform better, with FedGELA standing out as particularly effective. FedGELA excels in mitigating angle collapse for globally full classes while preserving feature space for locally missing classes, achieving the best performance under severe PCDD settings.

The rest of the contents is organized as follows. Section 2 introduces the preliminaries of this chapter, including the overview of federated learning via FedAvg and data heterogeneity problems. Section 3 presents the definition, some real applications, and the simulation way of partially class-disjoint data [11, 12, 18]. Section 3.3.2 analyzes the optimization difference from the view of LPM and shows two observations derived from the dilemma caused by PCDD. In Sections 4 and 5, we summarize some existing federated algorithms that might be helpful for PCDD settings and discuss experimental results on benchmark datasets in FedGELA [11]. We aspire for this survey to underscore the significance of PCDD scenarios in heterogeneous federated learning and to inspire future research in this rapidly evolving field.

## 2. Preliminaries

In this section, we outline the foundational concepts that underpin this chapter, including an overview of federated learning (FL) through the FedAvg framework, as discussed in Section 2.1, followed by an exploration of data heterogeneity in FL and a concise introduction to the PCDD problem in Section 2.2.

### 2.1 Federated learning via FedAvg

In traditional centralized training paradigms, clients typically upload their data to a central server, where a model is subsequently trained [25]. However, with the growing concern over data privacy, there has been a notable shift toward retaining sensitive data locally [26, 27]. In this context, federated learning has emerged as a prominent approach, garnering significant attention for its application in various tasks, including medical diagnosis [28], auto-driving [29] and visual recognition [30].

The vanilla federated learning via FedAvg consists of four steps [1]: (1) In round $t$, the server distributes the global model $w^t$ to clients that participate in the training; (2) Each local client receives the model and continues to train the model, *e.g.*, the $k$-th client conducts the following,

$$w_k^t \leftarrow w_k^t - \eta \nabla \ell_k \left( b_k^t; w_k^t \right), \tag{1}$$

where $\eta$ is the learning rate, and $b_k^t$ is a mini-batch of training data randomly sampled from the local dataset $\mathcal{D}_k$. After $E$ epochs, we acquire a new local model $w_k^t$; (3) The updated models are then collected to the server as $\{w_1^t, w_2^t, \dots, w_K^t\}$; (4) The server performs the following aggregation to acquire a new global model $w^{t+1}$,

$$w^{t+1} \leftarrow \sum_{k=1}^{K} p_k w_k^t, \tag{2}$$

where $p_k$ is the proportion of sample number of the $k$-th client to the sample number of all the participants, *i.e.*, $p_k = N_k \sum_{k'=1}^{K} N_{k'}$. When the predefined maximal round $T$ reaches, we will have the final optimized model $w^T$.

## 2.2 Data heterogeneity in federated learning

Statistical heterogeneity, a defining characteristic of non-IID data, introduces model bias within local clients. In traditional centralized training paradigms, this issue is typically mitigated through the use of a unified model trained via stochastic gradient descent [31]. However, in the context of federated learning, statistical heterogeneity poses a significant challenge when aggregating diverse client models. Specifically, prior research indicates that the presence of statistical heterogeneity leads to substantial differences in the gradients derived from various client models, thereby diminishing the overall performance of federated approachess [3–6, 12, 17, 18].

Data heterogeneity can typically be categorized into three types [3]: label distribution skew, feature distribution skew, and quantity skew. In label distribution skew, the label distributions $P(y_i)$ vary across clients. Feature distribution skew occurs when the feature distributions $P(x_i)$ differ among clients, despite the conditional knowledge $P(y_i|x_i)$ remaining consistent. Quantity skew refers to the variation in the size of local datasets $|D_i|$ across clients. In this chapter, we focus on a specific type of label distribution skew. Most previous studies addressing data heterogeneity have been designed for scenarios where clients contain most classes of samples, but with differences arising from covariate shifts, as depicted in **Figure 1(a)**. In practical settings, a common issue is that individual clients may only have access to a subset of the total classes of samples, a situation we refer to as partially class-disjoint data (PCDD), as illustrated in **Figure 1(b)**. For example, due to regional diversity [13], different hospitals may encounter both shared and distinct Thyroid diseases. These hospitals can collaborate within a federated learning framework to develop a comprehensive diagnostic model for thyroid diseases, but they face challenges related to PCDD. In the following sections, we will define the PCDD problem, introduce related algorithms, and compare and discuss these algorithms using benchmark datasets.

## 3. PCDD: Partially class-disjoint data

In this section, we first define partially class-disjoint data (PCDD) mathematically, present real-world applications of PCDD, and demonstrate how to simulate PCDD scenarios on public datasets with uniform class distribution. Additionally, we analyze the optimization challenges inherent to PCDD.

### 3.1 PCDD definition

To make it clear, we first define some notations of the partially disjoint data situation in federated learning. Let $C$ denote the collection of full classes, and $P$ denote the set of all local clients. Considering the real-world constraints like privacy or environmental limitation, each local client only owns the samples of partial classes. Formally, for the $k$-th client $P_k$, its corresponding local dataset $D_k$ can be expressed in the following

$$D_k = \left\{ \left(x_{k,i}, y_{k,i}\right) | y_{k,i} = c \in C_k \right\}, \text{where } C_k \subsetneq C. \tag{3}$$

The number of samples of the class $c$ ($c \in C_k$) in $P_k$ is $N_k^c$. In typical label distribution skew situations, the number of samples per class, $N_k^c$, varies among clients, while the total class number $C_k$ generally remains the same or similar in scale. However, in PCDD scenarios, $C_k$ differs significantly across clients.

### 3.2 Real PCDD application and simulation

There are numerous non-negligible real-world scenarios involving PCDD. Here, we highlight some public datasets suitable for further research in this area. The ISIC2019 [32–34] dataset serves as a region-driven subset representing types of thyroid diseases within hospital systems, where each hospital can only provide data for a portion of the total disease categories. In the context of landmark detection [35] involving thousands of categories with locally preserved data, most contributors possess images for only a subset of landmark categories specific to the regions they reside in or have traveled to, exemplifying a federated PCDD scenario. Similarly, in facial detection tasks, the CelebA [36] dataset comprises 202,599 face images of 10,177 celebrities. In this scenario, each celebrity, acting as a client with their facial images, can only provide data for several attributes out of the total 40 facial attributes. For quick evaluation and simulation of PCDD scenarios on public datasets with uniform label distribution, we introduce two widely used strategies: Dirichlet distribution partitioning and pathological partitioning. Pathological partitioning, controlled by the hyperparameter $\alpha$, directly induces PCDD scenarios by regulating the number of sample classes available to each client. Dirichlet distribution partitioning, governed by the hyperparameter $\beta$, controls the variance in sample distribution among clients, thereby introducing varying degrees of heterogeneity and enabling the simulation of more complex scenarios beyond PCDD. As illustrated in **Figure 3**, we present heatmaps of data distribution under Dirichlet distribution with different values of $\beta$ on two popular public datasets for machine learning: CIFAR10 and CIFAR100 [24]. A smaller $\beta$ value generates more severe PCDD conditions.

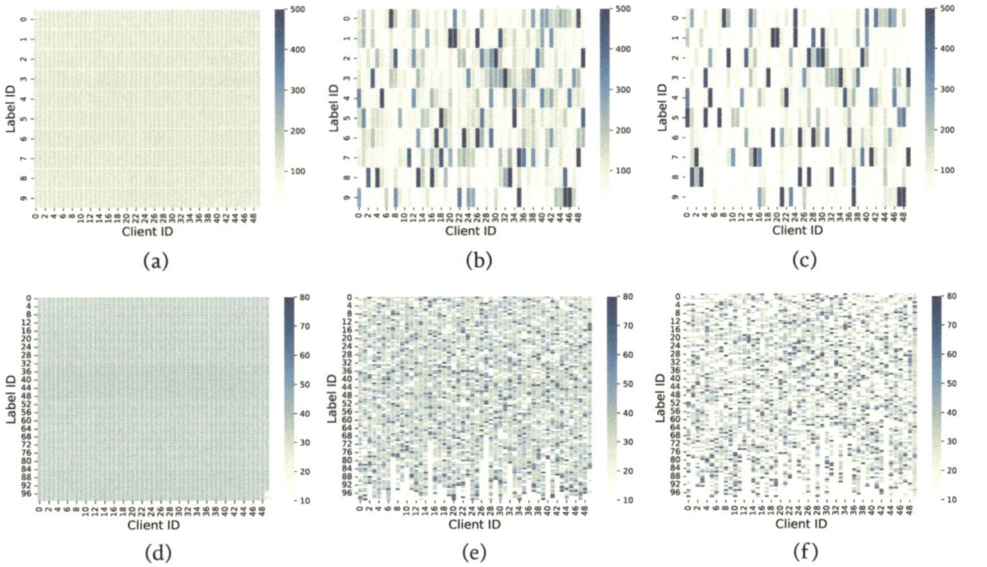


**Figure 3.**
*Heatmap of data distribution under Dirichlet distribution with different β from FedGELA [11]. The empty color denotes there is no sample of a category in a client, indicating the PCDD situation. (a) CIFAR10 (? = 10000). (c) CIFAR10 (? = 0.2) (d) CIFAR100 (? = 10000). (e) CIFAR100 (? = 0.5). (f) CIFAR100 (? = 0.2).*

## 3.3 PCDD challenges

Here we introduce the contradictions inherent in optimizing federated models in typical scenarios versus PCDD situations through the view of a layer-peeled model (LPM) [14–16] and discuss the corresponding observations.

### *3.3.1 LPM: Layer-peeled model*

A typical L-layer DNN parameterized by $w$ can be divided into the feature backbone parameterized by $w^{-L}$ and the classifier parameterized by $w^L$. From the view of layer-peeled model (LPM) [14–16], training $w$ with constraints on the weights can be considered as training the C-class classifier $w^L = \{w_1^L, \ldots, w_C^L\}$ and features $\mathbf{H} = \{h^1, \ldots, h^n\}$ of all $n$ samples output by last layer of the backbone with constraints $E_W$ and $E_H$ on them, respectively. On the balanced data, any solutions to this model form a simplex equiangular tight frame (ETF) that all last layer features $h_c^{i,*}$ and corresponding classifier $w_c^{L,*}$ of all classes converge as:

$$\frac{h_c^{i,*}}{\sqrt{E_H}} = \frac{w_c^{L,*}}{\sqrt{E_W}} = m_c^*, \tag{4}$$

where $m_c^*$ forms the ETF defined as $M = \sqrt{\frac{C}{C-1}}\mathbf{U}\left(\mathbf{I}_C - \frac{1}{C}\mathbf{1}_C\mathbf{1}_C^T\right)$. Here $M = [m_1^*, \cdots, m_C^*] \in \mathbb{R}^{d\times C}, \mathbf{U} \in \mathbb{R}^{d\times C}$ allows a rotation and satisfies $\mathbf{U}^T\mathbf{U} = \mathbf{I}_C$, and $\mathbf{1}_C$ is an all-ones vector. ETF is an optimal classifier and feature structure in the balanced case of LPM.

### *3.3.2 Optimization contradiction and observation*

From the view of LPM, the ideal global objective of federated learning is described as:

$$\min_{\mathbf{H}, w^L} \sum_{k=1}^{N} p_k \frac{1}{n_k} \sum_{c \in C_k} \sum_{i=1}^{n_{k,c}} \mathscr{L}_{CE}\left(h_{k,c}^i, w^L\right). \tag{5}$$

Assuming global distribution is balanced among classes, no matter whether local datasets have full or partial classes, the global objective with constraints on weights can be simplified as:

$$\min_{\mathbf{H}, w^L} \frac{1}{n} \sum_{c=1}^{C} \sum_{i=1}^{n_c} \mathscr{L}_{CE}\left(h_c^i, w^L\right), \text{s.t.} \left\|w_c^L\right\|^2 \leqslant E_W, \left\|h_c^i\right\|^2 \leqslant E_H. \tag{6}$$

Similarly, the local objective of k-th client with a set of classes $C_k$ can be described as:

$$\min_{\mathbf{H}_k, w_k^L} \frac{1}{n_k} \sum_{c \in C_k} \sum_{i=1}^{n_{k,c}} \mathscr{L}_{CE}\left(h_{k,c}^i, w_k^L\right), \text{s.t.} \left\|w_{k,c}^L\right\|^2 \leqslant E_W, \left\|h_{k,c}^i\right\|^2 \leqslant E_H. \tag{7}$$

When PCDD exists ($C_k \neq C$), we can see the contradiction between local and global objectives, which, respectively, forms two structures, shown in **Figure 2(a)** and **(b)**. Ideally, as shown in **Figure 2(a)**, global features and their corresponding classifier vectors shall maintain a proper structure to pursue the best separation of all classes. However, the angles of locally missing classes' classifier vectors will collapse, when trained on each client with partially class-disjoint data, as depicted in **Figure 2 (b)** and **(c)**. After aggregated in server or constrained by some FL methods, the structure in the local is restricted to meet the global structure, causing space waste for personal tasks shown in **Figure 2(d)**.

## 4. Recent innovations on solving PCDD

There are extensive works addressing statistical heterogeneity in federated learning. In the subsequent sections, we categorize related algorithms that may be effective in solving PCDD problems based on their primary objectives: generic federated learning (G-FL) and personalized federated learning (P-FL). G-FL focuses on generating an improved global model for the global task, whereas P-FL is more concerned with enhancing client-specific models for their respective tasks. We introduce G-FL algorithms in Section 4.1 and P-FL algorithms in Section 4.2. Recent studies that attempt to address data heterogeneity from both perspectives are discussed in Section 4.3. Based on observations related to angle collapse and the inefficient use of local feature space, we summarize relevant works in **Table 1**, distinguishing them based on whether they directly mitigate the angle collapse of classifier vectors or utilize locally wasted feature spaces under PCDD.

### 4.1 G-FL: Generic federated learning

Generic federated learning (G-FL) aims to produce a superior global model for the overarching task, and many of these approaches mitigate angle collapse by aligning local models or features with the global model. For instance, FedProx [6] constrains local model weights to remain close to the global model. FedAWS [17] employs a geometric regularizer to ensure that classes are well-distributed in the embedding space. FedRS [18] addresses angle collapse by constraining the logits of missing classes. MOON [5] and FedGen [10] leverage contrastive learning and generative learning, respectively, to align local representations with the global model. FedMR [12] proposes a manifold reshaping technique that adjusts class feature embeddings to calibrate the local feature space during training. FedLC [19] introduces logit calibration to adjust the logits of the local model, bringing them in line with the global model, which may indirectly alleviate angle collapse at the local level. However, all these methods attempt to enforce a global structure on the local models, which can lead to inefficient use of feature space for personalized tasks, as depicted in **Figure 2(d)**.

---

**Algorithm 1.** FedGELA

---

**Input**: $(N, K, n_k, c_k, \mathbf{H}^0, M, E_W, E_H, T, \eta, E)$
  Parallelly for all clients: $w_k^L \leftarrow \Phi_k \sqrt{E_W} M$
  **for** $t = 0, 1, \ldots, T-1$ **do**
    ⊳ on the server side
    $\mathbf{H}^t \leftarrow \sum_{k=1}^{K} p_k^t H_k^{t-1}$. sample $K$ clients from all $N$ clients.
    ⊳ on the k-th client side
    receive $\mathbf{H}^t$ from server, $\mathbf{H}_k^t \leftarrow \mathbf{H}^t$
    **for** $\tau = 0, 1, \ldots, E-1$ **do**
      sample a mini-batch $b_k^{tE+\tau}$ in local data
      $H_k^t \leftarrow H_k^t - \eta \nabla F_k\left(b_k^t, \Phi_k W_g^L; \mathbf{H}_k^t\right)$
    end for
    submit $\mathbf{H}_k^t$ to the server
  **end for**
**Output**: $\left(\mathbf{H}^T, W_g^L\right)$ and $\left(\mathbf{H}_k^T, \Phi_k W_g^L\right)$

---

### 4.2 P-FL: Personalized federated learning

P-FL algorithms seek to utilize the otherwise wasted feature space by encouraging angle collapse in the local classifiers. FedPER [21], for instance, introduces a base model with personalization layers specifically tailored to individual tasks. FedRep [7] shares only feature extractors among clients, while FedProto [8] submits only class prototypes, thereby reducing communication costs and aligning feature spaces. FedBN [20] employs local batch normalization to mitigate feature shift before model averaging. In FedBABU [9], the classifier is randomly initialized and fixed during federated training, with fine-tuning applied during evaluation for personalization. However, these approaches often compromise the generic performance across all classes.

### 4.3 Combining both P-FL and G-FL

Some recent studies have sought to address data heterogeneity by integrating the perspectives of both P-FL and G-FL. FedRod [22] attempts to bridge this gap by introducing a dual-head framework, incorporating logit adjustment in the global head to estimate the generic distribution. However, it falls short in addressing angle collapse. In contrast, FedGELA [11] can both mitigates angle collapse for globally full classes and utilizes feature space of locally missing classes by introducing a simplex equiangular tight frame (ETF). Since FedGELA is a representative algorithm to address both problems, we provide the detailed introduction about how it solves them in the following:

**FedGELA**. Given the global aim of achieving an unbiased classifier that treats all classes equally and provides them with the same discrimination and classifier angles, FedGELA curates the global model's classifier as a randomly initialized simplex ETF with scaling $\sqrt{E_w}$ at the start of federated training, which follows Eq. (8) as below

$$w^L = \sqrt{E_w}M. \tag{8}$$

Then the ETF is distributed to all clients to replace their local classifiers. In the theoretical analysis of FedGELA [11], by fixing the classifier as a randomly simplex ETF with scaling $\sqrt{E_W}$ and constraints $E_H$ on the last layer features, features output by last layer of backbone and their within class means will converge to the ETF similar to Eq. (4), which meets the requirement of global tasks. However, when PCDD exists in the local clients, naively combining ETF with FL does not meet the requirement of P-FL as analyzed in Eqs. (6) and (7). To utilize the wasted space for locally missing classes, in the training stage, FedGELA curates the length of ETF received from the server based on the local distribution as below:

$$w_k^L = \Phi_k w^L = \Phi_k \sqrt{E_w}M, \tag{9}$$

where $\Phi_k$ is the distribution matrix of k-th client. To meet the requirement that averaged classifier should be standard ETF: $w^L = \sum_{k=1}^{N} p_k w_k^L$ in the globally balanced case, its row vectors are all one's vector multiple statistical values of personal distribution: $\left(\Phi_k^T\right)_c = \frac{n_{k,c}}{n_k \gamma}\mathbf{1}$ ($\gamma$ is a constant, and $n_{k,c}$ and $n_k$ are the c-th class sample number and total sample number of the k-th client), respectively. FedGELA sets $\gamma$ to $\frac{1}{|C|}$. Finally, the local objective from Eq. (7) is adapted as:

$$\begin{aligned} \min_{\mathbf{H}_k} \quad & \frac{1}{n_k}\sum_{c=1}^{C}\sum_{i=1}^{n_{k,c}} -\log \frac{\exp\left(\Phi_{k,c} {w_c^L}^T h_{k,c}^i\right)}{\sum_{c' \in C_k} \exp\left(\Phi_{k,c'} {w_{c'}^L}^T h_{k,c}^i\right)}, \\ \text{s.t.} \quad & \|h^i\|^2 \leqslant E_H, \forall 1 \leqslant i \leqslant n_k. \end{aligned} \tag{10}$$

After introducing key parts of FedGELA, the total framework is illustrated in Algorithm 1. At the initializing stage, the server randomly generates an ETF as the global classifier and sends it to all clients while local clients adjust it based on the personal distribution matrix as Eq. (9). At the training stage, local clients receive global backbones and train with adapted ETF in parallel. After $E$ epochs, all clients submit personal backbones to the server. In the server, personal backbones are received and aggregated to a generic backbone, which is broadcast to all clients participating in the next round. At the inference stage, on the client side, a generic backbone is obtained with standard ETF to handle the world data while on the client side, a personal backbone with adapted ETF to handle the personal data.

## 5. Benchmark results and discussion

To compare existing methods, we here present the benchmark and experiments under PCDD in FedGELA [11] and discuss about the results, aiming to provide insights for further studies.

### 5.1 Benchmark setup

Here we show the results on three popular benchmark datasets SVHN [23], CIFAR10/100 [24] in federated learning from FedGELA [11]. As for data splitting, Dirichlet distribution with coefficient $\beta \in \{10000, 0.5, 0.2, 0.1\}$ is employed to simulate the situations of independently identical distribution and different levels of PCDD. Commonly used ResNet18 [37] model is used as the backbone for all datasets [2, 5, 8, 9, 37]. One layer of FC as the projection layer (the hidden size is 84 for SVHN and CIFAR10 and 512 for CIFAR100) is additionally employed for feature-based methods like MOON [5], FedMR [12], and FedProto [8]. For FedGELA, the model is a backbone, projection layer with a simplex ETF or adapted ETF. All methods are evaluated by PA and GA metrics. PA is the personalized accuracy, which is the mean of the accuracy computed on each client test dataset. GA is the generic accuracy on global test dataset (mixed clients' test datasets). Since there is no global model in P-FL methods, GA of them is the averaged accuracy of all best local models on global test dataset, which is the same as FedRod [22]. PA is the best results of personal models for P-FL methods while for G-FL methods, it is the results of the best global model tuned on personal task in 10 epochs. For FedRod and FedGELA, GA and PA can be directly obtained (without fine-tuning) during training. Training details can be found in the original paper of FedGELA [11].

### 5.2 Main results and discussion

As shown in **Table 2**, as the Dirichlet distribution coefficient $\beta$ decreases or the number of clients increases, the generic performance of FedAvg and all other methods significantly drops, while the personal performance of all methods improves considerably. This indicates that under PCDD conditions and in the presence of the straggler problem, the generic performance is constrained, but personal distributions are more easily captured. In addition, under severe PCDD settings, we have identified three main findings among existing methods:

*P-FL methods struggle with global tasks.* Particularly under severe PCDD conditions, P-FL methods fail in global tasks as they do not prioritize global convergence during training. The more these methods impose limitations on the shared components of the model, the poorer their aggregated model's performance becomes on general tasks.

*G-FL methods are limited in personalized tasks.* G-FL methods tend to perform better in generic tasks but are limited in personalized tasks, particularly in more complex scenarios such as CIFAR100. These methods constrain the model's ability to adapt to personalized distributions during local training, which enhances consistency during global optimization. However, these constraints also limit the client models' capacity to effectively distinguish local classes, leading to unsatisfactory personal performance.

*Methods for both P-FL and G-FL that can both mitigate angle collapse and utilize the wasted feature space perform better.* Methods like FedRod and FedGELA designed to address both P-FL and G-FL objectives generally outperform other baselines across all

| Dataset | Method | Full Participation (10, 10) | | | | | | Partial Participation (50, 10) | | | | | |
|---|---|---|---|---|---|---|---|---|---|---|---|---|---|
| | #Partition | IID | | $\beta = 0.5$ | | $\beta = 0.1$ | | IID | | $\beta = 0.5$ | | $\beta = 0.2$ | |
| | #Metric | PA | GA | PA | GA | PA | GA | PA | GA | PA | GA | PA | GA |
| SVHN | FedAvg | 93.01 | 92.61 | 93.95 | 91.24 | 98.10 | 75.24 | 91.44 | 91.29 | 92.70 | 89.29 | 95.31 | 84.70 |
| | FedProx | 93.12 | 93.12 | 93.71 | 92.15 | 97.98 | 75.13 | 91.67 | 91.66 | 92.71 | 89.98 | 95.13 | 85.68 |
| | MOON | 93.16 | 93.16 | 92.98 | 92.46 | 98.06 | 76.21 | 93.49 | 91.41 | 91.86 | 90.20 | 95.78 | 86.22 |
| | FedRS | 93.29 | 93.21 | 93.92 | 92.33 | 98.04 | 76.26 | 91.63 | 91.59 | 93.51 | 91.70 | 96.20 | 87.78 |
| | FedGen | 94.02 | 93.99 | 94.47 | 92.66 | 98.22 | 76.51 | 91.47 | 91.33 | 93.67 | 91.35 | 95.77 | 87.59 |
| | FedLC | 93.29 | 93.28 | 94.76 | 91.20 | 98.24 | 76.17 | 91.69 | 91.67 | 92.73 | 91.02 | 95.20 | 86.92 |
| | FedRep | 93.01 | 92.61 | 94.77 | 91.24 | 97.87 | 68.52 | 91.77 | 89.20 | 93.14 | 80.94 | 95.38 | 67.77 |
| | FedProto | 93.21 | 91.68 | 94.48 | 85.85 | 98.26 | 56.49 | 90.23 | 87.27 | 93.28 | 76.59 | 95.62 | 54.92 |
| | FedBABU | 93.26 | 93.08 | 95.20 | 92.04 | 98.16 | 75.52 | 93.69 | 91.05 | 93.54 | 90.49 | 95.70 | 84.42 |
| | FedRod | 93.50 | 93.22 | 95.47 | 92.09 | 98.06 | 76.24 | 92.04 | 91.65 | 93.96 | 91.20 | 95.68 | 86.98 |
| | **FedGELA** | **94.84** | **94.66** | **96.27** | **93.66** | **98.52** | **78.88** | **94.68** | **93.59** | **95.54** | **93.29** | **96.85** | **89.58** |
| CIFAR10 | FedAvg | 73.17 | 72.8 | 81.67 | 67.28 | 92.66 | 54.57 | 66.88 | 66.64 | 70.64 | 61.81 | 80.04 | 49.13 |
| | FedProx | 73.69 | 73.69 | 81.95 | 67.53 | 92.94 | 56.13 | 67.67 | 67.27 | 73.62 | 60.80 | 80.66 | 50.82 |
| | MOON | 73.29 | 73.29 | 82.27 | 68.34 | 92.90 | 55.61 | 67.58 | 67.58 | 74.64 | 61.81 | 83.42 | 52.19 |
| | FedRS | 73.56 | 72.94 | 81.59 | 68.10 | 92.57 | 58.19 | 66.76 | 66.52 | 72.21 | 58.95 | 81.11 | 51.66 |
| | FedLC | 73.05 | 73.00 | 81.99 | 67.97 | 92.48 | 57.02 | 67.46 | 67.13 | 72.57 | 61.31 | 82.14 | 55.15 |
| | FedGen | 73.72 | 73.49 | 82.22 | 69.33 | 92.79 | 58.04 | 68.74 | 68.02 | 75.52 | 62.44 | 81.07 | 53.46 |
| | FedRep | 73.42 | 73.23 | 83.30 | 47.96 | 92.92 | 38.32 | 67.85 | 67.74 | 77.28 | 42.64 | 84.52 | 33.22 |
| | FedProto | 67.06 | 66.74 | 81.03 | 46.99 | 93.17 | 32.13 | 61.85 | 52.76 | 72.89 | 37.47 | 81.73 | 26.07 |
| | FedBABU | 73.86 | 72.30 | 81.40 | 65.03 | 92.94 | 53.65 | 66.99 | 64.90 | 77.59 | 58.17 | 82.92 | 49.90 |
| | FedRod | 74.24 | 73.76 | 82.34 | 70.74 | 92.27 | 58.86 | 70.09 | 70.04 | 78.23 | 64.13 | 84.63 | 58.86 |

| Dataset | Method | Full Participation (10, 10) | | | | | | Partial Participation (50, 10) | | | | | |
|---|---|---|---|---|---|---|---|---|---|---|---|---|---|
| | #Partition | IID | | $\beta = 0.5$ | | $\beta = 0.1$ | | IID | | $\beta = 0.5$ | | $\beta = 0.2$ | |
| | #Metric | PA | GA | PA | GA | PA | GA | PA | GA | PA | GA | PA | GA |
| | **FedGELA** | **75.02** | **74.07** | **84.52** | **72.73** | **94.28** | **61.57** | **72.33** | **72.04** | **80.96** | **65.08** | **86.55** | |
| CIFAR100 | FedAvg | 65.27 | 65.27 | 65.59 | 63.96 | 76.43 | 59.17 | 55.16 | 55.29 | 55.36 | 54.15 | 58.85 | 53.39 |
| | FedProx | 65.71 | 65.71 | 65.31 | 64.18 | 75.95 | 59.93 | 56.86 | 56.89 | 56.89 | 56.08 | 59.27 | 55.25 |
| | MOON | 65.33 | 65.33 | 65.23 | 64.79 | 75.45 | 60.12 | 56.91 | 56.86 | 56.72 | 56.14 | 59.51 | 55.53 |
| | FedRS | 65.18 | 65.64 | 66.48 | 64.62 | 76.86 | 60.74 | 56.51 | 55.91 | 56.45 | 56.34 | 61.92 | 55.99 |
| | FedGen | 65.74 | 65.75 | 66.72 | 64.33 | 76.92 | 60.43 | 56.77 | 56.74 | 57.43 | 56.27 | 60.09 | 55.27 |
| | FedLC | 65.83 | 65.84 | 65.91 | 65.02 | 75.67 | 60.07 | 56.87 | 56.04 | 56.56 | 56.28 | 60.89 | 55.95 |
| | FedRep | 61.21 | 59.21 | 67.87 | 52.51 | 77.81 | 42.77 | 53.41 | 51.44 | 55.60 | 48.67 | 67.70 | 33.10 |
| | FedProto | 56.56 | 56.26 | 66.08 | 46.88 | 77.68 | 37.63 | 52.41 | 50.04 | 54.05 | 42.88 | 63.22 | 28.74 |
| | FedBABU | 65.63 | 65.28 | 71.30 | 64.54 | 80.33 | 60.99 | 56.91 | 54.57 | 60.14 | 54.40 | 68.44 | 54.24 |
| | FedRod | *66.17* | *66.17* | *72.05* | *65.19* | *80.46* | *61.01* | *57.76* | *57.01* | *63.90* | *56.53* | *72.37* | 54.67 |
| | **FedGELA** | **67.28** | **68.07** | **72.61** | **66.94** | **82.79** | **63.13** | **61.70** | **59.29** | **64.37** | **58.60** | **72.93** | **58.53** |

**Table 2.**
*Personal and generic performance on SVHN, CIFAR10, and CIFAR100 from FedGELA [11]. Dirichlet distribution with coefficient $\beta = 0.5$ for medium heterogeneity and $\beta = 0.1$ or $\beta = 0.2$ for high-level heterogeneity. To verify the straggler situation, all datasets are split into 10 or 50 clients for full participation or partial participation, and in each round, 10 clients are selected in the federated training.*

settings. Notably, FedGELA, which both mitigates angle collapse for globally comprehensive classes and utilizing the wasted feature space for locally existing classes, achieves the best performance. It provides fair and equal discrimination for all classes in the global task while being locally adapted to existing classes. FedGELA consistently surpasses all baselines, with an average performance improvement of 2.42, 5.2, and 5.7% over FedAvg, and 1.35, 1.64, and 1.81% over the best baseline across the three datasets, respectively.

These findings suggest that when designing federated algorithms, constraining local training can enhance global task performance but may limit the model's capacity for personal tasks. Conversely, allowing more flexibility in the local structure can hinder global model convergence, leading to suboptimal performance on global tasks. In PCDD settings, the divergence between global and local objectives becomes more pronounced. Therefore, designing a comprehensive federated algorithm that effectively balances the structural requirements of both global and personal tasks, as demonstrated by FedGELA, is crucial.

## 6. Conclusion

In this chapter, we introduce the problem of partially class-disjoint data in federated learning, which is both practical and challenging due to the angle collapse of classifier vectors in the global task and the inefficient use of feature space in personal tasks. We highlight the significant optimization differences between federated learning under PCDD conditions and traditional non-IID settings, and we examine recent advancements aimed at addressing these challenges to explore the development trajectory and future trends in this field. Furthermore, we present experimental results that reveal a more pronounced optimization divergence between global and local tasks under PCDD settings. Specifically, constraining local training can enhance global task performance but limits the model's capacity for personal tasks, while granting more flexibility to local structures can hinder the convergence of the global model, leading to suboptimal performance on global tasks. Therefore, designing a comprehensive federated algorithm that effectively balances the structural needs of both global and personal tasks is crucial for advancing FL in PCDD contexts. We hope this chapter clarifies the significance of PCDD scenarios in heterogeneous federated learning and serves as a catalyst for future research in this field.

## Acknowledgements

We would like to clarify that some contents are borrowed and extended from our previous accepted papers [11, 12] with the proper refinement. Please refer to these two papers for more details.

## Author details

Ziqing Fan and Jiangchao Yao*
Cooperative Medianet Innovation Center, Shanghai Jiao Tong University, Shanghai, China

*Address all correspondence to: sunarker@sjtu.edu.cn

## References

[1] McMahan B, Moore E, Ramage D, Hampson S, Arcas BA. Communication-efficient learning of deep networks from decentralized data. In: Artificial Intelligence and Statistics. Cambridge, MA: JMLR; 2017. pp. 1273-1282

[2] Fan Z, Wang Y, Yao J, Lyu L, Zhang Y, Tian Q. FedSkip: Combatting statistical heterogeneity with federated skip aggregation. In: 2022 IEEE International Conference on Data Mining. New York: IEEE; 2022. pp. 131-140

[3] Li Q, Diao Y, Chen Q, He B. Federated learning on non-iid data silos: An experimental study. In: 2022 IEEE 38th International Conference on Data Engineering (ICDE). New York: IEEE; 2022. pp. 965-978

[4] Fan Z, Hu S, Yao J, Niu G, Zhang Y, Sugiyama M, et al. Locally estimated global perturbations are better than local perturbations for federated sharpness-aware minimization. arXiv preprint arXiv:240518890. 2024

[5] Li Q, He B, Song D. Model-contrastive federated learning. In: Proceedings of the IEEE/CVF Conference on Computer Vision and Pattern Recognition. New York: IEEE; 2021. pp. 10713-10722

[6] Li T, Sahu AK, Zaheer M, Sanjabi M, Talwalkar A, Smith V. Federated optimization in heterogeneous networks. Proceedings of Machine Learning and Systems. 2020;**2**:429-450

[7] Collins L, Hassani H, Mokhtari A, Shakkottai S. Exploiting shared representations for personalized federated learning. In: International Conference on Machine Learning. Cambridge, MA: JMLR; 2021. pp. 2089-2099

[8] Tan Y, Long G, Liu L, Zhou T, Lu Q, Jiang J, et al. Fedproto: Federated prototype learning across heterogeneous clients. In: Proceedings of the AAAI Conference on Artificial Intelligence. Vol. 36. New York: AAAI; 2022. pp. 8432-8440

[9] Oh JH, Kim S, Yun S. FedBABU: Toward enhanced representation for federated image classification. In: 10th International Conference on Learning Representations, ICLR 2022. Appleton: ICLR; 2022

[10] Zhu Z, Hong J, Zhou J. Data-free knowledge distillation for heterogeneous federated learning. In: International Conference on Machine Learning. Cambridge, MA: JMLR; 2021. pp. 12878-12889

[11] Fan Z, Yao J, Han B, Zhang Y, Wang Y, et al. Federated learning with bilateral curation for partially class-disjoint data. In: Advances in Neural Information Processing Systems. 2024. pp. 32006-32019

[12] Fan Z, Yao J, Zhang R, Lyu L, Zhang Y, Wang Y. Federated learning under partially class-disjoint data via manifold reshaping. 2024. arXiv preprint arXiv:240518983

[13] Gaitan E, Nelson NC, Poole GV. Endemic goiter and endemic thyroid disorders. World Journal of Surgery. 1991;**15**(2):205-215

[14] Xiao L, Pennington J, Schoenholz S. Disentangling trainability and generalization in deep neural networks. In: International Conference on Machine Learning. Cambridge, MA: JMLR; 2020. pp. 10462-10472

[15] Zhu Z, Ding T, Zhou J, Li X, You C, Sulam J, et al. A geometric analysis of

neural collapse with unconstrained features. Advances in Neural Information Processing Systems. 2021; **34**:29820-29834

[16] Ji W, Lu Y, Zhang Y, Deng Z, Su WJ. An unconstrained layer-peeled perspective on neural collapse. In: International Conference on Learning Representations. Appleton: ICLR; 2021

[17] Yu F, Rawat AS, Menon A, Kumar S. Federated learning with only positive labels. In: International Conference on Machine Learning. Cambridge, MA: JMLR; 2020. pp. 10946-10956

[18] Li XC, Zhan DC. Fedrs: Federated learning with restricted softmax for label distribution non-iid data. In: Proceedings of the 27th ACM SIGKDD Conference on Knowledge Discovery & Data Mining. New York: ACM; 2021. pp. 995-1005

[19] Zhang J, Li Z, Li B, Xu J, Wu S, Ding S, et al. Federated learning with label distribution skew via logits calibration. In: International Conference on Machine Learning. Cambridge, MA: JMLR; 2022. pp. 26311-26329

[20] Li X, Jiang M, Zhang X, Kamp M, Dou Q. Fedbn: Federated learning on non-iid features via local batch normalization. arXiv preprint arXiv: 210207623. 2021

[21] Arivazhagan MG, Aggarwal V, Singh AK, Choudhary S. Federated learning with personalization layers. arXiv preprint arXiv:191200818. 2019

[22] Chen HY, Chao WL. On bridging generic and personalized federated learning for image classification. In: International Conference on Learning Representations. Appleton: ICLR; 2022

[23] Netzer Y, Wang T, Coates A, Bissacco A, Wu B, Ng AY. Reading digits in natural images with unsupervised feature learning. In: NIPS Workshop on Deep Learning and Unsupervised Feature Learning. San Diego, CA: NeurIPS; 2011

[24] LeCun Y, Bottou L, Bengio Y, Haffner P. Gradient-based learning applied to document recognition. Proceedings of the IEEE. 1998;**86**(11): 2278-2324

[25] Jordan MI, Mitchell TM. Machine learning: Trends, perspectives, and prospects. Science. 2015;**349**(6245): 255-260

[26] Shokri R, Shmatikov V. Privacy-preserving deep learning. In: Proceedings of the 22nd ACM SIGSAC Conference on Computer and Communications Security. New York: ACM; 2015. pp. 1310-1321

[27] Zhu L, Han S. Deep leakage from gradients. In: Federated Learning. Berlin: Springer; 2020. pp. 17-31

[28] Zhang R, Fan Z, Xu Q, Yao J, Zhang Y, Wang Y. Grace: A generalized and personalized federated learning method for medical imaging. In: International Conference on Medical Image Computing and Computer-Assisted Intervention. Berlin: Springer; 2023. pp. 14-24

[29] Liang X, Liu Y, Chen T, Liu M, Yang Q. Federated transfer reinforcement learning for autonomous driving. arXiv preprint arXiv: 191006001. 2019

[30] Hsu TMH, Qi H, Brown M. Federated visual classification with real-world data distribution. In: European Conference on Computer Vision. Berlin: Springer; 2020. pp. 76-92

[31] Verbraeken J, Wolting M, Katzy J, Kloppenburg J, Verbelen T,

Rellermeyer JS. A survey on distributed machine learning. ACM Computing Surveys (CSUR). 2020;**53**(2):1-33

[32] Codella NC, Gutman D, Celebi ME, Helba B, Marchetti MA, Dusza SW, et al. Skin lesion analysis toward melanoma detection: A challenge at the 2017 international symposium on biomedical imaging (ISBI), hosted by the international skin imaging collaboration (ISIC). In: 2018 IEEE 15th International Symposium on Biomedical Imaging (ISBI 2018). New York: IEEE; 2018. pp. 168-172

[33] Tschandl P, Rosendahl C, Kittler H. The HAM10000 dataset, a large collection of multi-source dermatoscopic images of common pigmented skin lesions. Scientific Data. 2018;**5**(1):1-9

[34] Combalia M, Codella NC, Rotemberg V, Helba B, Vilaplana V, Reiter O, et al. Bcn20000: Dermoscopic lesions in the wild. arXiv preprint arXiv: 190802288. 2019

[35] Weyand T, Araujo A, Cao B, Sim J. Google landmarks dataset v2-a large-scale benchmark for instance-level recognition and retrieval. In: Proceedings of the IEEE/CVF Conference on Computer Vision and Pattern Recognition. New York: IEEE; 2020. pp. 2575-2584

[36] Liu Z, Luo P, Wang X, Tang X. Deep learning face attributes in the wild. In: Proceedings of International Conference on Computer Vision (ICCV). New York: IEEE; 2015

[37] He K, Zhang X, Ren S, Sun J. Deep residual learning for image recognition. In: Proceedings of the IEEE Conference on Computer Vision and Pattern Recognition. New York: IEEE; 2016. pp. 770-778

Chapter 6

# Opportunistic Networking and the Future of Context-Aware Recommendations

*Lucas Nunes Barbosa*

## Abstract

In environments where internet connectivity is limited or disrupted, ensuring continuous access to personalized information presents significant challenges. This chapter introduces a distributed collaborative recommender system designed for opportunistic networks, which function without a centralized server. Mobile devices communicate directly, enabling localized data collection and processing through peer-to-peer interactions. This decentralized approach addresses issues of data sparsity, privacy, and scalability by keeping data processing on the user's device, thus minimizing third-party data storage. The system's flexibility allows it to dynamically adapt to varying network densities and mobility patterns, making it well-suited for remote areas, disaster recovery scenarios, and congested environments. Core elements such as communication protocols and recommendation algorithms are explored, demonstrating the system's potential to provide scalable, privacy-preserving, and efficient personalized content in resource-constrained conditions.

**Keywords:** distributed recommender systems, opportunistic networks, collaborative filtering, decentralized systems, peer-to-peer communication, privacy

## 1. Introduction

As mobile devices become indispensable tools for accessing personalized information, reliable internet connectivity remains a challenge, particularly in remote areas or during crises like natural disasters. This raises a key question: how can users continue to receive tailored content when traditional, centralized recommender systems are inaccessible?

This chapter addresses this issue by introducing a distributed collaborative recommender system that operates within opportunistic networks. Unlike conventional systems that rely on centralized servers for processing and delivering recommendations, this system allows mobile devices to communicate directly, sharing data and generating recommendations without any fixed infrastructure. This decentralized approach ensures continuous personalized content delivery even in the absence of internet access while enhancing user privacy, as data remains local to each device rather than being stored or processed by third parties.

Opportunistic networks, also known as mobile ad hoc networks, lack fixed infrastructure, relying on dynamic, intermittent connectivity between devices. These networks are particularly valuable in scenarios where stable internet access is unavailable, making them ideal for rural areas, disaster zones, or large public events where network congestion may occur. By leveraging the flexibility of these networks, the system facilitates decentralized data distribution and recommendations, overcoming common limitations like single points of failure, scalability issues, and privacy concerns.

This chapter explores how distributed recommender systems can be implemented effectively in opportunistic networks, offering a robust alternative to centralized models. The findings demonstrate the potential for such systems to deliver personalized content with greater resilience, scalability, and privacy, marking a significant advancement in recommendation technologies.

## 2. Conceptual overview

### 2.1 Recommender systems

Recommender systems help users navigate vast information spaces by predicting their preferences based on past behavior or those of similar users. These systems are integral in applications like e-commerce and content streaming, enhancing the user experience by filtering data and suggesting relevant items. The main types of recommender systems are:

- Collaborative filtering: This method uses the preferences of multiple users to generate recommendations. It can be user-based, where recommendations are made based on user similarity, or item-based, where similar items are suggested based on the user's history [1, 2].

- Content-based filtering: This approach analyzes item features to generate recommendations, learning a user's preferences through the characteristics of items they have interacted with [3, 4].

- Hybrid methods: These systems combine collaborative and content-based filtering to improve accuracy and robustness, leveraging the strengths of both approaches [5, 6].

### 2.2 Opportunistic networks

Opportunistic networks are mobile ad hoc networks that facilitate communication through dynamic, intermittent connectivity. These networks are especially valuable in environments where stable, continuous connections are unavailable, such as in remote areas or during emergencies.

- Store-carry-forward principle: Devices in opportunistic networks store data, carry it while mobile, and forward it upon encountering another device. This allows data transmission without requiring a direct, consistent connection between devices [7].

- Data forwarding strategies: These strategies assume devices will eventually encounter one another, making it possible to deliver data even with intermittent connectivity. This resilience makes opportunistic networks effective in scenarios where traditional networks fail [8].

The advent of *5G technology* further enhances opportunistic networks by providing higher data rates, lower latency, and increased reliability. This allows for efficient data transmission during brief device contacts and supports a large number of connected devices, making 5G a key enabler for large-scale opportunistic networks. The low latency and high reliability of 5G are critical for real-time applications, such as emergency response, smart cities, and IoT, where data needs to be transmitted quickly and consistently [9, 10].

### 2.3 Combining recommender systems with opportunistic networks

The integration of recommender systems with opportunistic networks offers a novel approach to personalized content delivery, taking advantage of the dynamic and spontaneous nature of these networks. By utilizing the unique properties of opportunistic networks, recommender systems can deliver tailored content based on user proximity, interaction patterns, and contextual information, even in environments with intermittent connectivity.

In traditional recommender systems, data sparsity is a common challenge, where the lack of sufficient user-item interactions limits the effectiveness of recommendations. Opportunistic networks, with their frequent and diverse interactions among nodes, can mitigate this issue by enabling the continuous collection of collaborative filtering data as devices encounter each other. For example, in a social event, an opportunistic network could dynamically recommend music, videos, or services based on the preferences of nearby users, enhancing the overall user experience [11, 12].

However, the decentralized nature of these networks introduces challenges such as privacy, scalability, and resource efficiency when dealing with sensitive user data. The decentralized nature raises concerns about privacy and security, especially when handling sensitive user preferences. Federated Learning (FL) offers a solution by enhancing both privacy and scalability in this context [13, 14]. FL enables devices in an opportunistic network to collaboratively train a shared prediction model while keeping user data localized. Each device processes its own data and shares only model updates (e.g., gradients) rather than raw data with other devices or a coordinating server. This drastically reduces the need for centralized data collection, ensuring user privacy and reducing the risk of data breaches [11].

For instance, in a healthcare setting, an opportunistic network could facilitate the sharing of medical resources or recommendations among patients and healthcare providers without compromising patient confidentiality. Secure data-sharing mechanisms, such as encryption and privacy-preserving algorithms, are essential to ensure that personal health data remains secure during transmission [15].

Devices in opportunistic networks, such as smartphones and IoT devices, often operate with limited battery life. Therefore, it is crucial that the recommender system is optimized for low power consumption to extend device usability. For example, in a smart city scenario, opportunistic networks could be used to recommend transportation options or local services to citizens in real time. The recommender system would need to balance the frequency of recommendations with energy consumption, possibly by using energy-efficient protocols or limiting recommendations to moments when devices are already active for other purposes [16, 17].

In addition to addressing technical challenges, the integration of recommender systems with opportunistic networks opens up new possibilities for context-aware recommendations. These systems can leverage contextual information such as location, time of day, and social settings to provide more relevant and timely suggestions. For example, in a retail environment, an opportunistic network could detect when a user enters a store and immediately provide personalized product recommendations or discounts based on the user's purchase history and current location within the store.

Key advantages of FL in opportunistic networks include:

- Enhanced privacy: Since no raw data is shared between devices or with central servers, user information remains secure. This is crucial in sensitive contexts like healthcare or social networking.

- Improved scalability: FL distributes the computational load across devices, allowing the system to scale more efficiently as the number of devices increases while reducing strain on individual devices.

- Reduced communication overhead: By transmitting only model updates, FL minimizes the data exchanged across the network, which is particularly beneficial in bandwidth-limited or intermittent environments.

*2.3.1 Scenarios of use*

The integration of recommender systems with opportunistic networks opens up numerous possibilities across various domains. Below are several key scenarios where this combination proves particularly useful:

1. Disaster response: In disaster-stricken areas where traditional communication networks are down, opportunistic networks can play a crucial role in coordinating rescue efforts. A recommender system can prioritize and suggest critical resources such as food, water, and medical supplies to rescuers based on real-time data collected from nearby devices. This ensures that aid is delivered to the areas where it is most needed, improving the efficiency and effectiveness of relief operations.

2. Tourism and travel: Travelers in foreign cities could benefit from opportunistic networks that recommend nearby attractions, restaurants, or events based on their preferences and the recommendations of other travelers they encounter. The system can function even in areas with limited internet connectivity, using interactions between tourist devices to disseminate information and provide timely, context-aware suggestions.

3. Social networking: At large events such as conferences or festivals, opportunistic networks can enhance social networking by recommending connections with other attendees who share similar interests or professional backgrounds. The system could also suggest meeting points or relevant sessions to attend, fostering meaningful real-time interactions.

These scenarios illustrate the potential to provide personalized, contextually relevant recommendations in dynamic, resource-constrained environments by combining the strengths of recommender systems with the flexibility of opportunistic networks.

### *2.3.2 Advantages of federated learning in opportunistic networks*

Federated learning (FL) offers several key advantages when integrated into opportunistic networks, enhancing both privacy and scalability while reducing communication overhead. These advantages are crucial in environments with intermittent connectivity and resource constraints.

- Enhanced privacy: Since no raw data is shared between devices or with central servers, user information remains secure. This is especially important in sensitive contexts such as healthcare or social networking, where privacy is paramount [18].

- Improved scalability: FL distributes the computational load across devices, allowing the system to scale more efficiently as the number of devices increases. This ensures that the system remains functional even in high-density environments without placing excessive strain on individual devices [19].

- Reduced communication overhead: By transmitting only model updates (such as gradients) instead of raw data, FL minimizes the amount of information exchanged across the network. This is particularly beneficial in bandwidth-limited or intermittent environments [20].

For instance, in disaster recovery scenarios, FL allows devices to collaboratively learn from local conditions—such as damage assessments and medical needs—while maintaining data privacy. The model can then provide tailored recommendations, directing rescue efforts and medical supplies based on real-time inputs from the surrounding environment.

Similarly, in high-density environments like tourist hotspots or large events, FL can dynamically adapt to user preferences and interactions, safeguarding privacy while continuously refining recommendations for attractions, restaurants, or social connections.

### *2.3.3 Challenges of federated learning in opportunistic networks*

While Federated Learning provides significant benefits, it also introduces several challenges that must be addressed to ensure the system's effectiveness in real-world applications.

- Synchronization: Opportunistic networks are inherently asynchronous, which complicates the synchronization of model updates. Research should explore adaptive synchronization techniques to enable functionality despite intermittent connections and varying device availability.

- Device resource constraints: Devices within these networks, such as smartphones and IoT devices, often operate with limited processing power and battery life. FL must be optimized for energy efficiency to ensure that these devices can continue to function effectively over extended periods, especially in resource-constrained settings such as disaster zones.

- Communication efficiency: While FL reduces raw data transmission, model updates still need to be shared across the network. Ensuring efficient communication without overwhelming the network is crucial to maintaining performance, particularly in bandwidth-limited or resource-constrained environments.

## 3. Application of distributed representations in recommender systems

Distributed representations, particularly those learned through neural networks like word embeddings, have transformed how recommender systems capture and encode complex relationships between users and items. These representations are highly effective at handling sparse data and generalizing from limited feedback, enabling more accurate and contextually relevant recommendations. When combined with the adaptive nature of opportunistic networks, distributed representations allow for personalized content delivery, even in resource-constrained environments. This section highlights the applications and benefits of integrating distributed representations into recommender systems within opportunistic networks.

### 3.1 Enhancing data exchange and processing in opportunistic networks

Opportunistic networks, known for their dynamic and intermittent connectivity, pose challenges for data exchange. Distributed representations address these challenges by compressing information into compact forms, facilitating efficient transmission across the network.

In environments with intermittent connectivity, such as remote areas or disaster recovery scenarios, rapid and efficient data transmission is critical. Distributed representations enable only the most relevant information to be exchanged, reducing bandwidth usage and ensuring recommendations can still be generated with minimal communication opportunities.

Additionally, these compact representations help conserve bandwidth and energy, both of which are limited in opportunistic networks. By reducing the data that needs to be transmitted, the system remains sustainable and energy-efficient, extending device usability over longer periods.

### 3.2 Personalized content delivery in dynamic environments

Integrating distributed representations with opportunistic networks enables highly personalized content delivery, even in environments with unreliable or limited internet connectivity.

- Mobile social networks: In constantly shifting environments where users frequently interact with others, such as large social events, distributed representations capture evolving user preferences. The system dynamically updates recommendations based on limited interactions, providing timely and relevant suggestions. For example, at a social event, it could recommend networking

*DOI: http://dx.doi.org/10.5772/intechopen.1007561*

opportunities or activities based on the preferences of attendees who have interacted throughout the day.

- E-learning platforms: In educational contexts, distributed representations enhance personalized learning experiences. The system can track students' progress and adapt recommendations based on their evolving needs, even in environments with sporadic connectivity, such as remote classrooms. This ensures that students receive tailored learning materials aligned with their individual learning paths.

- Smart cities: In smart city environments, distributed representations enable personalized services, such as traffic management or public transportation recommendations. By using real-time data from a network of vehicles and mobile devices, the system provides efficient urban management tailored to individual needs. For instance, commuters can receive real-time updates on optimal routes to avoid traffic congestion based on data aggregated from nearby vehicles.

### 3.3 Critical scenarios for opportunistic recommender systems

In critical environments such as disaster zones, underdeveloped healthcare regions, and large public events, opportunistic networks provide significant advantages for disseminating essential information. However, challenges like scalability and data privacy persist. Federated Learning (FL) offers an effective solution by allowing devices to collaboratively learn from local data while keeping sensitive information decentralized, making it particularly suitable for resource-constrained environments.

- Disaster scenarios: Reliable communication is vital for sharing critical information such as the location of safe zones and medical aid stations. Using Federated Learning, devices can locally train models on disaster-related data and share only model updates, reducing reliance on centralized communication. This allows crucial information to be exchanged quickly, even with intermittent connectivity, while safeguarding privacy.

- Healthcare in underdeveloped regions: In areas with limited healthcare infrastructure, Federated Learning enables healthcare workers to collaborate on treatment recommendations while keeping patient data local. Devices can exchange model updates to share best practices and medical resources without compromising confidentiality. This approach improves the quality of care while scaling across regions with limited connectivity.

- High-density events: At large-scale events such as festivals or rallies, Federated Learning helps deliver real-time, personalized recommendations without overwhelming the network. Devices locally process interactions and share model updates, allowing efficient delivery of suggestions—such as nearby services or stage recommendations—while maintaining privacy and minimizing data transmission.

- Public safety during gatherings or protests: In large public gatherings, FL can securely share real-time safety information, such as safe routes or hazardous areas, while preserving user anonymity. This decentralized approach enhances public safety by ensuring critical updates are delivered to all participants, even when traditional communication infrastructure is compromised.

## 3.4 Future directions and challenges

While the integration of distributed representations within opportunistic networks offers numerous benefits, several challenges must be addressed to fully realize the potential of the proposed framework across diverse real-world scenarios.

### *3.4.1 Scalability and network density*

The performance of opportunistic networks is heavily dependent on the density of nodes. In sparsely populated areas, such as *rural communities* or *disaster-stricken zones*, the limited number of interactions between devices can hinder the dissemination of information and affect the overall effectiveness of the system. For example, in a *natural disaster scenario*, the network may lack sufficient users to continuously exchange critical data like safe zones or medical aid locations. Future research should explore techniques to optimize the framework's ability to operate efficiently in low-density areas. One possible solution could involve leveraging Federated Learning to aggregate data across remote users while reducing the reliance on frequent peer-to-peer connections.

Conversely, in high-density areas, such as political rallies or concerts, the network could become overwhelmed with connections, leading to congestion and slower data exchange. Developing algorithms that can dynamically adjust to varying network densities and prioritize relevant information, especially in real-time events, will be essential for the scalability of the system in different environments.

### *3.4.2 Privacy and security*

Privacy and security remain significant challenges, especially given the peer-to-peer nature of opportunistic networks. In scenarios like political rallies, where anonymity and the protection of personal data are crucial, robust encryption methods and privacy-preserving algorithms are needed to ensure that sensitive information is not compromised during data exchanges. Similarly, in disaster recovery operations, protecting the privacy of individuals sharing medical data or other critical resources must be prioritized, even when communication infrastructure is unstable.

In addition to encryption, incorporating Federated Learning can enhance privacy by keeping user data localized on devices and only sharing model updates instead of raw data. This approach is particularly beneficial in high-density events, where data exchanges occur frequently and privacy risks are higher due to the increased number of interactions.

### *3.4.3 Energy efficiency*

Devices in opportunistic networks often have limited battery life, making energy efficiency a critical consideration, particularly in resource-constrained environments. For instance, in disaster zones, where users may not have access to reliable charging facilities, optimizing the system for low power consumption is crucial to maintaining device usability. Future developments should explore energy-efficient communication protocols, such as store-carry-forward techniques that minimize the frequency of data exchanges to conserve battery life.

In high-activity environments, like urban gatherings or festivals, the system can be optimized to limit recommendations to moments when devices are already active (e.g., during interactions with other users or when the device is being used for other tasks), thereby reducing unnecessary energy consumption.

#### *3.4.4 Adoption of emerging technologies*

Emerging technologies like 5G and edge computing present opportunities to enhance the capabilities of opportunistic networks. For instance, 5G's low latency and high bandwidth would allow for faster and more reliable data exchanges during crowded events or urban environments, where real-time recommendations for entertainment, transportation, or services are essential. The high capacity of 5G networks would also enable the system to support a large number of connected devices simultaneously, making it ideal for high-density environments like public gatherings.

Similarly, edge computing can reduce the load on individual devices by offloading some of the data processing tasks to nearby edge servers. In disaster recovery scenarios, edge computing could help aggregate and distribute critical information, such as rescue operations or medical aid locations, without relying entirely on the capabilities of individual mobile devices.

### 3.5 Use case simulations and performance metrics

To comprehensively evaluate the proposed distributed recommender system, simulations must be conducted to address specific challenges encountered in real-world environments. These simulations will focus on network performance under varying conditions such as node density, mobility, latency, privacy, and energy efficiency. The objective of these simulations is to assess the system's scalability, adaptability, and operational efficiency in real-world situations where the traditional communication infrastructure may be compromised or overwhelmed.

Simulations offer an opportunity to replicate real-world conditions in a controlled environment, allowing researchers to measure key performance metrics and make data-driven improvements to the system. The One Simulator, an established tool for modeling opportunistic networks, will be used for these tests due to its ability to mimic dynamic and diverse network environments effectively.

Each simulation will focus on different real-world scenarios, such as natural disasters, political rallies, and urban concerts, each presenting unique challenges for the distributed recommender system. These use cases aim to test the system's ability to maintain efficient communication and provide reliable recommendations across varying conditions.

#### *3.5.1 Natural disaster scenario*

In the aftermath of a natural disaster, such as an earthquake, hurricane, or flood, communication infrastructure often becomes unreliable or is completely destroyed. Survivors and rescue teams must rely on alternative forms of communication to exchange critical information, such as the locations of safe zones, medical aid stations, and rescue efforts. The proposed distributed recommender system leverages opportunistic networks to ensure that even in low-density, disconnected environments, users can still share and receive vital information.

This scenario presents a challenging environment characterized by low device availability, limited power, and unpredictable mobility patterns. The system must maintain data persistence, prioritize critical information, and minimize delays in data delivery, even in fragmented networks with sparse user encounters. Devices must act as carriers of essential information, holding it until they encounter other nodes and can forward the data, ensuring that everyone in the affected area has access to up-to-date, life-saving recommendations.

#### *3.5.2 Political rally scenario*

Political rallies often attract large crowds of participants who gather in public spaces to advocate for specific causes. These environments are characterized by high node density, where participants exchange information such as event schedules, crowd movement updates, and relevant news, all while seeking to maintain privacy and anonymity. Furthermore, political rallies are highly dynamic, with large crowds moving in unpredictable ways, making centralized communication systems prone to congestion or failure.

In this scenario, the distributed recommender system operates within a dense, highly mobile environment, ensuring that participants can access event-specific recommendations without compromising their privacy. The system must efficiently distribute relevant information in real time while ensuring that user identities and data remain anonymized. Additionally, it should prioritize ephemeral data—only storing information for the duration of the event, ensuring that no traces remain once the rally concludes.

#### *3.5.3 Urban concert scenario*

Urban concerts and large-scale public events present environments with high concentrations of people in relatively confined spaces. In such settings, attendees are often looking for real-time recommendations on nearby performances, food stands, transportation options, or merchandise booths. Network congestion is a frequent issue, as many devices attempt to connect to limited communication infrastructure simultaneously.

In this scenario, the distributed recommender system must function efficiently within a crowded, high-density network, handling a large volume of data exchanges while minimizing battery consumption. It must provide accurate and timely recommendations to users based on their location, preferences, and interactions with nearby devices. Furthermore, the system should leverage emerging technologies like 5G to manage network congestion and ensure the swift transmission of data across the crowded event space, enabling users to have a seamless experience despite the high volume of participants and data exchanges.

### 3.6 Suggested exploration areas and metrics

To ensure the comprehensive evaluation and optimization of the proposed distributed recommender system, several key areas warrant further exploration. These areas focus on addressing the critical challenges posed by each use case scenario, allowing for the measurement of performance across different network conditions,

*DOI: http://dx.doi.org/10.5772/intechopen.1007561*

and providing insights into how the system can be refined. The following subsections outline the suggested exploration areas and metrics that should guide future research.

#### *3.6.1 Node density and mobility*

In real-world scenarios, the density and mobility of nodes (devices) significantly influence network performance. For instance, in natural disaster scenarios, node density tends to be low, with few survivors or rescue workers spread over a large area. Conversely, political rallies and urban concerts typically involve high-density environments with large crowds moving dynamically. Researchers should simulate environments with varying node densities to assess how the system adapts to both sparse and congested networks. In low-density scenarios, the system's ability to maintain data persistence and exchange critical information is tested, while high-density settings challenge its capacity to handle congestion without sacrificing performance. The main metrics to consider include the rate of data exchange, time to deliver recommendations, and the system's resilience in maintaining communication across both sparse and highly mobile nodes.

#### *3.6.2 Data persistence and redundancy*

In critical environments, such as disaster zones, it is crucial to ensure that vital information remains available until it is received by all relevant nodes. In large events, the temporary nature of information exchange requires careful management to retain data only as long as needed. Researchers should explore data persistence in different scenarios to determine how long crucial information, such as rescue locations or event updates, remains in the network. Furthermore, the effectiveness of redundancy mechanisms in preventing data loss while minimizing unnecessary duplication should be evaluated. Metrics such as persistence time, successful data delivery rates, and overhead caused by redundant data transmissions provide valuable insights into the system's ability to balance data retention and efficiency.

#### *3.6.3 Latency and time-sensitive information*

In scenarios like natural disasters, where lives may depend on the rapid dissemination of information, minimizing latency is essential. In contrast, latency in settings like concerts or rallies can affect user experience by delaying real-time recommendations. Future research should investigate the latency of data transmission across different network environments, with particular attention to time-sensitive data. Optimizing routing protocols and developing adaptive mechanisms that prioritize urgent information over less critical data are promising areas for development. Key metrics include average latency from data generation to receipt and the system's ability to prioritize and expedite high-urgency information.

#### *3.6.4 Battery consumption and energy efficiency*

In resource-constrained environments, such as disaster zones or extended public events, devices may have limited access to charging facilities. As a result, the system must optimize power consumption to extend device operability without compromising communication. Energy-efficient communication protocols should be tested to reduce battery consumption, with techniques such as low-power listening modes or limiting data transmissions to critical moments offering potential improvements. Adaptive algorithms that adjust data-sharing frequency based on battery status can also be explored. Performance indicators include battery life over time, energy consumed per transmission, and the overall power efficiency of the system under varying operating conditions.

#### *3.6.5 Privacy and anonymity*

In certain scenarios, such as political rallies, privacy is paramount. Participants may wish to share information without revealing personal details or exposing themselves to tracking. Ensuring anonymity while facilitating effective communication is a key challenge. Privacy-preserving mechanisms should be integrated into the system to protect data shared in sensitive environments from unauthorized access. This includes exploring encryption techniques, anonymized data exchange, and ensuring that event-related data is deleted once its relevance ends. The effectiveness of privacy measures can be assessed through the success rate of anonymized data exchanges, the ability to protect user identities, and the system's compliance with data retention policies.

#### *3.6.6 Scalability and emerging technologies*

As emerging technologies such as 5G and edge computing continue to evolve, the distributed recommender system can benefit from these innovations, particularly in managing data traffic and reducing latency in high-density environments. Researchers should investigate how the integration of 5G networks and edge computing infrastructure can enhance the system's scalability, especially in scenarios with large numbers of users. By leveraging edge servers for local data processing, the load on individual devices can be reduced. Scalability should be measured by the system's ability to maintain performance as the number of nodes increases, alongside latency reductions and the efficiency of local data processing through edge infrastructure.

## 4. Conclusion

The integration of recommender systems with opportunistic networks marks a major step forward in personalized content delivery, particularly in environments with unreliable or intermittent connectivity. By leveraging distributed representations, these systems efficiently process and transmit data even under constrained conditions. The inherent "store-carry-forward" principle of opportunistic networks ensures that data can be dynamically shared and utilized across devices, enhancing the system's adaptability.

This combination opens up new opportunities for delivering personalized experiences in diverse applications, ranging from mobile social networks to smart cities. As both recommender systems and opportunistic networks evolve, we can expect more sophisticated, real-time solutions that operate effectively even in challenging environments.

The integration of Federated Learning further strengthens this approach, addressing key challenges like scalability, privacy, and energy efficiency. This novel framework not only improves on the limitations of centralized systems but also offers a promising future for delivering resilient, privacy-preserving, and scalable recommendations. As these technologies continue to develop, they will undoubtedly pave the way for more robust, efficient, and secure recommender systems in the future.

## Acknowledgements

The author acknowledges the use of ChatGPT and Grammarly for language polishing of the manuscript.

## Author details

Lucas Nunes Barbosa
Universidade Federal de Lavras, Lavras, Brazil

*Address all correspondence to: lnbasrbosa.ufla@gmail.com

## References

[1] Breese JS, Heckerman D, Kadie C. Empirical analysis of predictive algorithms for collaborative filtering. In: Proceedings of the Fourteenth Conference on Uncertainty in Artificial Intelligence. San Francisco, CA, USA: Morgan Kaufmann Publishers Inc.; 1998. pp. 43-52

[2] Cai Y, Gao H, Liao J, Li X, Xu Y, Xiong J. A personalized recommendation model based on collaborative filtering and federated learning for cultural tourism attractions in Fujian-Taiwan. In: 2023 International Conference on Software and System Engineering (ICoSSE). Marseille, France: IEEE; 2023. pp. 69-77

[3] Capuano N, Fenza G, Loia V, Nota FD. Content-based fake news detection with machine and deep learning: A systematic review. Neurocomputing. 2023;**530**:91-103

[4] Pazzani MJ, Billsus D. Content-based recommendation systems. In: Brusilovsky P, Kobsa A, Nejdl W, editors. The Adaptive Web. Lecture Notes in Computer Science. Vol. 4321. Berlin, Heidelberg: Springer; DOI: 10.1007/978-3-540-72079-9_10

[5] Burke R. Hybrid recommender systems: Survey and experiments. User Modeling and User-Adapted Interaction. 2002;**12**(4):331-370. DOI: 10.1023/A:1021240730564

[6] Walek B, Fajmon P. A hybrid recommender system for an online store using a fuzzy expert system. Expert Systems with Applications. 2023;**212**:118565

[7] Pelusi L, Passarella A, Conti M. Opportunistic networking: Data forwarding in disconnected mobile ad hoc networks. IEEE Communications Magazine. 2006;**44**(11):134-141. DOI: 10.1109/MCOM.2006.248176

[8] Conti M, Giordano S, May M, Passarella A. From opportunistic networks to opportunistic computing. IEEE Communications Magazine. 2010;**48**(9):126-139. DOI: 10.1109/MCOM.2010.5560599

[9] Li S, Da Xu L, Zhao S. 5G internet of things: A survey. Journal of Industrial Information Integration. 2018;**10**:1-9. DOI: 10.1016/j.jii.2018.01.005

[10] Rahimi H, Zibaeenejad A, Safavi AA. A novel IoT architecture based on 5G-IoT and next generation technologies. In: 2018 IEEE 9th Annual Information Technology, Electronics and Mobile Communication Conference (IEMCON). Vancouver, BC, Canada: IEEE; 2018. pp. 415-421

[11] Sarwar B, Karypis G, Konstan J, Riedl J. Item-based collaborative filtering recommendation algorithms. In: Proceedings of the 10th International Conference on World Wide Web. New York, NY, USA: ACM; 2001. pp. 285-295. DOI: 10.1145/371920.372071

[12] Zanotti G, Horvath M, Barbosa LN, Gemmell J. Infusing collaborative recommenders with distributed representations. In: Proceedings of the 1st Workshop on Deep Learning for Recommender Systems. New York, NY, USA: ACM; 2016. pp. 35-42. DOI: 10.1145/2988450.2988455

[13] Javeed D, Saeed MS, Kumar P, Jolfaei A, Islam S, Islam AN. Federated learning-based personalized recommendation systems: An overview on security and privacy challenges.

IEEE Transactions on Consumer Electronics. 2023;**70**(1):2618-2627

[14] Jie Z, Chen S, Lai J, Arif M, He Z. Personalized federated recommendation system with historical parameter clustering. Journal of Ambient Intelligence and Humanized Computing. 2023;**14**(8):10555-10565

[15] Zakhary S, Radenkovic M, Benslimane A. Efficient location privacy-aware forwarding in opportunistic mobile networks. IEEE Transactions on Vehicular Technology. 2014;**63**(2):893-906. DOI: 10.1109/TVT.2013.2287342

[16] Asadi A, Wang Q, Mancuso V. A survey on device-to-device communication in cellular networks. IEEE Communications Surveys & Tutorials. 2014;**16**(4):1801-1819. DOI: 10.1109/COMST.2014.2319555

[17] Mikolov T, Sutskever I, Chen K, Corrado GS, Dean J. Distributed representations of words and phrases and their compositionality. Advances in Neural Information Processing Systems. 2013;**26**:3111-3119

[18] Qin Y, Li M, Zhu J. Privacy-preserving federated learning framework in multimedia courses recommendation. Wireless Networks. 2023 May;**29**(4):1535-1544

[19] Schoinas I, Triantafyllou A, Ioannidis D, Tzovaras D, Drosou A, Votis K, et al. Federated learning: Challenges, SoTA, performance improvements and application domains. IEEE Open Journal of the Communications Society. 2024;**5**:5933-6017

[20] Vyas J, Das D, Chaudhury S. Federated learning based driver recommendation for next generation transportation system. Expert Systems with Applications. 2023;**225**:119951

Section 2

# Support Vector Machines

Chapter 7

# Introductory Chapter: Recent Trends and Progress in Support Vector Machines

*Robertas Damaševičius*

## 1. Introduction

Rooted in the principles of statistical learning theory and optimization, support vector machines (SVMs) have emerged as a fundamental technique characterized by their efficacy in high-dimensional data classification, regression, and outlier detection tasks [1]. The essence of SVMs lies in their ability to construct optimal hyperplanes in a high-dimensional space, which serves as the decision boundaries that distinctly categorize data points into different classes [2]. The versatility of SVMs is further amplified through the ingenious use of kernel functions, which enables the transformation of input data into higher-dimensional spaces, thus facilitating the linear separation of data points that might be nonlinearly separable in the original input space. This kernel trick has been the cornerstone of SVMs, allowing them to adapt and thrive in a multitude of problem spaces with varying complexities and dimensions [3].

Over recent years, the pursuit of innovation within the field of SVMs has led to significant breakthroughs, notably through the development of novel SVM kernel functions [4], optimization techniques leveraging heuristic methods [5], and the strategic hybridization with other computational paradigms such as fuzzy logic [6], reinforcement learning [7], quantum computing [8], and deep learning [9]. These advancements have not only extended the boundaries of SVMs' applicability but have also addressed some of the intrinsic challenges such as scalability, computational efficiency, and the handling of nonlinear and high-dimensional data.

The integration of SVMs with cutting-edge technologies has opened new avenues for research and application. For instance, the synergy between SVMs and deep learning architectures promises to further enhance the interpretability and generalization capabilities of machine learning models [10], while the advent of quantum computing offers a glimpse into future possibilities where SVMs could solve complex optimization problems with unprecedented speed and efficiency [11].

The primary aim of this study is to systematically explore and analyze the recent advancements and hybridization strategies within the domain of SVMs, focusing on the integration with fuzzy logic, reinforcement learning, quantum computing, and deep learning. By delving into each of these hybridization approaches, the study seeks to uncover the strengths, limitations, and applicability of these enhanced SVM models across various computational tasks and domains. Through this comprehensive examination, the study endeavors to provide a nuanced understanding of how SVMs can be optimized and applied more effectively in the face of modern data-driven challenges.

## 2. Recent achievements in the evolution of SVMs

### 2.1 Novel SVM kernel functions

Kernel functions play a pivotal role in SVMs as they implicitly map input data into a higher-dimensional space, enabling the linear separation of data points that are not linearly separable in the original input space. The choice of kernel function highly impacts the performance of an SVM model, making the exploration of novel kernels a critical endeavor for enhancing SVM's applicability and effectiveness. Here are some directions that have been explored in recent research for novel SVM kernel functions:

- Approaches that learn the kernel function directly from the data rather than selecting from a predefined set of kernel functions aim to optimize the kernel in a way that best suits the specific data distribution and task at hand, potentially improving classification or regression performance [12].

- These kernels combine the properties of two or more standard kernels (e.g., linear, polynomial, and radial basis function (RBF)) to leverage their strengths and mitigate their weaknesses. Hybrid kernels can be particularly effective in domains where different types of features (e.g., linear and nonlinear) are present [13].

- Kernels designed with domain knowledge in mind, tailored to capture the underlying patterns and relationships specific to particular fields such as bioinformatics, text processing or image analysis. These kernels integrate domain-specific metrics or similarity measures into the kernel function [14].

- For data represented as graphs, graph kernels compute the similarity between graphs, enabling SVMs to be applied to structured data. These kernels are particularly useful in social network analysis, bioinformatics (e.g., protein structure classification), and chemical compound analysis [15].

- Based on spectral analysis, these kernels are designed to capture the frequency components of the data. Spectral kernels can be particularly useful for time series analysis, audio processing, and any application where the frequency domain representation of the data provides valuable insights [16].

- With the advent of quantum computing, researchers have begun exploring quantum-enhanced kernel functions that leverage quantum computing resources to define and compute similarity measures in a quantum Hilbert space. These kernels hold the promise of exponential speedup in computing similarities for certain types of data and tasks [17].

The development of novel SVM kernel functions faces several challenges, including ensuring generalizability to avoid overfitting [18], computational efficiency [19], and the interpretability of the resulting models [20]. Furthermore, the integration of domain knowledge [21] and the adaptability of kernels to evolving data distributions [22] are critical areas for future research. Researchers continue to explore novel mathematical formulations [23], computational techniques [24], and domain-specific insights [25] to develop SVM kernel functions that can more effectively capture complex patterns and relationships in data. The ultimate goal is to enhance the versatility, accuracy, and efficiency of SVM models across a wide range of applications. For example, the new kernel proposed in [26] uses radial basis function (RBF) and RBF city block kernels that enable SVM to learn complex decision boundaries.

### 2.2 Quantum computing enhanced SVMs

Quantum computing enhanced support vector machines (QSVMs) represent a fascinating convergence of quantum computing and machine learning, leveraging the principles of quantum mechanics to enhance the computation of SVMs, particularly in terms of speed and scalability. The underlying idea is to utilize the parallelism and unique computational capabilities of quantum computers to address some of the limitations faced by classical SVMs, especially when dealing with large-scale and complex datasets [8, 17]. Quantum computers can process a vast amount of information simultaneously due to quantum parallelism, arising from the principle of superposition. This ability can be harnessed to evaluate multiple states (or solutions) simultaneously, potentially reducing the time required for tasks, such as the optimization of the SVM decision boundary [27]. These quantum phenomena can be exploited to efficiently explore and evaluate the solution space for the SVM optimization problem, enabling the identification of the optimal hyperplane with fewer computational steps compared to classical methods [28]. Quantum algorithms can utilize amplitude amplification, a process that improves the probability of finding the correct solution, thereby reducing the number of iterations needed to achieve a desired accuracy in the optimization process [29]. For example, a standard support vector machine (SVM), combined with the quantum-behaved mechanism, a quantum-behaved genetic algorithm-SVM (QBGA-SVM) is proposed in [30]

The benefits are summarized as follows:

- The primary advantage of QSVMs is the potential for significant speedup in the training and prediction phases, especially for tasks that are computationally intensive on classical computers. This can make QSVMs particularly appealing for big data applications and complex feature spaces.

- By leveraging quantum computing's parallelism, QSVMs can potentially handle larger datasets and higher-dimensional feature spaces more efficiently than classical SVMs, breaking through the bottlenecks of memory and processing power.

- Quantum algorithms may offer new ways to navigate the optimization landscape of SVMs, potentially finding better solutions that minimize the classification error more effectively or efficiently explore the kernel trick.

The challenges are:

- Current quantum computers are in the "Noisy intermediate-scale quantum" (NISQ) era, characterized by a limited number of qubits and high error rates. This makes the practical implementation of QSVMs challenging.

- Developing quantum algorithms that outperform their classical counterparts for specific machine learning tasks, including SVMs, requires overcoming significant theoretical and practical hurdles.
- Efficiently encoding classical data into quantum states (qubits) is a nontrivial task that is crucial for the effective implementation of QSVMs.
- Exploring quantum-specific feature mappings that can leverage the high-dimensional Hilbert space of quantum systems to reveal complex patterns in data.

Despite these challenges, QSVMs hold great promise for the future of machine learning and computational science. Ongoing research in quantum computing and algorithm development continues to pave the way for these advancements, with the potential to revolutionize how we approach complex data analysis and classification problems. As quantum technology matures and becomes more accessible, we can expect to see further integration of quantum-enhanced methods across various domains of machine learning.

## 2.3 Integration of deep learning with SVM

The integration of deep learning with SVMs has been a significant area of exploration in recent years, aiming to combine the best attributes of both techniques for enhanced model performance, especially in classification tasks. Deep learning provides powerful feature extraction and representation learning capabilities, while SVMs are renowned for their efficiency in high-dimensional spaces and for their robust decision boundaries. This synergy has led to several noteworthy achievements and progress.

One of the most common integrations involves using deep neural networks (DNNs) for feature extraction or representation learning, followed by an SVM for the final classification. This approach leverages the deep learning models' ability to learn hierarchical feature representations from raw data (such as images, text, or audio), which are then used as inputs to an SVM. The SVM benefits from this rich feature set, often leading to improved classification accuracy compared to using traditional features or using DNNs with standard output layers [31]. This method has been particularly effective in domains, such as image and speech recognition, where deep learning excels at extracting complex patterns [10, 32].

Another innovative approach is training deep neural networks using hinge loss, which is the loss function used by linear SVMs. This method, often referred to as using an "SVM layer" at the output of a neural network, combines the representation learning capabilities of deep learning with the margin maximization principle of SVMs. By doing so, the network aims to not only classify training examples correctly but also maximize the margin between classes, potentially leading to better generalization on unseen data. This technique has shown promise in various classification tasks, including object recognition and sentiment analysis [31].

Recent research has also explored models that jointly learn the feature representation and the SVM classifier in a unified framework. These approaches often use a combination of neural network layers for feature transformation and a layer that directly incorporates the optimization objective of an SVM (such as margin maximization). Joint learning models can lead to better alignment between the feature extraction process and the classification objective, optimizing both concurrently for improved overall performance [33].

In specific domains, the integration of deep learning with SVMs has led to notable achievements. For example, in bioinformatics, combining convolutional neural networks (CNNs) with SVMs has improved the accuracy of protein structure prediction and gene expression analysis [34]. In computer vision, hybrid models have enhanced object detection and image classification tasks, particularly in scenarios with limited labeled data or where fine-grained classification is necessary [35].

## 3. Conclusions

The exploration of the recent achievements and advancements in SVMs has yielded significant insights into the evolution of this robust machine learning methodology. Through a detailed examination of novel kernel functions, innovative heuristic optimization methods, and the integration of SVMs with various computational paradigms such as fuzzy logic, reinforcement learning, quantum computing, and deep learning, this study has underscored the adaptability and expanding applicability of SVMs across a myriad of domains. The conclusions drawn from this investigation not only illuminate the path traversed but also chart the course for future endeavors in enhancing the SVM framework.

The development of novel kernel functions has emerged as a cornerstone in the advancement of SVMs, offering a nuanced approach to mapping input data into higher-dimensional spaces. This innovation facilitates the SVMs' ability to elegantly navigate and classify nonlinear and complex data structures, thereby significantly broadening the scope of SVM applicability. The investigation into these kernels reveals a promising trajectory for the design of more adaptive and data-specific functions that could further optimize classification performance and model generalization.

The application of novel heuristic optimization methods to SVM training has demonstrated potential in overcoming some of the traditional challenges associated with model scalability and computational efficiency. These methods, characterized by their ability to find optimal or near-optimal solutions within reasonable time frames, have shown to enhance the SVMs' performance, particularly in handling large-scale and high-dimensional datasets. This area of research holds substantial promise for the development of more sophisticated optimization algorithms that could streamline SVM training processes and improve model accuracy.

The hybridization of SVMs with other computational paradigms has unveiled a fertile ground for innovation. The integration with fuzzy logic, for example, enhances SVMs' ability to deal with uncertainty and imprecision in data, while the synergy with reinforcement learning introduces dynamic adaptability and decision-making capabilities into the SVM framework. The advent of quantum computing and its application to SVMs open up unprecedented possibilities for computational speedup and efficiency, heralding a new era of machine learning where classical boundaries are continuously pushed. The fusion with deep learning, leveraging deep neural networks for feature extraction coupled with the precision of SVM classifiers, represents a powerful combination for tackling complex pattern recognition tasks.

## Author details

Robertas Damaševičius
Vytautas Magnus University, Kaunas, Lithuania

*Address all correspondence to: robertas.damasevicius@gmail.com

## References

[1] Cristianini N, Ricci E. Support Vector Machines. Boston, MA: Springer US; 2008. pp. 928-932

[2] Vapnik V. The Nature of Statistical Learning Theory. New York, NY: Springer; 1995

[3] Scholkopf B, Smola AJ. Learning with Kernels: Support Vector Machines, Regularization, Optimization, and beyond. Cambridge, MA: MIT Press; 2002

[4] Hofmann T, Scholkopf B, Smola AJ. Kernel methods in machine learning. Annals of Statistics. 2008;**36**(3):1171-1220

[5] Suykens JAK, Vandewalle J. Least squares support vector machine classifiers. Neural Processing Letters. 1999;**9**(3):293-300

[6] Lin C-T, Lin C-J. A fuzzy support vector machine. IEEE Transactions on Systems, Man, and Cybernetics, Part B (Cybernetics). 2002;**32**(4):379-384

[7] Sutton RS, Barto AG. Reinforcement Learning: An Introduction. 2nd ed. Cambridge, MA: MIT Press; 2018

[8] Rebentrost P, Mohseni M, Lloyd S. Quantum support vector machine for big data classification. Physical Review Letters. 2014;**113**(13):130503

[9] Goodfellow I, Bengio Y, Courville A. Deep Learning. Cambridge, MA: MIT Press; 2016

[10] LeCun Y, Bengio Y, Hinton G. Deep learning. Nature. 2015;**521**(7553):436-444

[11] Biamonte J, Wittek P, Pancotti N, Rebentrost P, Wiebe N, Lloyd S. Quantum machine learning. Nature. 2017;**549**(7671):195-202

[12] Lanckriet GRG, Cristianini N, Bartlett P, El Ghaoui L, Jordan MI. Learning the kernel matrix with semidefinite programming. Journal of Machine Learning Research. 2004;**5**(Jul):27-72

[13] Gonen M, Alpaydın E. Multiple kernel learning algorithms. Journal of Machine Learning Research. 2011;**12**(Jul):2211-2268

[14] Vert J-P, Tsuda K, Schölkopf B. Kernel Methods in Computational Biology. Cambridge, MA: MIT Press; 2004

[15] Vishwanathan SVN, Schraudolph NN, Kondor R, Borgwardt KM. Graph kernels. Journal of Machine Learning Research. 2010;**11**(Apr):1201-1242

[16] Cuturi M. Fast global alignment kernels. In: Proceedings of the 28th International Conference on Machine Learning (ICML-11). WI, United States: Omnipress; 2011. pp. 929-936

[17] Schuld M, Killoran N. Quantum machine learning in feature hilbert spaces. Physical Review Letters. 2019;**122**(4):040504

[18] Burges CJC. A tutorial on support vector machines for pattern recognition. Data Mining and Knowledge Discovery. 1998;**2**(2):121-167

[19] Joachims T. Training linear svms in linear time. In: Proceedings of the 12th ACM SIGKDD International Conference on Knowledge Discovery and Data Mining. New York, NY, United States: Association for Computing Machinery; 2006. pp. 217-226

[20] Doshi-Velez F, Kim B. Towards a rigorous science of interpretable machine learning. arXiv preprint arXiv:1702.08608. 2017

[21] Drucker H, Burges CJC, Kaufman L, Smola A, Vapnik V. Support vector regression machines. In: Advances in Neural Information Processing Systems. Cambridge, MA, United States: MIT Press; 1997. pp. 155-161

[22] Kivinen J, Smola AJ, Williamson RC. Online learning with kernels. IEEE Transactions on Signal Processing. 2004;**52**(8):2165-2176

[23] Shawe-Taylor J, Cristianini N. Kernel Methods for Pattern Analysis. Cambridge, England: Cambridge University Press; 2004

[24] Chang C-C, Lin C-J. Libsvm: A library for support vector machines. ACM Transactions on Intelligent Systems and Technology (TIST). 2011;**2**(3):27

[25] Leslie C, Eskin E, Noble WS. The spectrum kernel: A string kernel for SVM protein classification. In: Proceedings of the Pacific Symposium on Biocomputing. World Scientific; 2002. pp. 564-575

[26] Shamim Reza M, Hafsha U, Amin R, Yasmin R, Ruhi S. Improving svm performance for type II diabetes prediction with an improved non-linear kernel: Insights from the PIMA dataset. Computer Methods and Programs in Biomedicine. 2023;**4**:100118

[27] Nielsen MA, Chuang IL. Quantum Computation and Quantum Information. 10th Anniversary ed. Cambridge, England: Cambridge University Press; 2010

[28] Havlicek V, Antonio D, et al. Supervised learning with quantum-enhanced feature spaces. Nature. 2019;**567**:209-212

[29] Brassard G, Hoyer P, Mosca M, Tapp A. Quantum Amplitude Amplification and Estimation. Vol. 305. American Mathematical Society; 2002. pp. 53-74

[30] Li Q, Ouyang A, Peng X, Xijun H. QBGA-SVM for face recognition of livable cities. International Journal of Pattern Recognition and Artificial Intelligence. 2023;**37**(04)

[31] Tang Y. Deep learning using linear support vector machines. arXiv preprint arXiv:1306.0239. 2013

[32] Hinton G, Deng L, Dong Y, Dahl GE, Mohamed A-R, Jaitly N, et al. Deep neural networks for acoustic modeling in speech recognition. IEEE Signal Processing Magazine. 2012;**29**(6):82-97

[33] Weston J, Chopra S, Bordes A. A unified architecture for natural language processing: Deep neural networks with multitask learning. In: Proceedings of the 25th International Conference on Machine Learning (ICML'08). New York, NY, United States: Association for Computing Machinery; 2012

[34] Zeng M, Xiao F, Wang J. Convolutional neural networks with svm for protein structure prediction. Molecular BioSystems. 2016;**12**

[35] Razavian AS, Azizpour H, Sullivan J, Carlsson S. CNN features off-the-shelf: An astounding baseline for recognition. In: Proceedings of the IEEE Conference on Computer Vision and Pattern Recognition Workshops. Curran Associates; 2014

Chapter 8

# Machine Learning for Sustainable Shipping: Predicting Vessel $CO_2$ Emissions Using Random Forest Models

*Carol Anne Hargreaves and Briana Wan Nee Toh*

## Abstract

Predicting fuel consumption in the shipping industry is a critical task that supports optimized operations, driving both economic and environmental benefits as global demand for shipping continues to grow. However, accurately forecasting Carbon Dioxide ($CO_2$) emissions is challenging due to the complexity and volume of operational data. In this study, we developed and evaluated the Random Forest model to measure the prediction accuracy. The Random Forest model achieved a high predictive accuracy, with a Mean Absolute Percentage Error (MAPE) of 0.046, demonstrating its robustness in capturing the non-linear relationships in the data. Feature importance analysis within the Random Forest model highlighted vessel length, gross tonnage, width, and draft as key predictors of fuel consumption, offering valuable insights into $CO_2$ emissions-reduction strategies. These findings underscore the potential of machine learning to empower data-driven decisions in the maritime sector. Future work will explore further optimization of the Random Forest model, incorporate additional predictive features, and investigate real-time applications to enhance operational efficiency and sustainability. By making accurate $CO_2$ emission predictions, this research contributes to the industry's efforts to achieve sustainable and environmentally responsible shipping practices.

**Keywords:** decarbonization, $CO_2$ emissions prediction, sustainability, maritime industry, machine learning, Random Forest model

## 1. Introduction

The growth of the shipping sector has intensified public concerns about decarbonization due to its significant environmental impact, particularly in terms of energy consumption and greenhouse gas (GHG) emissions. International shipping accounts for 2.4% of global anthropogenic GHG emissions, a percentage expected to rise in the coming years [1]. Discussions were held on the recent literature regarding technical and operational strategies to reduce fuel consumption for new and existing ships (hull and propeller design) [2]. Nadery et al. [3]

numerically investigated a new pre-swirl stator (PSS) configuration on the ship propulsion's performance. The KP505 propeller and the KRISO container ship (KCS) were used, and the PSS was installed before the propeller to adjust the wake inflow and to increase the performance of the propeller. The numerical results indicated that the PSS with these parameters worked well at low ship speed and increased the efficiency and decreased the delivered power.

The International Maritime Organization's (IMO's) 2050 targets will be achieved via radical technology shift together with the aid of social pressure, financial incentives, regulatory and legislative reforms at the local, regional, and international level. This has driven research interest in accurately predicting Carbon Dioxide ($CO_2$) emissions, as operational data hold immense potential to provide timely insights into a ship's $CO_2$ efficiency [4].

Such data can help experts identify and address key factors contributing to $CO_2$ emissions, supporting efforts to reduce emissions through informed operational strategies [4]. A precise understanding of the relationship between fuel consumption and influencing factors is essential to optimize ship operations, improve energy efficiency, and develop effective navigation plans [5]. However, predicting fuel consumption efficiency is challenging due to the complexity of operational data, which are often unstructured, collinear, and non-stationary [4]. In this context, machine learning models offer promising solutions to process these data intricacies and generate reliable predictions.

## 2. Literature review

A common strategy for reducing fuel emissions in shipping is speed optimization, or "slow steaming" [6–8]. Using noon report data, Bal Beşikçi et al. [6] proposed an Artificial Neural Network (ANN) model for on-site optimization, which was integrated into a Decision Support System (DSS) to provide real-time fuel-efficient guidance for ship operations. Tay et al. [8] developed a Hidden Markov Model (HMM) to predict fuel consumption based on environmental conditions, enabling decision-makers to optimize ship speed for maximum fuel efficiency. Meanwhile, Bassam et al. [7] compared a range of regression techniques, including Multiple Linear Regression (MLR), tree ensemble models, and Support Vector Machines (SVMs). Their study underscores the inherent collinearity and non-linearity in ship operational data [4], highlighting the value of non-parametric models like tree-based regression and Gaussian Process Regression (GPR) for capturing complex data patterns effectively.

Another prominent research area involves estimating a ship's propulsion power to enhance operational efficiency [9]. Dos Santos Ferreira et al. [9] explored six algorithms to model the relationship between propulsion power and fuel consumption, leveraging ship operational variables, such as Speed Over Ground, Course Over Ground, Speed through Water, Shaft Revolutions Per Minute (RPM), mean draft, and trim. Their study found that ensemble models, specifically gradient-boosted trees and random forests, delivered superior precision in fuel consumption prediction compared to least squares methods and Multilayer Perceptron Neural Networks, supporting their applicability for future fuel efficiency studies [9].

In recent years, shipborne emissions have become a growing environmental threat. The International Maritime Organization has implemented various rules and regulations to resolve this concern. The Ship Energy Efficiency Management Plan (SEEMP), Energy Efficiency Design Index (EEDI), and Energy Efficiency Operational Indicator (EEOI) are examples of guidelines that increase energy efficiency and reduce shipborne emissions. The main engine shaft power (MESP) and fuel consumption (FC) are the critical components used in ship energy efficiency calculations.

A study by Tayfun Uyanık et al. [10] aimed to predict the MESP and FC of a container ship with the help of data-driven methodologies utilizing actual voyage data to assist in the calculation process of the ship's energy efficiency indexes appropriately. The algorithms' prediction success was measured using the Root Mean Square Error (RMSE), Mean absolute Error (MAE), and R-Squared ($R^2$) error metrics. When the simulation results were analyzed, the Deep Neural Network and Bayes algorithms predicted MESP best with 0.000001 and 0.000002 RMSE, 0.000987 and 0.000991 MAE, and 0.999999 $R^2$, respectively, while the Multiple-Linear Regression and Kernel Ridge algorithms estimated FC best with 0.000208 and 0.000216 RMSE, 0.001375 and 0.001471 MAE, and 0.999999 $R^2$, respectively.

Collectively, these studies reveal a growing preference for machine learning and advanced regression methods in the prediction of fuel consumption and emissions, with a particular emphasis on handling the non-linear and collinear nature of operational data. This body of work lays the groundwork for developing robust models that improve fuel efficiency, reduce emissions, and support sustainable practices in the shipping industry.

## 3. Objective of study

Despite extensive research into the factors influencing carbon emissions in the shipping industry, the impact of ship draft and length on emissions remains under-explored. Most studies have centered on variables, such as ship speed, fuel type, and environmental conditions, with limited attention to how structural characteristics might affect emissions efficiency.

Three responses that reduce energy consumption and $CO_2$ emissions in maritime transport are slower speeds, larger vessels, and slender hull designs (Dr Elizabeth Lindstad, et al. [11]). She also demonstrated that increasing the length of a 63,000 Dead Weight Tonnage (DWT) supramax vessel from 200 m to 220 m, thereby creating a "slender supramax" with a reduced block coefficient (Cb) from 0.875 to 0.806, can yield significant power consumption savings, 15–20% on typical northern European sea routes, while maintaining the same operational speed ("Half Measures: Could "Slender" Ships Be the Answer to IMO's GHG Targets?," n.d.). This evidence underscores the potential of ship length as a critical design factor in reducing emissions, providing a compelling case for investigating how vessel design elements, such as slenderness and draft, might contribute to achieving emissions reductions.

This study aims to address this gap by focusing on the role of draft and length in shipping emissions, thereby broadening the scope of emission-reducing strategies beyond traditional operational factors. By understanding the influence of these design attributes, the research has the potential to inform more sustainable ship designs and contribute to industry-wide decarbonization efforts.

## 4. Methodology

### 4.1 Data collection and description

This study draws on a comprehensive dataset comprising two main components: Automatic Identification System (AIS) data and vessel emissions information.

Focusing on $CO_2$ emissions data from 2021, we sourced emissions data from the European Union (EU) Monitoring, Reporting, and Verification (EU MRV) platform [12], which offers standardized insights into emissions generated by vessels operating in EU waters.

The dataset, referred to as vessel info, includes key characteristics such as gross tonnage and age of ships, with each vessel identifiable through its unique International Maritime Organization (IMO) number. For the AIS data, we utilized information from MarineCadastre.gov, extracting vessel traffic data from the first and last days of each month in 2021. After initial processing, we integrated these data with the EU MRV emissions and vessel information. This integration, based on matching IMO numbers, ensured a clean and unified dataset.

Our final dataset provides operational, structural details and emissions data of each vessel, including Length, Draft, Gross Tonnage, $CO_2$ emissions per distance traveled, Distance traveled, time spent at sea, fuel consumption, and $CO_2$ emissions by voyage. This dataset allows us to explore not only the operational metrics tied to emissions but also how vessel-specific attributes may influence $CO_2$ output, enabling a more robust analysis of emission trends and potential efficiencies.

### 4.2 Preprocessing the data

In this study, we applied one-hot encoding to process the categorical variables such as ship_type and AgeGroup. One-hot encoding is a widely used technique for handling categorical variables in machine learning. It transforms each unique category value into a new binary column, where the presence of a category is indicated by a value of "1" and its absence by a "0" [13]. This approach prevents any unintended intercorrelation between variables, ensuring each category is represented independently and avoids misinterpretation.

For example, if a ship is classified as a Bulk Carrier in the ship_type column, a new column specifically for Bulk Carrier will show a value of "1," while all other ship types will display a "0" in this column. This one-hot encoding method was similarly applied to the AgeGroup variable, allowing each age category to be represented as a distinct binary column.

### 4.3 Model used: Random Forest

The Random Forest method, introduced by Breiman [14], improves model accuracy by creating an ensemble of decision trees, each trained on randomly selected subsets of data. This randomness—either in the choice of features or in the combination of features at each node—reduces the likelihood of overfitting while allowing the model to capture complex patterns. Even as the number of trees grows, the Random Forest model's generalization error stabilizes, converging due to the Strong Law of Large Numbers, which limits overfitting [14].

In Random Forests, predictions are aggregated from numerous decision trees, which enhance robustness and reduce variance compared to a single decision tree model [15]. This approach is also resilient to noise and outliers, making it well suited for real-world datasets with irregularities [14].

A key feature of Random Forests is bagging (bootstrap aggregating), where each tree is trained on a bootstrapped sample of the training data. This process involves drawing samples with replacement, creating multiple training sets that increase model robustness. Bagging generates a collection of estimators on these diverse samples and averages their predictions to form a final output, improving stability and reducing variance [16].

The procedure of bootstrap aggregating is given by the following steps [14]:

1. *Generate Bootstrap Samples*: For each tree $b$ in the ensemble, generate a bootstrap sample $\{(y_1^b, x_1^b), ,, \ldots, ,(x_N^b, y_N^b)\}$ by randomly drawing with replacement from the training data, where $b = 1, \ldots, B$.

2. *Train Each Tree*: For each bootstrap sample, fit a decision tree $\hat{f}_b(x)$ by minimizing the L2 loss function:

$$\min_{\hat{f}_b(x)} \sum_{i=1}^{N} \left( y_i^b - \hat{f}_b\left(x_i^b\right) \right)^2 \tag{1}$$

3. *Aggregate Predictions*: Once all trees are trained, aggregate their predictions to obtain the final output. The bagging estimate is calculated as:

$$\hat{f}(x)_{bagging} = \frac{1}{B} \sum_{b=1}^{B} \hat{f}_b(x) \tag{2}$$

By combining the outputs of multiple decision trees, Random Forests achieve a balance of accuracy and robustness, avoiding reliance on any single decision tree's prediction while reducing generalization error. This ensemble approach makes Random Forests a powerful choice for predictive tasks in data-driven fields.

### 4.4 Model optimization method: Grid search cross-validation

To optimize the model, we employed Grid Search Cross-Validation (CV) to systematically identify the best hyperparameters. In this approach, a set of hyperparameters is passed on to the GridSearchCV function along with predetermined values for each parameter. We define a dictionary, where each hyperparameter is assigned a list of possible values to explore [17].

The Grid Search process uses cross-validation to evaluate the model's performance across all possible combinations of these hyperparameters, ensuring a thorough search of the parameter space. For each combination, metrics such as accuracy and loss are computed, allowing us to assess the model's effectiveness for different parameter settings. Finally, the hyperparameter combination that yields the best performance, as indicated by the highest accuracy or lowest loss, is selected [17].

### 4.5 Model performance indicators

To assess the performance of our models in predicting $CO_2$ emissions, we employed three key performance indicators: Mean Absolute Percentage Error (MAPE), Root Mean Square Error (RMSE), and Mean Absolute Percent Accuracy (Accuracy). These indicators provide insight into the accuracy and reliability of the models by comparing the actual and predicted $CO_2$ emissions per distance, denoted as $y_i$ and $y_i$, respectively [18].

1. *Mean absolute percentage error (MAPE)*: MAPE measures the average percentage error between the actual and predicted values, offering a normalized metric that highlights model accuracy over multiple observations. It is calculated by dividing the absolute error for each instance by the observed value, as shown in Eq. (3) [19]:

$$\mathrm{MAPE} = \frac{100}{n} \times \sum_{i=1}^{n} \left| \frac{y_i - \hat{y}_i}{y_i} \right| \tag{3}$$

2. *Root mean square error (RMSE)*: RMSE is widely used to evaluate model performance due to its interpretability; it uses the same units as the predicted variable, which allows it to directly reflect the model's prediction accuracy. RMSE is derived from the mean square error (MSE) by taking the square root of the average squared differences between the actual and predicted values [7]:

$$MSE = \frac{1}{n} \sum_{i=1}^{n} \left( y_i - \hat{y}_i \right)^2 \tag{4}$$

$$\mathrm{RMSE} = \sqrt{MSE} \tag{5}$$

3. *Mean absolute percent accuracy* (*accuracy*): Accuracy is computed as the complement of MAPE, representing the percentage of accuracy in predictions relative to observed values [20]:

$$Accuracy = 100\% - MAPE \tag{6}$$

Together, these performance indicators provide a comprehensive evaluation of the models, allowing us to gauge both the absolute error magnitude (via RMSE) and percentage accuracy (via MAPE and Accuracy) of the $CO_2$ emissions predictions.

## 5. Results and analysis

### 5.1 Initial Random Forest model

In the initial Random Forest model, we utilized GridSearchCV to optimize the "n_estimators" hyperparameter on the training and validation sets. This tuning process helped to identify the optimal number of trees for improved performance. Based on feature importance analysis, we selected the top six most influential features and created a refined dataset, X_new, containing only these features to enhance model efficiency and reduce computational complexity.

With the optimal hyperparameters from the grid search, we fitted the RandomForestRegressor model using X_new. This approach allowed us to leverage the most relevant features, potentially improving model accuracy and stability by focusing on factors most closely associated with the target variable.

**Table 1** presents the accuracy results of the initial Random Forest model in predicting $CO_2$ emissions. The model demonstrated high predictive accuracy, achieving an accuracy rate of 95.4%. Additionally, the Mean Absolute Percentage Error (MAPE) was

| Evaluation metric for initial model | RMSE | MAPE | Accuracy |
|---|---|---|---|
| Training set | 28.271 | 0.046 | 95.4% |

**Table 1.**
*Initial random forest model accuracy results.*

0.046, indicating that the model's predictions deviated minimally from the actual values. These results suggest that the Random Forest model, with tuned hyperparameters and feature selection, is highly effective in accurately estimating vessel $CO_2$ emissions.

## 5.2 Feature importance for Random Forest model

Permutation Importance (PIMP) is an effective method for feature selection, particularly valuable in enhancing the interpretability of models by quantifying the significance of each variable [21]. This approach has proven especially useful in evaluating the impact of features within a Random Forest model. By applying permutation importance, we calculate p-values for each feature, derived through a permutation test that normalizes biased measures.

To preserve the relationships between features, the permutation test is applied to the outcome variable rather than directly to the features themselves. This allows us to correct the inherent bias in feature significance estimates produced by Random Forests, providing a more accurate measure of each variable's contribution to the model's predictions [21]. The resulting feature importance scores, as shown below, offer valuable insights into the variables that are most influential in predicting $CO_2$ emissions.

**Table 2** presents the feature importance scores derived from the Random Forest model using permutation importance. These scores reflect the relative impact of each feature on predicting $CO_2$ emissions, with higher values indicating a stronger influence on the model's predictions.

| Feature | Importance |
|---|---|
| Length | 1.121203 |
| grossTonnage | 0.086251 |
| Width | 0.036428 |
| Draft | 0.018683 |
| ship_type_Container ship | 0.013443 |
| AgeGroup_6–10 | 0.005324 |
| AgeGroup_11–15 | 0.002319 |
| AgeGroup_16–20 | 0.001167 |
| ship_type_Bulk carrier | 0.001013 |
| AgeGroup_0–5 | 0.000391 |
| ship_type_General cargo ship | 0.000074 |
| AgeGroup_21–25 | 0.000057 |
| ship_type_Oil tanker | 0.000051 |
| AgeGroup_6–10 | 0.000040 |

**Table 2.**
*The feature importance scores derived from the random forest model.*

The analysis of feature importance scores in our Random Forest model identified several key variables that significantly influence $CO_2$ emissions. The most impactful feature was vessel length (importance score: 1.121203), suggesting that vessel length is a critical factor in emissions prediction. This is followed by gross tonnage (importance score: 0.086251), which indicates that vessel weight also plays a substantial role in determining emissions levels. Vessel width (importance score: 0.036428) emerged as another important feature, highlighting the relevance of overall vessel dimensions in emissions-related predictions. Additionally, draft (importance score: 0.018683), though less influential than the top three features, still showed a notable contribution to $CO_2$ emissions, underscoring the importance of a vessel's depth in the water as a factor.

In contrast, certain features exhibited minimal importance scores, suggesting they may not add substantial predictive value to the model. For example, specific ship types (Bulk Carrier, General Cargo Ship, Oil Tanker) demonstrated very low scores, ranging from 0.000074 to 0.001013. This indicates that, apart from Container Ships, vessel type does not strongly impact $CO_2$ emissions predictions. Similarly, age group classifications (e.g., AgeGroup_11–15, AgeGroup_16–20) yielded low importance scores (0.000057 or below), implying that a vessel's age may have negligible influence on emissions in this dataset.

Based on these findings, we recommend focusing on the most influential features, such as Length, Gross Tonnage, Width, and Draft, for $CO_2$ emissions prediction. Conversely, features, such as specific ship types (excluding Container Ships) and age groups, may be deprioritized or ignored in future modeling efforts, given their minimal impact. This approach can streamline the model, improving computational efficiency while maintaining predictive accuracy. These insights provide a data-driven foundation for prioritizing design and operational factors that contribute most to emissions, offering valuable guidance or emissions-reduction strategies within the shipping industry.

## 6. Discussion and conclusion

The findings of this study underscore the importance of vessel dimensions and design characteristics, such as length, gross tonnage, and width, as key determinants of $CO_2$ emissions in the maritime sector. These insights suggest that optimizing vessel design could lead to significant reductions in emissions. For instance, longer, more streamlined vessels have been shown to experience reduced hydrodynamic drag, which in turn lowers fuel consumption. This finding aligns with prior research that advocates for "slender" vessel designs as an emissions-reduction strategy. Therefore, future vessel designs could incorporate these structural adjustments to enhance fuel efficiency and reduce $CO_2$ output.

For existing vessels, retrofitting options, such as hull shape modifications and the installation of bulbous bows optimized for different speeds, could provide immediate emissions benefits. Operational optimization also emerged as a critical factor, particularly through speed and draft management. Speed optimization, or "slow steaming," has consistently demonstrated its potential to reduce fuel consumption, and the results of this study highlight its continued relevance. Maritime companies should consider implementing speed optimization protocols across their fleets, particularly on longer voyages, to maximize fuel efficiency. Similarly, draft management, tailored to cargo load and route conditions, can help reduce resistance, leading to lower emissions.

The high predictive accuracy of the Random Forest model used in this study indicates that advanced machine learning techniques hold promise for real-time decision-making in emissions reduction. Integrating predictive analytics into onboard systems could allow vessel operators to make data-driven decisions that optimize speed, route, and other operational factors, ultimately minimizing $CO_2$ emissions. This approach could be particularly valuable in voyage planning, where models can suggest optimal speeds and routes that balance emissions reduction with timely delivery. By leveraging predictive insights, shipping companies could develop dynamic, adaptive strategies to maintain efficiency in various operational scenarios.

Together, these insights and proposed actions provide a multifaceted approach to reducing $CO_2$ emissions in the maritime sector. By focusing on both immediate operational adjustments and longer-term investments in sustainable practices, the maritime industry can make meaningful progress toward environmental sustainability while enhancing operational efficiency and remaining competitive in an increasingly eco-conscious global market.

## 7. Future work

We propose the implementation of digital platforms for tracking and monitoring vessel emissions data to allow companies to set measurable targets and assess progress toward achieving their $CO_2$ emission goals. Such transparency will not only enhance a company's reputation but can also align with the growing market demand for sustainability in maritime operations. In the long term, companies should consider investing in green technologies, including wind-assisted propulsion systems, hybrid engines, and solar power integration, which offer sustainable alternatives to traditional fuel-reliant propulsion. We strongly suggest collaborations with industry stakeholders to shape policies and standards for sustainable practices to accelerate industry-wide adoption of effective $CO_2$ emissions-reduction strategies.

## Conflict of interest

The authors declare no conflict of interest.

## Author details

Carol Anne Hargreaves* and Briana Wan Nee Toh
National University of Singapore (NUS), Singapore, Singapore

*Address all correspondence to: carol.hargreaves@nus.edu.sg

## References

[1] Spinelli F, Mancini S, Vitiello L, Bilandi RN, De Carlini M. Shipping decarbonization: An overview of the different stern hydrodynamic energy saving devices. Journal of Marine Science and Engineering. 2022;**10**(5):574. DOI: 10.3390/jmse10050574

[2] Mallouppas G, Yfantis E. Decarbonization in shipping industry: A review of research, technology development, and innovation proposals. Journal of Marine Science and Engineering. 2021;**9**:415, 10.3390/jmse9040415

[3] Nadery A, Ghassemi H, Chybowski L. The effect of the PSS configuration on the hydrodynamic performance of the KP505 propeller behind the KCS. Ocean Engineering. 2021;**234**:109310, 10.1016/j.oceaneng.2021.109310

[4] Reis MS, Rendall R, Palumbo B, Lepore A, Capezza C. Predicting ships' $CO_2$ emissions using feature-oriented methods. Applied Stochastic Models in Business and Industry. 2019;**36**(1):110-123. DOI: 10.1002/asmb.2477

[5] Jeon M, Noh Y, Shin Y, Lim OK, Lee I, Cho D. Prediction of ship fuel consumption by using an artificial neural network. Journal of Mechanical Science and Technology. 2018;**32**(12):5785-5796. DOI: 10.1007/s12206-018-1126-4

[6] Bal Beşikçi E, Arslan O, Turan O, Ölçer A. An artificial neural network-based decision support system for energy efficient ship operations. Computers & Operations Research. 2016;**66**:393, 10.1016/j.cor.2015.04.004-401

[7] Bassam AM, Phillips AB, Turnock SR, Wilson PA. Ship speed prediction based on machine learning for efficient shipping operation. Ocean Engineering. 2022;**245**:1-11. DOI: 10.1016/j.oceaneng.2021.110449

[8] Tay ZY, Hadi J, Chow F, Loh DJ, Konovessis D. Big data analytics and machine learning of harbour craft vessels to achieve fuel efficiency: A review. Journal of Marine Science and Engineering. 2021;**9**(12):1351. DOI: 10.3390/jmse9121351

[9] Dos Santos Ferreira R, Padilha De Lima JV, Caprace JD. Comparative analysis of machine learning prediction models of container ships propulsion power. Ocean Engineering. 2022;**255**:111439, 10.1016/j.oceaneng.2022.111439

[10] Uyanık T, Yalman Y, Kalenderli Ö, Arslanoğlu Y, Terriche Y, Chun-Lien S, et al. Data-driven approach for estimating power and fuel consumption of ship: A case of container vessel. Mathematics. 2022;**10**:1-21. DOI: 10.3390/math10224167

[11] Lindstad DE, Eskeland GS. Low carbon maritime transport: How speed, size and slenderness amount to substantial capital energy substitution. Transportation Research Part D Transport and Environment. 2015;**41**(3):244-256. DOI: 10.1016/j.trd.2015.10.006

[12] THETIS-MRV. Available from: https://mrv.emsa.europa.eu/#public/eumrv

[13] Al-Shehari T, Alsowail R. An insider data leakage detection using one-hot encoding, synthetic minority oversampling and machine learning techniques. Entropy. 2021;**23**(10):1258. DOI: 10.3390/e23101258

[14] Breiman L. Random forests. Machine Learning. 2001;**45**(1):5-32. DOI: 10.1023/a:1010933404324

[15] Couronné R, Probst P, Boulesteix A. Random forest versus logistic regression: A large-scale benchmark experiment. BMC Bioinformatics. 2018;**19**(1):1-14. DOI: 10.1186/s12859-018-2264-5

[16] Lee T, Ullah A, Wang R. Bootstrap Aggregating and Random Forest. Springer EBooks; 2020. pp. 389-429. DOI: 10.1007/978-3-030-31150-6_13

[17] Great Learning Team. An Introduction to GridSearchCV | What is Grid Search | Great Learning. Great Learning Blog: Free Resources What Matters to Shape Your Career!. 2022. Available from: https://www.mygreatlearning.com/blog/gridsearchcv/#:~:text=GridSearchCV%20is%20a%20technique%20for,the%20parameters%20must%20be%20entered

[18] Panapakidis IP, Sourtzi V, Dagoumas A. Forecasting the fuel consumption of passenger ships with a combination of shallow and deep learning. Electronics. 2020;**9**(5):776. DOI: 10.3390/electronics9050776

[19] Khair U, Fahmi H, Hakim SA, Rahim R. Forecasting error calculation with mean absolute deviation and mean absolute percentage error. Journal of Physics: Conference Series. 2017;**930**:012002. DOI: 10.1088/1742-6596/930/1/012002

[20] Singh S. Two Sides of the MAPE Coin. Supply Chain Link Blog - Arkieva. 2019. Available from: https://blog.arkieva.com/two-sides-of-the-mape-coin/

[21] Altmann A, Tolosi L, Sander O, Lengauer T. Permutation importance: A corrected feature importance measure. Computer Applications in the Biosciences. 2010;**26**(10):1340-1347. DOI: 10.1093/bioinformatics/btq134

Chapter 9

# Perspective Chapter: Lattice Function-Based Support Vector Machine for Shape-Constrained Classification

*Geng Deng, Yaoguo Xie, Xindong Wang and Qiang Fu*

## Abstract

Shape-constrained classification is an important and evolving topic within machine learning, offering insights into enhancing model accuracy and interpretability through the integration of shape information from input features. In this paper, we present a novel Lattice Support Vector Machine (Lattice-SVM) classifier, which accommodates user-defined shape constraints, including monotonicity and convexity/concavity. Lattice-SVM constructs a nonparametric nonlinear discriminant hyperplane by integrating lattice functions. We optimize the model parameters using the Pegasos algorithm for SVM, which incorporates stepwise projections to ensure the feasibility of the shape constraints. Through a series of simulation studies and real-world examples, we illustrate how Lattice-SVM enhances classification performance and effectively captures nonlinear effects by leveraging the shape information of input features.

**Keywords:** lattice regression, Pegasos SDG algorithm, support vector machine, shape-constrained classification, lattice-SVM

## 1. Introduction

In the field of machine learning, classification stands out as a widely discussed subject aiming to utilize an object's features to identify the class to which the target belongs. Real-world problems frequently exhibit shape-restricted relationships in classification tasks. This shape information includes characteristics like monotonicity and convexity/concavity between input features and the target variable. For instance, the default probability of a loan typically decreases as a borrower's credit score (FICO) rises; the incidence of certain diseases may increase with age; cost functions might exhibit concavity with rising prices; and the utility functions of risk-averse agents could be concave. Conventional classifiers, such as Linear Discriminant Analysis (LDA), logistic regression, and Support Vector Machine (SVM), fall short in effectively leveraging this prior shape information to enhance model prediction accuracy, and they can also pose challenges to model interpretability. Recent research on classification problems with monotonicity has gained notable attention. For instance, a comprehensive review of contemporary monotonic classifiers, encompassing monotonic tree methods, SVM, monotonic neural networks (NN), and so on, is provided in [1].

SVM, a fundamental supervised learning tool for classification and regression analysis [2], was initially introduced by Cortes and Vapnik [3]. It continues to hold significance as a robust and widely embraced method, standing as a cornerstone in contemporary machine learning practices. Recent applications of SVM include the integration of Inception V3 deep convolutional neural network with SVM in human posture detection [4] and prediction of Chinese tax revenue [5] using least-squares SVM. SVM, in its conventional form, constructs a hyperplane to effectively separate distinct classes within the data. While the traditional SVM employs a linear separating hyperplane, advancements in the field have introduced parametric kernel transformations that create nonlinear hyperplanes. Nevertheless, extant SVM models are confined to parametric formulations and do not account for tailored shape constraints. This limitation, characterized by the absence of domain-specific shape information, may pose model overfitting issues. Thus, a more refined methodology, capable of incorporating monotonic or more generic shape information, is preferred in practical applications.

The concept of monotonic classification has been extensively explored in various research, spanning diverse machine learning methodologies, including k-Nearest Neighbor (k-NN) [6], tree methods [7], SVM [8], Extreme Learning Machine (ELM) [9], and neural networks (NN) [10]. Pioneering this exploration, Best and Chakravarti [11] introduced isotonic regression, as an early instance of shape-restricted inference. Since its inception, researchers have developed numerous methods and algorithms for incorporating monotonic constraints into machine learning models. For example, Gutierrez et al. [12] proposed an ordinal classification/regression to handle target variables with ordered categorical values. Zhu et al. [9] introduced a generalized form of ELM to address monotonic classification problems. Hu et al. [13] contributed a rank entropy-based decision tree method accommodating monotonicity constraints. Additionally, in the realm of finance, Potharst and Feelders [14] presented a monotonically constrained tree method to model house pricing problems. Chen and Samworth [15] discussed incorporating shape-restricted constraints to Generalized Additive Models (GAM). Barley et al. [16] introduced Partially Monotone SVM (PM-SVM), which provided a more general way of generating monotonicity constraints. Xu et al. [17] enhanced this GAM model using quantile-based knots in mortgage loan default modeling, featuring automatically spline knot selection.

In this paper, we propose a novel Lattice-SVM model, inspired by the widely adopted lattice approach. The proposed Lattice-SVM leverages a lattice-based discriminant hyperplane, accommodating shape constraints such as monotonicity and convexity/concavity tailored for unimodal input data. We formulate a nonlinear discriminant hyperplane using an additive model structure (1-D lattice function) to effectively handle the main feature effects. Optimization of the target function is based on the Pegasos Stochastic Gradient Descent (SGD) algorithm [18, 19]. Furthermore, we employ a sequential projection algorithm to map the solution to shape-constrained feasible regions.

The lattice-based model represents a nonparametric approach, with the lattice being entirely defined by the lattice grid and the values at the grid points. The inclusion of shape constraint serves as a regularization mechanism, augmenting the robustness of the model fitting process. Garcia and Gupta [20] originally introduced the lattice regression, a statistical method that has found application across diverse domains [21]. Notably, Google introduces the TensorFlow Lattice (TFL) library [22], a lattice-based predictive model that incorporates shape-constrained features, complementing the renowned TensorFlow library. In our research, the Pegasos algorithm, combined with the sequential projection technique, is motivated by the same conceptual approach as TFL. Deng et al. [23] extended this idea, applying the 1-D lattice transformation to develop a Lattice-LDA classifier capable of handling various monotonicity and convexity/concavity shape information.

The traditional method of incorporating monotonic constraints into classifiers varies depending on the model being used. Tree-based classifiers such as XGBoost [24] and LightGBM [25] maintain monotonic constraints by refraining from creating new splits on features that violate these constraints. Monotonic Extreme Learning Machine (ELM) [9], on the other hand, directly enforces the gradient of the model output with respect to input features to be either positive or negative during the model parameter optimization process. However, many classifiers marketed as "monotonic" do not offer the capability to model second-order convex or concave shape constraints.

Classifiers that incorporate second-order constraints are often categorized as shape-constrained classifiers rather than monotonic classifiers. For instance, the shape-constrained Generalized Additive Model (GAM) [8] utilizes active-set optimization by splining each input feature. However, this method comes with a rigid optimization framework and is limited to accommodating only a few shape types, such as monotonic and convex/concave, while neglecting other more generic shapes like s-shape or mixtures of convex and concave shapes. In contrast, the lattice-based approach (TFL [22], Lattice LDA [23], Lattice-SVM) emerges as highly versatile due to its ability to flexibly model complex shape constraints and interaction effects (via two-dimensional and high-dimensional lattices). Nevertheless, a notable drawback of this method is its computational expense, especially when dealing with large lattice grids. Additionally, specifying the knot locations requires prior knowledge and expertise from the modeler.

We present a summary outlining the pros and cons of various shape-constrained classifiers in **Table 1** below.

| Classifiers | Pros | Cons |
|---|---|---|
| Tree-based method (XGBoost, Light GBM) | Powerful classification models | Do not model second order shape constraints |
| Monotonic ELM | Monotonic classifier based on efficient ELM | Do not model second order shape constraints |
| Shape-constrained GAM | 1. Computationally efficient algorithm based on GAM<br>2. Automatic knot selection<br>3. Model second order shape constraints | Do not model complex shape constraints such as s-shape. |
| Lattice-based classifiers (TFL, Lattice LDA, Lattice SVM) | 1. Flexible to model complex shape constraints<br>2. Flexible to model interaction effects | 1. Computationally expensive<br>2. Requires specifying knot set |

**Table 1.**
*Comparison of shape-constrained classifiers.*

The subsequent sections of this paper are structured as follows. Section 2 provides an introduction to the standard SVM theory. Following that, Section 3 delves into a comprehensive discussion of the Lattice-SVM methodology, with the application of the Pegasos algorithm to solve the optimization problem, as detailed in Section 3.3. Sections 4 and 5 present simulation and real-data studies, respectively, demonstrating that the Lattice-SVM methodology produces superior classification results when compared to other classifiers, including the standard SVM and tree methods. Finally, in Section 6, we present the conclusion of this research, along with a discussion of future research directions.

## 2. Standard linear SVM

In this section, we provide a brief overview of notations and algorithms for the standard linear SVM solver.

The training dataset is denoted as $\{(x_l, y_l)\}, l = 1, 2, \ldots, N$. Each object $x_l$ includes $d$ features, $x_l \in \mathbb{R}^d$; and each label $y_l$ is selected from a two-class set, $y_l \in \{-1, 1\}$. The standard SVM aims to construct a linear separating hyperplane

$$\{\boldsymbol{x}, f(\boldsymbol{x}) = \boldsymbol{x}^T\boldsymbol{\beta} + \beta_0 = 0\} \tag{1}$$

with the objective to separate data into two classes. The coefficients $\boldsymbol{\beta}$ and $\beta_0$ represent the model parameters to be estimated, and the new label prediction is determined as $\hat{y} = \text{sign}(f(x) \geq 0)$.

Formally, the linear SVM is formulated as an optimization problem that maximizes the margin of the band region $1/\|\boldsymbol{\beta}\|$, defined by two shifted hyperplanes $\{\boldsymbol{x}, f_{\pm}(\boldsymbol{x}) = \boldsymbol{x}^T\boldsymbol{\beta} + \beta_0 = \pm 1\}$. Refer to **Figure 1** for an illustration of the separating band of a linear SVM classifier. In situations when data are non-separable, SVM introduces new slack variables $\xi = (\xi_1, \xi_2, \ldots, \xi_N)$ and a penalty hyperparameter $C$ as a new penalizing error term in the objective function. Notably, $\xi_l$ becomes positive whenever the data point $x_l$ is incorrectly classified, as depicted in **Figure 1**.

$$\min_{\boldsymbol{\beta}, \beta_0} \frac{1}{2}\|\boldsymbol{\beta}\|^2 + C\sum_{l=1}^{N} \xi_l \tag{2}$$

$$\text{subject to:} \quad \xi_l \geq 0, \quad y_l(x_l^T\boldsymbol{\beta} + \beta_0) \geq 1 - \xi_l, \quad \forall l$$

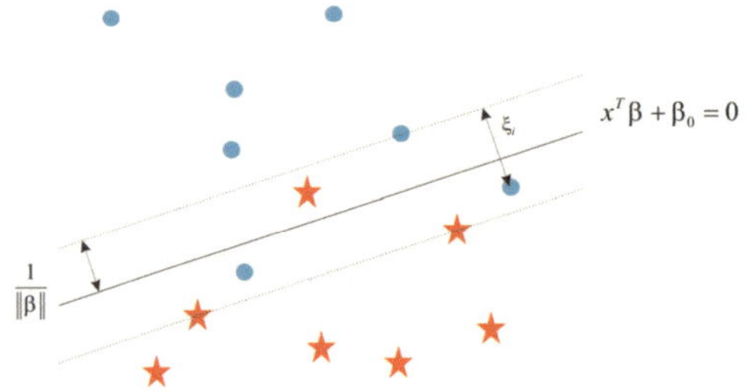


**Figure 1.**
*Illustration of linear SVM.*

SVM is typically solved efficiently through its Lagrange dual problem, which is effectively a constrained quadratic programming problem. Alternatively, another class of methods involves directly optimizing the primal problem using the gradient decent type of algorithms. In SVM, the primal problem requires a slight modification to transform it into an unconstrained optimization problem with a hinge loss function

$$\min_{\boldsymbol{\beta},\beta_0} F(\boldsymbol{\beta},\beta_0) = \frac{\lambda}{2}\|\boldsymbol{\beta}\|^2 + \frac{1}{N}\sum_{l=1}^{N} \max\{0, 1 - y_l(x_l^T\boldsymbol{\beta} + \beta_0)\} \tag{3}$$

Here, the new parameter $\lambda = \frac{1}{NC}$ is a transformation of $C$, also serving the purpose as a regularization parameter for misclassifications. In our study, the primary algorithm is the sub-gradient decent method, the Pegasos algorithm [18, 19]. Since the hinge loss function is non-differentiable, the Pegasos algorithm's iteration utilizes the subgradient of the primal objective function.

## 3. Lattice-SVM for shape-constrained classification

We propose an innovative Lattice-SVM methodology that extends the conventional linear hyperplane to a lattice-based hyperplane, accommodating the shape constraints. The fundamental concept involves constructing the hyperplane through additive modules comprised of 1-D lattice functions.

Recall that in the standard SVM, the linear separating hyperplane is defined as:

$$\left\{\boldsymbol{x}, f(\boldsymbol{x}) = \boldsymbol{x}^T\boldsymbol{\beta} + \beta_0 = \sum_{i=1}^{d} x_i\beta_i + \beta_0 = 0\right\}, \tag{4}$$

where $d$ is the number of features.

In Lattice-SVM, we introduce a nonlinear function, $f(\cdot)$, defined as an additive form of the main effects, akin to the GAMI-Net concept in [26, 27], where the authors proposed a complex xNN structure and lattice modules for the main effects.

In the new Lattice-SVM model, the discriminant hyperplane is given by:

$$f(\boldsymbol{x}) = \sum_{i=1}^{d} r_i(x_i) + \beta_0 \tag{5}$$

where $r_i(x_i)$ is the main effect component, and $\beta_0$ is the bias term (intercept). For model identification purposes, each $r_i$ is assumed to have a zero mean over empirical distribution of the training data.

In this study, we primarily investigate five types of shape constraints, including linear, monotone increasing/decreasing, and convex/concave, as summarized in **Table 2**. In Lattice-SVM, the model is component-wise shape-restricted, implying that each main module $r_i(x_i)$ adheres to a specific shape constraint. These five shapes represent simple and fundamental types of shapes, readily expandable to more complex combinations such as convex increasing/decreasing or S-shapes.

In the following subsections, we will elaborate on the process of constructing the 1-D function $r_i(x_i)$ by applying the lattice transformation. Following this, we will present the formulation of the Lattice-SVM optimization problem and solve it using the Pegasos algorithm.

| Shape # | Shape type | Shape label |
|---|---|---|
| 1 | Linear | l |
| 2 | Monotone increasing | in |
| 3 | Monotone decreasing | de |
| 4 | Convex | cvx |
| 5 | Concave | ccv |

**Table 2.**
*Supported shape constraints.*

## 3.1 Lattice transformation

The concept of lattice transformation was originally introduced in a sequence of papers on Lattice regression [20]. The lattice regression model is essentially interpolating a parametric function on a regular grid of knots. Once the function values on the grid knots are defined, the function within the lattice cell is calculated simply by taking the weighted average of the vertex values of the cell. The lattice transformation maps the original data to a higher dimensional sparse matrix of weights. Instead of directly processing the source data, the transformed weight matrix effectively becomes the new model input. Google's TFL also adopts the lattice transformation and the 1-D lattice function as a fundamental model component.

The lattice transformation is designed to address generic high-dimensional problems. It is important to note that constructing a high dimensional lattice of $(x_1, x_2, \ldots, x_d)$ is computationally expensive. In our Lattice-SVM model, we mitigate the challenge by applying 1-D lattice transformation to each function $r_i(x_i)$ in Eq. (5).

### *3.1.1 1-D lattice transformation of $r_i(x_i)$*

For the main effect $r_i(x_i)$, it is assumed there are $K_i$ knots in the $x_i$ dimension, where the knots are defined as

$$X_{1,i} \leq X_{2,i} \leq \ldots \leq X_{K_i,i} \tag{6}$$

$X_{1,i}$ and $X_{K_i,i}$ represent the minimum and maximum bounds of the domain of $x_i$. Although the placement of the knots is customizable, it is typically set as (equal spaced) quantiles of the data and unchanged throughout the model estimation. Consequently, each 1-D lattice of $x_i$ is fully defined using $K_i$ knot values or $K_i$ parameters.

The 1-D lattice is essentially a piecewise linear function.[1] Without loss of generality, we omit the subscript $i$ in this subsection, simplifying the function form to $r(x)$. We describe how to approximate the function $r(x)$ using an interpolation of look-up table values on the knots. **Figure 2** provides an illustration of the piecewise linear, or 1-D lattice approximation.

The predetermined $K$ knots $X_1, X_2, \ldots, X_K$ define $K-1$ buckets in the entire domain of $x$. Suppose $x$ is a data point in one bucket $[X_k, X_{k+1})$, it can be expressed as the weighted average of the preceding and subsequent knots

[1] In TensorFlow Lattice, the piecewise linear function is referred as a calibrator.

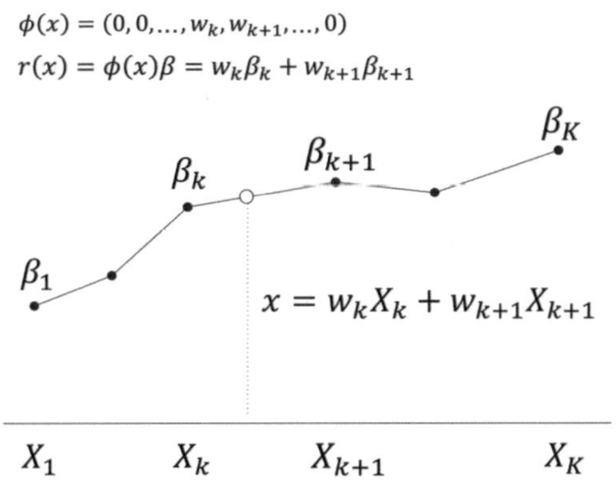


**Figure 2.**
*Piecewise linear function construction of $r(x)$ (equivalent to one-dimensional lattice).*

$$x = w_k X_k + w_{k+1} X_{k+1} \tag{7}$$

where the linear weights are simply computed as

$$w_k = \frac{X_{k+1} - x}{X_{k+1} - X_k} \text{ and } w_{k+1} = 1 - w_k \tag{8}$$

Let parameter vector $\boldsymbol{\beta}$ be the knot values of the piecewise linear function, or $\beta_k = r(X_k)$. The values of the parameter $\boldsymbol{\beta}$ regulate the shape of the piecewise linear function. The function value of $r(x)$ is therefore the weighted average of the knot values

$$r(x) = w_k\beta_k + w_{k+1}\beta_{k+1} \tag{9}$$

To ensure consistency across all buckets, we introduce a weight vector $\phi(\boldsymbol{x})$ of length $K$ for any given $x$, including zero weights in the other buckets

$$\boldsymbol{\phi}(x) = (0, 0, \ldots, w_k, w_{k+1}, 0, \ldots, 0) \tag{10}$$

such that

$$x = \phi(\boldsymbol{x})^T (X_1, X_2, \ldots, X_K) \tag{11}$$

and define the piecewise function $r(x)$ of the entire domain as

$$r(x) = \phi(\boldsymbol{x})^T \boldsymbol{\beta} \tag{12}$$

The weight vector $\phi(\boldsymbol{x})$ is the lattice transformation or mapping function.

Note that the vector $\beta$ defines the look-up table values on each knot $r(X_k) = \beta_k$. To make function $r(x)$ satisfy domain-knowledge shape constraints, it is essentially realized by altering the values of $\boldsymbol{\beta}$. For instance, ensuring a monotone increasing piecewise linear function, $r(x)$, necessitates that $\boldsymbol{\beta}$ be monotone increasing, expressed as:

$$\beta_k \leq \beta_{k+1}, \quad k = 1, 2, \ldots, K - 1 \tag{13}$$

The ordering constraint on $\boldsymbol{\beta}$ ensures monotonicity in the piecewise linear function. Similar adjustments to the values in $\boldsymbol{\beta}$ can be made to satisfy more intricate shape constraints, such as convex or concave shapes. The utilization of knot values in $\boldsymbol{\beta}$ to control the function's shape is a distinctive feature of the lattice transformation.

### 3.2 Solving the optimization problem

This subsection describes the methodology to address the optimization problem. Let parameter set $(\boldsymbol{\beta}_1, \cdots, \boldsymbol{\beta}_d)$ be the parameter for modules $(i = 1, 2, \ldots, d)$. $\beta_0$ is the bias term (intercept). In the proposed Lattice-SVM model, the discriminant hyperplane is defined as:

$$f(\boldsymbol{x}, \boldsymbol{\beta}) = \sum_{i=1}^{d} r_i(x_i, \boldsymbol{\beta}_i) + \beta_0 \tag{14}$$

Upon the application of the lattice transformation on input $\boldsymbol{x}$ to $\boldsymbol{\phi}(\boldsymbol{x})$, which is a matrix of weights, the original input with $1 + d$ dimensions is transformed to a much larger dimension: $1 + \sum_{i=1}^{d} K_i$ number of covariates. Given the hyperplane defined by $\{\boldsymbol{x}, f(\boldsymbol{x}, \boldsymbol{\beta}, \beta_0) = 0\}$, the lattice SVM's objective function is the primal objective. Lattice-SVM requires additional shape constraints $g_i\left(\boldsymbol{\beta}^{(i)}\right) \geq 0, i = 1, \ldots, d$.

The optimization problem setup of the new shape-constrained Lattice-SVM is therefore formulated as a new constrained optimization problem:

$$\arg\min_{\boldsymbol{\beta}, \beta_0} F(\boldsymbol{\beta}, \beta_0) \tag{15}$$

$$\text{subject to}: \; g_i\left(\boldsymbol{\beta}^{(i)}\right) \geq 0, i = 1, \ldots, d$$

### 3.3 The Pegasos algorithm: stochastic subgradient descent for SVM

In this section, we provide a brief overview of the main structure of the Pegasos algorithm and delve into the implementation details.

For illustration purposes, we first omit the bias term $\beta_0$. At iteration $t$ of the algorithm, one needs to select a random training sample $\left(x_{l_t}, y_{l_t}\right)$ by picking an index $l_t \in \{1, \cdots, N\}$, or a random mini-batch of indexes $A_t$. The objective function (3) is then approximated as

$$F(\boldsymbol{\beta}, A_t) = \frac{\lambda}{2} \|\boldsymbol{\beta}\|^2 + \frac{1}{k} \sum_{l \in A_t} \max\{0, 1 - y_l x_l^T \boldsymbol{\beta}\} \tag{16}$$

where $k$ indexes are selected from a random subset $A_t \subset [N] = \{1, \cdots, N\}$, $|A_t| = k$, at each iteration. As noted, $k = N$ makes the optimization equivalent to the original problem (3). The subsamples in this case are referred as mini-batches.

Given the subsample set $A_t$, the subgradient of the objective function is derived as

$$\nabla F_t = \lambda \boldsymbol{\beta} - \frac{1}{k} \sum_{l \in A_t} \mathbf{1}(y_l (x_l^T \boldsymbol{\beta}) < 1) y_l x_l, \tag{17}$$

where $\mathbf{1}(\cdot)$ is the indicator function.

As mentioned earlier, the original SVM problem (3) typically includes a bias (intercept) term, $\beta_0$, which is a scale parameter. The bias term is essential when the distribution of the target $y$ is uneven, a common occurrence in practice. However, simply adding the bias parameter $\beta_0$ to the model makes the objective function non-strictly convex, diminishing the efficiency of algorithm.

Several approaches have been proposed in the original paper to treat the additional bias parameter $\beta_0$. One method involves introducing an optimization sub-problem for $\beta_0$ at each iteration given $\boldsymbol{\beta}$. This effectively redefines the new objective function as

$$\min_{\boldsymbol{\beta}} F(\boldsymbol{\beta}, A_t) = \frac{\lambda}{2} \|\boldsymbol{\beta}\|^2 + G(\boldsymbol{\beta}, S), \tag{18}$$

where

$$G(\boldsymbol{\beta}, S) = \min_{\beta_0} \frac{1}{N} \sum_{l=1}^{N} \max\left\{0, 1 - y_l\left(x_l^T \boldsymbol{\beta} + \beta_0\right)\right\} \tag{19}$$

At each iteration, a subgradient of $F(\boldsymbol{\beta}, A_t)$ needs to be found, and a steep decent step of $\boldsymbol{\beta}$ is performed. Solving the optimization subproblem is a generalized weighted median problem, but this adaptation is effective only for $k = N$.

We outline the main structure of the Pegasos algorithm as follows.

---

**Algorithm 1**: Pegasos algorithm with projection

---

Initialize $\boldsymbol{\beta}_1 = 0 \in \mathbb{R}^d$

**for** each iteration $t = 1, \cdots, T$ **do**

Select $A_t \in [m]$, where $|A_t| = k$ uniformly at random.

Optimize $\beta_0$ in the optimization subproblem (19) given $\boldsymbol{\beta}_t$.

Set $\gamma_t = \frac{1}{\lambda t}$, $A_t^+ = \left\{l \in A_t : y_l x_l^T \boldsymbol{\beta} < 1\right\}$. Update the parameter vector by applying the projection algorithm

$$\boldsymbol{\beta}_{t+1} = \text{proj}\left((1 - \gamma_t \lambda)\boldsymbol{\beta}_t + \frac{\gamma_t}{k} \sum\nolimits_{l \in A_t^+} y_l x_l\right), \text{ s.t. } g_i\left(\boldsymbol{\beta}^{(i)}\right) \geq 0 \tag{20}$$

Stop if convergence is obtained, or the max number of iteration $T$ is reached.

**end for**

---

The constraints $g_i\left(\boldsymbol{\beta}^{(i)}\right) \geq 0$ are shape constraints specifying the shape of each individual feature. We introduce a stepwise projection function $\text{proj}(\cdot)$ in the Pegasos algorithm to accommodate the shape constraints in the Lattice-SVM problem (14). As mentioned before, the Pegasos with projection is also motivated by the algorithm implemented in TFL [22].

In this research, we consider the following two basic types of projection algorithms designed to handle monotone shapes and convex/concave shapes:

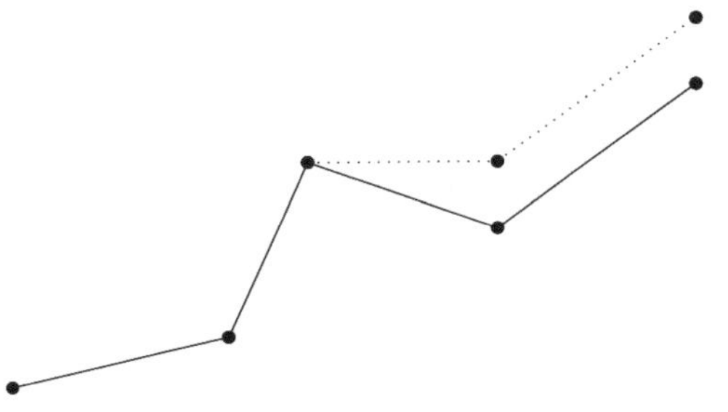

**Figure 3.**
*Projection for a monotone increasing solution.*

- Monotone increasing or decreasing shapes

The details of the algorithm are presented below. **Figure 3** illustrates an example of the projection for a monotone increasing shape constraint by adjusting the step difference $\Delta\beta_k \geq 0$.

---

**Algorithm 2**: Monotone projection algorithm $\hat{\boldsymbol{\beta}} = \text{proj}(\boldsymbol{\beta})$.

---

Given a vector $\boldsymbol{\beta} = (\beta_1, \beta_2, \dots, \beta_K)$.
Compute the step difference between the values

$$\Delta\beta_k = \beta_{k+1} - \beta_k, k = 1, 2, \dots, K - 1 \tag{21}$$

Update and output $\hat{\boldsymbol{\beta}}$

$$\hat{\beta}_{k+1} = \beta_1 + \sum\nolimits_{i=1}^{k-1} \min/\max(\Delta\beta_i, 0), k = 1, 2, \dots, K - 1 \tag{22}$$

" max " is applied to monotone increasing shape and " min " to monotone decreasing shape.

---

- Convex or concave shapes

The algorithm for projecting a vector as a convex (or concave) shape is based on Dykstra's alternating projections algorithm. See Algorithm 3 for detailed steps.

---

**Algorithm 3**: Convex and Concave projection algorithm $\hat{\boldsymbol{\beta}} = \text{proj}(\boldsymbol{\beta})$.

---

Given a vector $\boldsymbol{\beta} = (\beta_1, \beta_2, \dots, \beta_K)$
Compute the step difference between the values

$$\Delta\beta_k = \beta_{k+1} - \beta_k, k = 1, 2, \dots, K - 1 \tag{23}$$

Compute the step difference of the knot locations

$$\Delta X_k = X_{k+1} - X_k, k = 1, 2, \dots, K - 1 \tag{24}$$

Update $\Delta\hat{\boldsymbol{\beta}}$ in two steps

$$\Delta\hat{\beta}_k = \min/\max\left(\Delta\beta_k, \frac{\Delta X_k(\Delta\beta_k + \Delta\beta_{k+1})}{\Delta X_k + \Delta X_{k+1}}\right), k = 1, 3, \ldots \tag{25}$$

$$\Delta\hat{\beta}_k = \max/\min\left(\Delta\beta_k, \frac{\Delta X_{k+1}(\Delta\beta_k + \Delta\beta_{k+1})}{\Delta X_k + \Delta X_{k+1}}\right), k = 2, 4, \ldots \tag{26}$$

" min and max " is applied to the convex shape, and " max and min " is applied to the concave shape

Output $\hat{\boldsymbol{\beta}}$

$$\hat{\beta}_{k+1} = \beta_1 + \sum\nolimits_{i=1}^{k-1} \Delta\hat{\beta}_k, k = 1, 2, \ldots, K-1 \tag{27}$$

In practice, when applying Dykstra's alternating projection algorithm, multiple updates are required at each iteration. As suggested by the authors in TFL [22], while Dykstra's algorithm provides proper projection with respect to the L2 norm, it approaches it from the "wrong" side, necessitating approximate projections strictly into the feasible space. To ensure the values fall into the feasible region defined by the constraints, the author set the default number of projection times to eight.

From our experience, we notice that about 10 rounds of the Dykstra's updates can provide good approximations for convex/concave shapes. In the subsequent simulation and real-data analysis, we use a large default value (50) as the maximum number of rounds of updates.

## 4. Simulation studies

We created two simulation examples to demonstrate the performance of Lattice-SVM. In both examples, the targeting $y$ labels $\{-1, 1\}$ were simulated based on two-dimensional nonlinear separating planes $f(x_1, x_2)$, subject to complex shape constraints. The Lattice-SVM classifier was implemented in MATLAB, and the simulation tests were conducted in a computer equipped with an Intel i7-10850H processor and 32GB of RAM.

1. The first example applies a convex function for the domain $x_1, x_2 \in [0, 1]$. The separating plane is defined as

$$f_1(x_1, x_2) = r_1(x_1) + r_2(x_2) = (x_1 - 0.5)^2 + (x_2 - 0.5)^2, \tag{28}$$

which is "convex" for both $x_1$ and $x_2$.

2. The second example uses the same domain $x_1, x_2 \in [0, 1]$ and defines the separating plane as

$$f_2(x_1, x_2) = r_1(x_1) + r_2(x_2) = \log(4x_1 + 0.05) + log\,(x_2 + 0.05), \tag{29}$$

which is "concave increasing" for both $x_1$ and $x_2$, and the value 0.05 is added to the log function to prevent negative infinity values when either $x_1$ or $x_2$ is 0.

When configuring Lattice-SVM, the knot set includes equal-spaced percentiles. For the first example, we used 99 knots, spanning percentiles 0.01–0.99, and for the second example, we used 19 knots, covering percentiles 0.05–0.95, alongside the inclusion of minimum and maximum points for each feature. We generated 5000 samples from a binomial distribution of the underlying function $f(x_1, x_2)$ and set the parameter $\lambda$ to 0.01.

**Figures 4** and **5** present the true underlying function compared with recovered lattice function by Lattice-SVM. In both examples, we normalized the probability $f_1$ and $f_2$ to a range of $(0, 1)$ and scaled the Lattice-SVM-fitted curve to match the range of the actual functions $r_1$ and $r_2$.

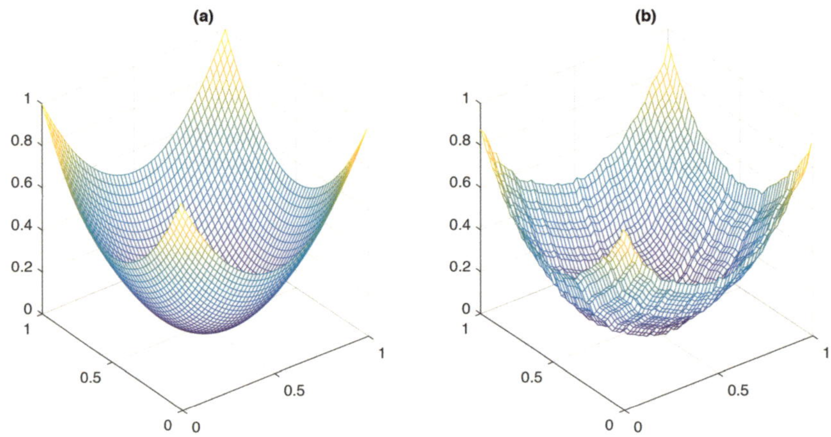


**Figure 4.**
*(a) Theoretical form of separating plane* $f_1(x_1, x_2) = (x_1 - 0.5)^2 + (x_2 - 0.5)^2$, *(b) 2-D Lattice-SVM spline approximation of* $f_1$.

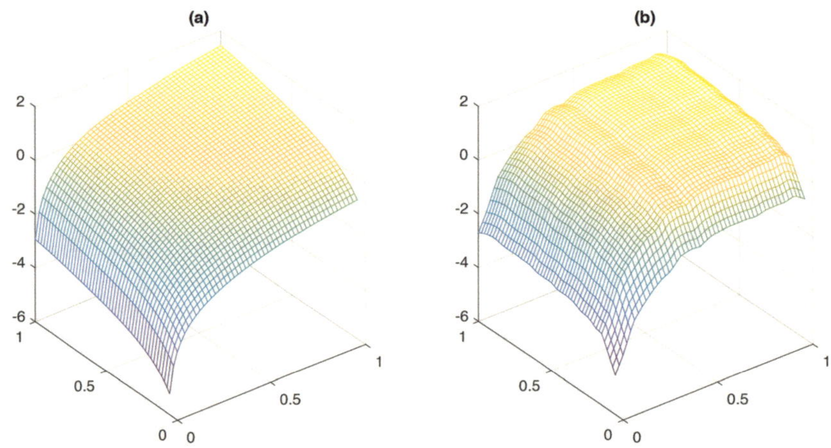


**Figure 5.**
*(a) Theoretical form of separating plane of* $f_2(x_1, x_2) = \log(4x_1 + 0.05) + \log(x_2 + 0.05)$, *(b) 2-D Lattice-SVM spline approximation of* $f_2$.

From the 2-D plots in both examples, it is evident that Lattice-SVM can accurately capture the underlying function and its shape, outperforming conventional linear classifiers. Further enhancement of model fit can be achieved by increasing the sample size or employing denser knot sets, albeit at the expense of additional computational iterations. However, this approach may also lead to overfitting with an excessive number of knots. Drawing from our simulation and real-data analyses, we find that employing approximately 10 to 20 knots provides Lattice-SVM with satisfactory performance.

## 5. Real world data analysis

Next, we applied Lattice-SVM to real world data to evaluate its performance. We compared the model predicting accuracy between Lattice-SVM and several commonly used classifiers, including SVM (Linear), SVM (Gaussian kernel), Classification tree, Classification tree with Adaptive Boosting [28], and PM-SVM [16].

The datasets were sourced from the UCI Machine Learning Repository [29]. We selected four datasets, including the Wisconsin Breast Cancer (WBC), the Abalone, the Auto MPG, and the Car Evaluation data. The data statistics are summarized in **Table 3**, with all entries containing missing values removed. To configure the classification problem, we restricted the target to two classes (1 and $-$ 1) for each dataset. Specifically, for the WBC data, the target class with "malignant" was set to 1 and with "benign" was set to $-1$. For the Abalone data, the target "Rings" is a continuous variable ranging from 1 to 29. We split it using the threshold at 10, where $Rings \geq 10$ was set to 1, and $Rings < 10$ was set to $-1$. For Auto MPG, we set the target $mpg \geq 20$ to be 1, and $mpg < 20$ to be $-1$. While for the Car Evaluation data, the target class with "unacc" (unacceptable) was set to $-1$, and the other three classes with "acc" (acceptable), "good," and "vgood" (very good) to be 1. It is also noted that when we applied PM-SVM, the constrained set was generated based on Randomized Conjunctive (CJ1) algorithm [8].

In our analysis, each example underwent 10-fold cross-validation. Each validation round utilized 90% of the source data as the training set and the remaining 10% as the test set. The same training and testing data were used for each cross-validation partition when evaluating other classifiers. It is noted that when employing a tree with Adaptive Boosting, we selected 100 learning cycles for each training dataset. To ensure a fair comparison among input features, we standardized each feature to have a zero mean and a standard deviation of one before optimizing Lattice-SVM. Subsequently, we transformed the results back to their original scale. Regarding knot selection, we utilized nine knots for all examples, spanning percentiles 0.1 to 0.9, in addition to the minimum and maximum points for each feature.

| Dataset | # Obs | # Features | # Original Classes | Source |
|---|---|---|---|---|
| Wisc Breast Cancer (WBC) | 683 | 9 | 2 | UCI |
| Abalone | 4177 | 7 | Continuous | UCI |
| Auto MPG | 392 | 7 | Continuous | UCI |
| Car | 1728 | 6 | 4 | UCI |

**Table 3.**
*Data description in the real-world examples.*

We evaluated the model performance by computing the average accuracy across test datasets obtained from cross-validation. In each iteration, accuracy was determined as the sum of the True Positive Rate (TP) and the True Negative Rate (TN), calculated as one minus the mean misclassification rate of the 0/1 loss function. The results, including both average accuracy and standard deviation, are presented in **Table 4**.

From the WBC example, we assigned 1 (orange) to the target "class = malignant" and − 1 (blue) to "class = benign." The data contained approximately 35% of the records with the attribute = 1. In this example, we selected Clump Thickness to be "convex increasing," Cell Shape Uniformity to be "monotone increasing," Bland Chromatin to be "concave increasing," and the rest of the features to have "linear" shapes. The fitted results in **Table 4** indicate that the Lattice-SVM model achieves an average prediction accuracy of approximately 0.9723, outperforming popular nonlinear classifiers such as SVM (with Gaussian kernel), PM-SVM, and decision trees. Moreover, the bar plot of each feature and its marginal approximation function $\hat{r}_i(x_i)$ are shown in **Figures 6** and 7, respectively. Notably, we observe that for Clump Thickness, the slope becomes steeper when it exceeds 8, while for Bland Chromatin, the slope gets steeper when it falls below 4, offering enhanced fitting and insights into the relationship between the probability of breast cancer and the input variables.

For the Abalone example, the target "Rings" (Rings plus 1.5 gives the age in years) indicates the age of abalone. We assigned 1 (orange) to the target "Rings ≥10" and − 1 (blue) to "Rings <10;" about 50% of the records have the attribute = 1. The dataset contains seven input features, including length (longest shell measurement), diameter (perpendicular to length), height (with meat in shell), whole weight (whole abalone), shucked weight (weight of the meat), viscera weight (gut weight after bleeding), and shell weight (after being dried). We notice that several input features exhibit high correlations, potentially causing multicollinearity issues in the additive model structure. To mitigate this, we removed input features with correlation greater than 0.9, retaining only three features: height, viscera weight, and shell weight. In this example, we set shell weight to be "concave increasing" and the other two to be "linear." As shown in **Table 4**, specifying the shape constraint solely for shell weight markedly enhances predictive accuracy, enabling the Lattice-SVM model to outperform SVM, PM-SVM, and decision tree methods. Moreover, from **Figures 8** and **9**, it is evident that each input feature exhibits a positive correlation with age (Rings), with the slope for shell weight steepening when it falls below 0.3 and leveling off when it exceeds 0.5.

| Dataset | Lattice-SVM | SVM | SVM (Gaussian) | Tree | Tree (AdaBoost) | PM-SVM |
|---|---|---|---|---|---|---|
| WBC | 0.9723 | 0.9664 | 0.9664 | 0.9253 | 0.9605 | 0.9605 |
| | ± 0.0210 | ± 0.0206 | ± 0.0181 | ± 0.0357 | ± 0.0217 | ± 0.0265 |
| Abalone | 0.7556 | 0.7529 | 0.6818 | 0.7046 | 0.7539 | 0.7548 |
| | ± 0.0180 | ± 0.0198 | ± 0.0479 | ± 0.0147 | ± 0.0182 | ± 0.0188 |
| Auto MPG | 0.9158 | 0.9132 | 0.9106 | 0.8928 | 0.9031 | 0.9055 |
| | ± 0.0380 | ± 0.0367 | ± 0.0423 | ± 0.0266 | ± 0.0411 | ± 0.0384 |
| Car | 0.8941 | 0.8860 | 0.9769 | 0.9798 | 0.9514 | 0.9693 |
| | ± 0.0273 | ± 0.0177 | ± 0.0105 | ± 0.0106 | ± 0.0132 | ± 0.0086 |

**Table 4.**
*Classification performance based on average accuracy and standard deviation of 0/1 loss.*

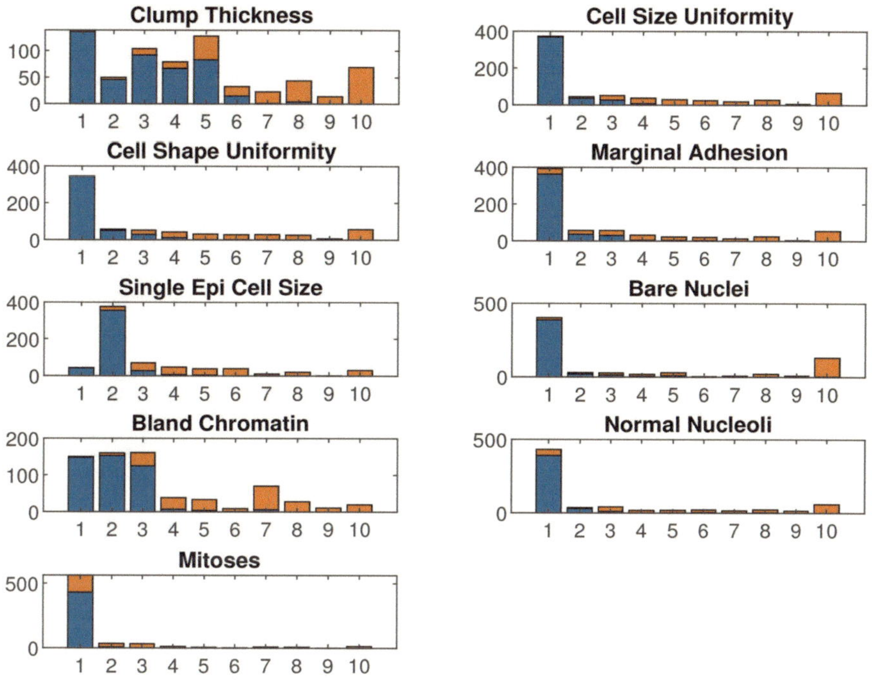


**Figure 6.**
*Bar plot of each feature in the WBC example: Orange: "malignant" (1), Blue: "benign" (−1).*

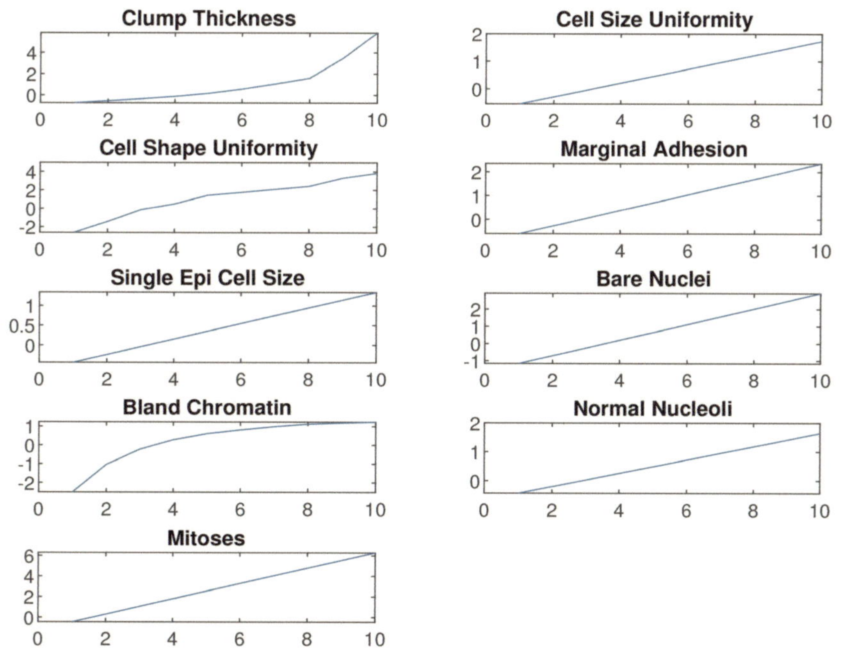


**Figure 7.**
*Plot of each marginal approximation function $\hat{r}_i(x_i)$ in the WBC example.*

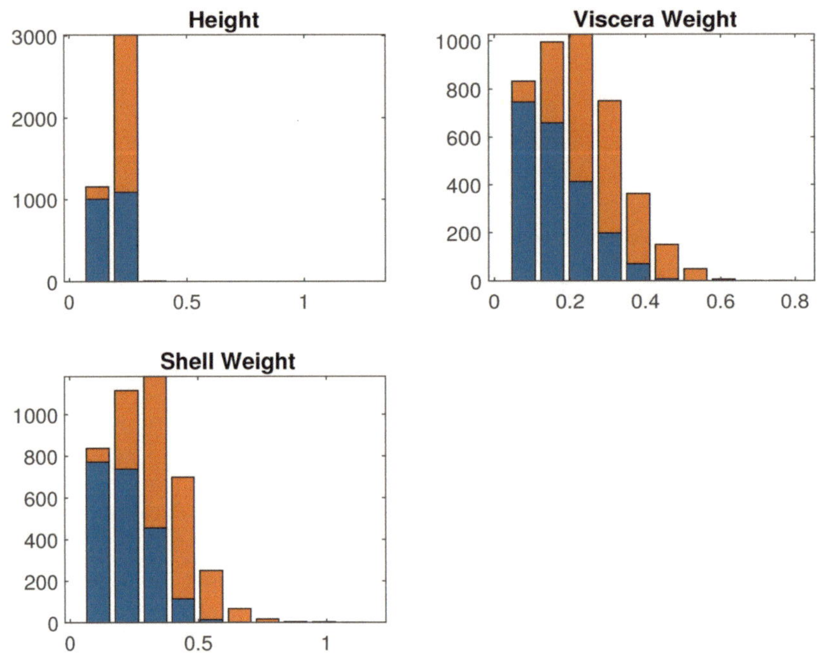


**Figure 8.**
*Bar plot of each feature in the Abalone example: Orange: "Rings ≥10" (1), Blue: "Rings <10" (−1).*

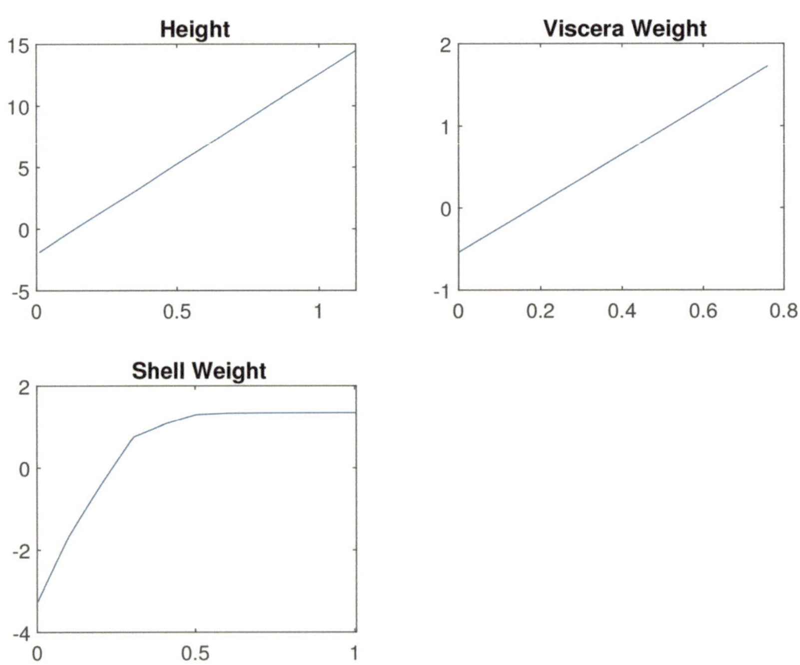


**Figure 9.**
*Plot of each marginal approximation function $\hat{r}_i(x_i)$ in the Abalone example.*

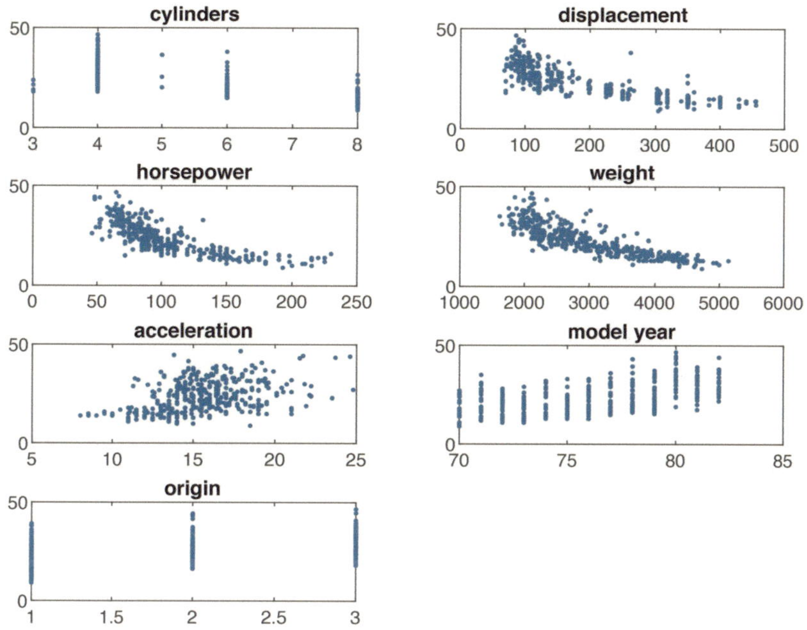


**Figure 10.**
*Distribution of each feature in the Auto MPG example.*

For the Auto MPG example, as mentioned above, the target "mpg" was split at 20. The dataset contains seven input features, including cylinders, displacement, horsepower, weight, acceleration, model year, and the origin. **Figure 10** gives the marginal approximation function of each input feature. From the plot, one can easily identify the shape information, and in this analysis, we set cylinders, weight, and model year to be linear shape; displacement and horsepower to be "convex decreasing;" and acceleration and origin to be "monotone increasing," From **Table 4**, the Lattice-SVM model has an average prediction accuracy of approximately 0.9158 and outperforms the other classifiers. Moreover, it can be seen that for displacement, the slope is steeper when it is less than 200, and similarly for horsepower, the slope is steeper when the value is less than 150. While for acceleration, when the value is between 13 and 17, the slope is steeper than outside this range.

The fourth example is the Car Evaluation data. The target is to evaluate the cars' condition to be unacceptable, acceptable, good, or very good. We note that in this example, with appropriate shape information, the Lattice-SVM method can reach an average prediction accuracy of 0.8941 and only performs better than linear SVM, while SVM with Gaussian kernel and tree methods have much higher accuracy. Given the sub-optimal performance of Lattice-SVM in this case, the marginal distribution and the approximation functions are not presented. One potential reason is that Lattice-SVM still follows the GAM structure and may not handle the non-linear relationship with interaction effects or other complex structures like trees or neural networks. This implies some limitations for the Lattice-SVM method and the GAM structure, which will be discussed further (**Figure 11**).

An advantage of Lattice-SVM observed in real-data analysis is its interpretability. Upon specifying the shape constraint, users can readily visualize the fitted marginal effect of each input feature through plots, facilitating a more intuitive understanding of

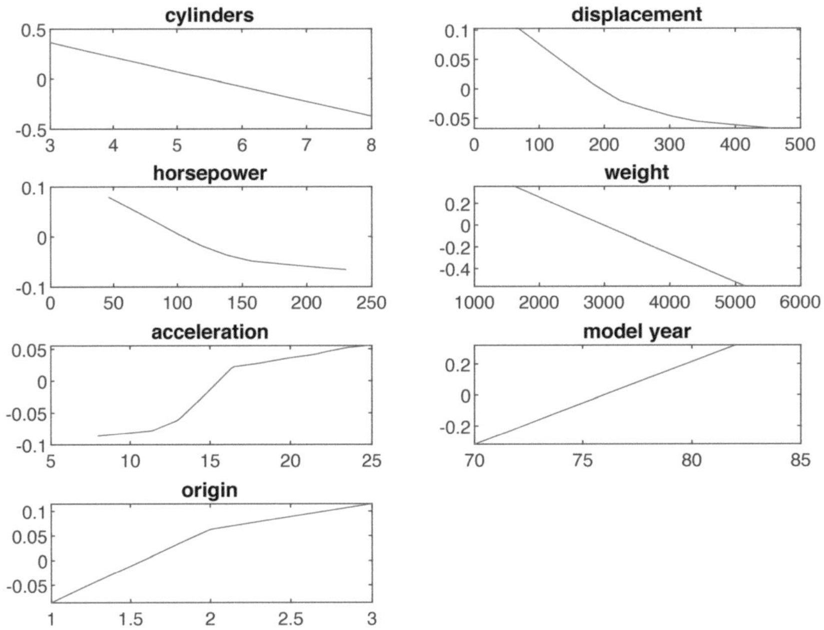


**Figure 11.**
*Plot of each marginal approximation function $\hat{r}_i(x_i)$ in the Auto MPG example.*

the relationship between inputs and targets. It is worth noting that while employing more knots may yield more granular-fitted results, it demands greater computational resources and may lead to overfitting. Based on our experience, we recommend using 10 to 20 knots for the Lattice-SVM model to achieve both higher accuracy and computational efficiency. Additionally, it is also possible to add interaction effects, modeled by a high-dimensional lattice. However, this could substantially increase the number of parameters to optimize, making the optimization solver computationally expensive.

While the choice between convex and concave may seem intriguing initially, incorrectly selecting the opposite type (e.g., using convex types for concave data) can cause the algorithm to degenerate to a linear line without applying transformations at any knots (provided with sufficient amount of data). Therefore, careful consideration and understanding of the data's characteristics are essential when choosing the appropriate shape constraint.

The Pegasos is a stochastic subgradient algorithm that is subject to the stochastic index set selection and subgradient calculation accuracy. Generally speaking, the computational efficiency is not as good as the solvers for traditional linear SVM and kernel-based SVM, which apply quadratic programming algorithm for the SVM dual problem. This is observed even for the standard Pegasos algorithm. Regarding the projection algorithms embedded in the main Pegasos algorithms, they typically produce robust shape-constrained mappings in our experiments.

## 6. Conclusions

In this paper, we have introduced a new Lattice Support Vector Machine (Lattice-SVM) classifier, designed to incorporate user-defined shape constraints such as monotonicity and convexity/concavity, thereby enhancing model accuracy and interpretability. Employing an additive format of lattice functions, the Lattice-SVM method effectively addresses nonlinear problems. Optimizing the model utilizes the Pegasos algorithm for SVM, integrating customized stepwise projections to ensure the specified shape constraints.

By incorporating appropriate shape constraints, users can refine model fitting and reduce prediction bias. Our research demonstrates the efficacy and robustness of the Lattice-SVM model through simulation studies and real-world examples. Notably, this method exhibits greater stability in the presence of random errors or noise in the data while maintaining model interpretability compared to other machine learning tools such as SVM or decision trees. The incorporation of shape information into the model fitting process facilitates a better understanding of the underlying relationship between specific inputs and the target variable.

Upon modification, Lattice-SVM can be easily extended to handle multi-class problems and regression with shape constraints. Let $M$ be the number of classes, one common technique involves creating $M$ one-versus-rest classifiers and selecting the class that best classifies the data with the largest margin. Alternatively, a set of one-versus-one classifiers can be built, and the class with the highest number of votes is chosen. The latter approach involves constructing $M(M-1)/2$ classifiers.

There are several directions to enhance the Lattice-SVM model. Utilizing higher-dimensional lattices could enable capturing interactions or more complex joint effects among input features. Additionally, developing an automatic procedure to determine the optimal number of knots on each feature by incorporating penalty terms could further refine the model. Given that Lattice-SVM optimization relies on the Pegasos algorithm, which is a stochastic gradient descent method, future research could focus on optimizing the selection of regularization parameters and stopping rules to strike a balance between model accuracy and computational efficiency.

## Conflict of interest

The authors declare no conflict of interest.

## Disclaimer

The opinions in this paper are strictly those of the authors and do not represent the views of Wells Fargo & Company, or any of their subsidiaries or affiliates.

## Author details

Geng Deng[1*], Yaoguo Xie[2], Xindong Wang[1] and Qiang Fu[1]

1 Corporate Model Risk, Mc Lean, VA, USA

2 Corporate Model Risk, Charlotte, NC, USA

*Address all correspondence to: geng.deng@wellsfargo.com

## References

[1] Cano J-R, Gutiérrez PA, Krawczyk B, Woźniak M, García S. Monotonic classification: An overview on algorithms, performance measures and data sets. Neurocomputing. 2019;**341**: 168-182

[2] Hastie T, Tibshirani R, Friedman J. The Elements of Statistical Learning. New York, NY: Springer; 2009

[3] Cortes C, Vapnik V. Support-vector networks. Machine Learning. 1995; **20**(3):273-297

[4] Ogundokun RO, Maskeliūnas R, Misra S, Damasevicius R. Hybrid Inceptionv 3-SVM-based approach for human posture detection in health monitoring systems. Algorithms. 2022; **15**(11):410

[5] Zhang D, Zheng S, Fu W. Research on the prediction model of Chinese tax revenue based on GM (1,1) and LSSVM. Information Technology and Control. 2023;**52**(4):811-818

[6] Duivesteijn W, Feelders A. Nearest neighbour classification with monotonicity constraints. ECML/PKDD Lecture Notes in Computer Science. 2008;**5211**:301-316

[7] Qian Y, Xu H, Liang J, Wang J, Liu B. Fusing monotonic decision trees. IEEE Transactions on Knowledge and Data Engineering. 2015;**27**(10): 2717-2728

[8] Chen C, Li ST. Credit rating with a monotonicity-constrained support vector machine model. Expert Systems with Applications. 2014;**41**(16): 7235-7247

[9] Zhu H, Tsang E, Wang XZ, Ashfaq R. Monotonic classification extreme learning machine. Neurocomputing. 2017;**225**:205-213

[10] Daniels H, Velikova M. Monotone and partially monotone neural networks. IEEE Transactions on Neural Networks. 2010;**21**(6):906-917

[11] Best MJ, Chakravarti N. Active set algorithms for isotonic regression; a unifying framework. Mathematical Programming. 1990;**47**:425-439

[12] Gutierrez P, Perez-Ortiz M, Sanchez-Monedero J, Fernandez-Navarro F, Hervas-Martinez C. Ordinal regression methods: Survey and experimental study. IEEE Transactions on Knowledge and Data Engineering. 2015;**28**(1):127-146

[13] Hu Q, Che X, Zhang L, Zhang D, Guo M, Yu D. Rank entropy-based decision trees for monotonic classification. IEEE Transactions on Knowledge and Data Engineering. 2011; **24**(11):2052-2064

[14] Potharst R, Feelders AJ. Classification trees for problems with monotonicity constraints. ACM SIGKDD Explorations Newsletter. 2002;**4**(1):1-10

[15] Chen Y, Samworth RJ. Generalized additive and index models with shape constraints. Journal of Royal Statistical Society, Series B. 2016;**78**(4):729–754

[16] Bartley C, Liu W, Reynolds M. Effective monotone knowledge integration in kernel support vector machine. In: Proceedings of the 12th International Conference on Advanced Data Mining and Applications. Cham: Springer; 2016. pp. 3-18

[17] Xu G, Deng G, Wang X, Fu K. Automatic spline knot selection in

modeling mortgage loan default using shape constrained regression. The Journal of Structured Finance. 2021; **27**(3):18-36

[18] Shalev-Shwartz S, Singer Y, Srebro N. Pegasos: Primal estimated sub-gradient solver for SVM. Mathematical Programming. 2011;**127**(1):3-30

[19] Spall JC. Introduction to Stochastic Search and Optimization: Estimation, Simulation, and Control. Hoboken, NJ: John Wiley & Sons; 2005

[20] Garcia E, Gupta M. Lattice regression. Advances in Neural Information Processing Systems (NIPS). 2009;**22**:1-9

[21] Garcia EK, Arora R, Gupta MR. Optimized regression for efficient function evaluation. IEEE Transactions on Image Processing. 2012;**21**(9): 4128-4140

[22] Gupta M, Cotter A, Pfeifer J, Voevodski K, Canini K, Mangylov A, et al. Monotonic calibrated interpolated look-up tables. Journal of Machine Learning Research. 2016;**17**(109):1-47

[23] Deng G, Xie Y, Wang X, Fu Q. Lattice linear discriminant analysis for shape constrained classification. Fuzzy Systems and Data Mining VIII: Proceedings of FSDM. 2022;**2022**(358): 80-96

[24] Chen T, Guestrin C. Xgboost: A scalable tree boosting system. In: Proceedings of the 22nd ACM SIGKDD International Conference on Knowledge Discovery and Data Mining, KDD'16. San Francisco: ACM; 2016

[25] Ke G, Meng Q, Finley T, Wang T, Chen W, Ma W, et al. Light GBM: A highly efficient gradient boosting decision tree. Advances in Neural Information Processing Systems. 2017; **30**:3146-3154

[26] Deng G, Xu G, Yang Z, Liang Y, Wang X, Fu Q, et al. The anatomy of mortgage default using shape-constrained explainable machine learning model. The Journal of Financial Data Science. 2023;**5**(4):66-85

[27] Yang Z, Zhang A, Sudjianto A. GAMI-net: An explainable neural network based on generalized additive models with structured interactions. Pattern Recognition. 2021;**120**:108192

[28] Freund Y, Schapire RE. A decision-theoretic generalization of on-line learning and an application to boosting. Journal of Computer and System Sciences. 1997;**55**:119-139

[29] Dua D, Graff C. UCI machine learning repository, 2017

Chapter 10

# Private SVM Inference on Encrypted Data

*Ahmad Al Badawi*


## Abstract

This tutorial chapter provides a comprehensive guide to implementing privacy-preserving Support Vector Machine (SVM) inference using Fully Homomorphic Encryption (FHE). We demonstrate a practical solution for secure and private SVM inference on encrypted data, enabling sensitive data analysis while maintaining confidentiality. Through a step-by-step implementation on a real-world dataset, we cover data preparation, SVM model training, and homomorphic inference. Our experimental results on a commodity laptop show that our approach achieves high accuracy with a reasonable latency of nearly 6 seconds for SVM inference. This chapter serves as a valuable resource for practitioners and researchers seeking to apply privacy-preserving techniques to SVM solutions, with significant implications for applications like medical diagnosis, financial prediction, and recommender systems, where data privacy is crucial. By following this tutorial, readers can gain hands-on experience with privacy-preserving SVM inference using FHE.


**Keywords:** encrypted SVMs inference, machine learning as a service, privacy-preserving machine learning, homomorphic encryption, implementation

## 1. Introduction

Support Vector Machines (SVMs) have become indispensable tools in supervised machine learning, playing a crucial role in solving a wide range of problems. These algorithms are widely employed for both classification and regression tasks. Their effectiveness lies in their ability to find optimal decision boundaries by maximizing the margin between different classes making them particularly useful when dealing with complex datasets [1–9].

A significant challenge arises when applying SVMs to problems involving sensitive data, which poses substantial privacy risks. This is particularly concerning in scenarios where datasets contain personal and sensitive information, such as medical records, financial transactions, or user preferences. In these cases, maintaining data privacy becomes crucial to prevent unauthorized access, misuse, or exploitation. Furthermore, stringent privacy regulations like the General Data Protection Regulation (GDPR) impose strict constraints on handling sensitive data, limiting its use beyond specific purposes like storage and logging and prohibiting its use for analysis without privacy-aware methods [10, 11]. Therefore, developing machine learning algorithms,

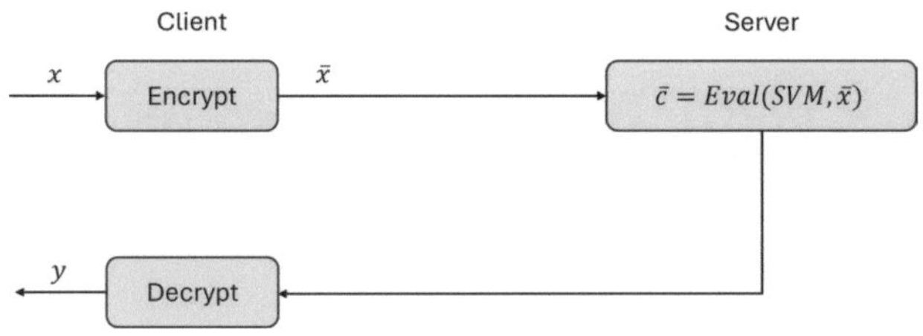


**Figure 1.**
*Privacy-preserving MLaaS protocol with FHE.*

including SVMs, that effectively utilize sensitive data while ensuring privacy remains a critical and active research area [12–19].

One promising solution to balancing data utility and privacy is Fully Homomorphic Encryption (FHE) [20], a cryptographic method that allows an untrusted party to perform operations directly on encrypted data without decryption. This ensures that sensitive information remains confidential throughout the analysis process, making it remarkably useful in cloud computing environments where sensitive data might be shared with the cloud provider. FHE offers a solution for utilizing sensitive data while preserving user privacy. It allows us to extract insights from the data without ever decrypting it, effectively overcoming the limitations imposed by privacy regulations and concerns.

This chapter specifically addresses the challenge of Machine Learning as a Service (MLaaS) when the analysis algorithm is an SVM [21, 22]. As shown in **Figure 1**, in this scenario, two main actors are involved: (1) a user with sensitive data records and (2) a public server that owns a pre-trained SVM model. The user encrypts their data using their FHE secret key and sends it, along with the FHE public material, to the server. The server can then evaluate the pre-trained SVM model on the encrypted user input using FHE evaluation methods. This generates an encrypted insight that is transmitted back to the user. Only the user who possesses the FHE secret key can decrypt the result and gain insight.

We provide a comprehensive guide that empowers the reader to implement private SVM inference using homomorphic encryption. Our main goal is to provide readers with the knowledge and tools necessary to implement private SVM inference while preserving data confidentiality via FHE. This chapter caters to readers with varying levels of cryptographic expertise, assuming only a basic understanding of SVMs.

The remainder of this chapter is structured as follows. Section 2 reviews the state of the art on private machine and deep learning under FHE. Section 3 reviews the core methods employed in the presented solution. Section 4 details the design and implementation of the proposed solution. Section 5 presents the experimental results. Section 6 concludes the work and explores potential avenues for future research.

## 2. Literature review

Gentry's seminal work [20] realized the first FHE scheme, enabling arbitrary computations on encrypted data without compromising privacy. This new cryptographic capability has seen far-reaching implications, particularly in cloud-based machine and deep learning applications. Numerous studies have investigated the potential of FHE-based private machines and deep learning.

The exploration of machine learning models under FHE began with linear classifiers [23], followed by a series of works adapting other common models, including Convolutional Neural Networks (CNN) [12], SVMs [14, 15], logistic regression [17, 24, 25], and Transformers [26, 27] and many others. These advancements have paved the way for secure and private machine learning applications, ensuring the protection of sensitive data while maintaining computational capabilities.

Notably, the majority of research in this domain has concentrated on the inference phase of the machine or deep learning process, largely due to its relative simplicity and lower computational intensity compared to the training phase. However, a growing body of recent studies has begun to explore the feasibility of machine and deep learning training under FHE, yielding promising preliminary results. These investigations encompass various aspects, including logistic regression training [28], SVM training [29], CNNs training [30], shallow neural networks training [16], and transfer learning [31, 32], which paves the way for more comprehensive advancements in secure machine learning.

In this chapter, we focus on the evaluation of the inference phase of SVM models under FHE, presenting the reader with a comprehensive overview of cutting-edge tools and expert optimization techniques to facilitate this process. Our primary objective is to provide practitioners with the knowledge and expertise necessary to develop and implement their own secure SVM inference models, enabling them to protect their sensitive data while maintaining its utility.

## 3. Preliminaries

In this section, we provide an overview of the basic concepts and theoretical foundations that underpin our subsequent discussion, establishing a solid basis for the developments presented in this chapter.

### 3.1 Notations

We adopt the following notation conventions throughout this chapter: scalar quantities are denoted by lowercase letters, e.g., $a$; vector quantities are denoted by lowercase boldface letters, e.g., $\mathbf{a}$; and matrix quantities are denoted by uppercase boldface letters, e.g., $\mathbf{A}$. The dot-product between two vectors $\mathbf{u}$ and $\mathbf{v}$ is denoted by $\langle \mathbf{u} \cdot \mathbf{v} \rangle$. The point-wise addition and multiplication between two vectors are denoted by $\oplus$ and $\otimes$, respectively. We will be working with various sets of numbers such as the set of integers denoted as $\mathbb{Z}$, the set of reals $\mathbb{R}$, and the set of complex numbers $\mathbb{C}$. Encrypted quantities are distinguished by an over-bar symbol, e.g., $\overline{a}$ to denote an encryption of the scalar quantity $a$.

### 3.2 CKKS FHE scheme

The Cheon-Kim-Kim-Song (CKKS) scheme [33] is a FHE scheme ideally well-suited for handling encrypted real or complex quantities. Due to the wide use of real-number computations in machine learning algorithms, including SVMs, CKKS stands out as one of the most efficient FHE schemes for implementing machine learning algorithms.

Similar to other FHE schemes, CKKS operates under the honest-but-curious threat model, which assumes that all participants in a CKKS computation will follow the underlying protocol but may attempt to monitor and analyze the system to extract sensitive information. As long as participants adhere to the protocol, CKKS guarantees the confidentiality of secret keys and encrypted messages, provided that the participants' computational power does not exceed a predefined security level. For instance, CKKS may offer a 128-bit security level, ensuring that any attempt to break the system, recover the secret key, or decrypt encrypted messages would require computational resources exceeding this threshold. The security level of CKKS is primarily determined by the selection of cryptographic parameters, which must be chosen carefully to ensure a secure instantiation of CKKS that meets a specified security requirement. The careful choice of parameters is crucial to maintain the confidentiality and integrity of encrypted data and prevent potential security breaches.

It is crucial to understand the concept of noise, also referred to as error, which is inherent in CKKS and numerous other FHE schemes. This noise is a fundamental component of the Learning With Errors (LWE) problem [34], the primary mathematical framework underlying CKKS and many other FHE schemes. The security of CKKS is predicated on the presence of this noise, which is introduced during the encryption process. As homomorphic computations are performed on encrypted data, the noise accumulates and must be managed through specific CKKS primitives. Fortunately, many of existing CKKS libraries automate this noise maintenance process and abstracts it from the user.

### *3.2.1 CKKS instantiation*

The CKKS scheme is instantiated by specifying various user-defined parameters. Firstly, the multiplicative depth, denoted as $d$, must be selected, which determines the maximum number of sequential multiplications in the computation graph. It is essential to note that increasing the multiplicative depth can result in higher computational overhead, as CKKS internally manipulates larger mathematical objects. Consequently, minimizing the multiplicative depth is crucial to reduce the CKKS parameters, decrease computational overhead, and enhance the overall performance of the CKKS application.

Secondly, the user should specify the precision of the underlying CKKS computation by defining the scaling factor parameter, denoted as $\sigma$ (measured in bits). This parameter controls the precision of the computation and is typically selected within the range of 45–60 bits in most existing CKKS implementations. By adjusting $\sigma$, users can trade-off between computational efficiency and precision, with higher values resulting in more accurate computations at the cost of increased computational overhead.

Thirdly, the user can specify the CKKS security parameter, denoted as $\lambda$ (measured in bits), which determines the security level of the CKKS scheme. This parameter controls the computational overhead and overall performance of the CKKS application, with higher values of $\lambda$ providing increased security at the cost of reduced performance. Typical values for $\lambda$ include 128, 192, and 256 bits, which correspond to common security levels. It is essential to note that increasing $\lambda$ will result in higher computational overhead, leading to decreased overall performance of the CKKS application.

Upon defining the aforementioned parameters, the user can instantiate the CKKS scheme, which entails calculating the encryption keys, comprising the public key $(pk)$ and secret key $(sk)$, as well as the public evaluation keys, including the multiplication key $(evk)$, set of rotation keys $\left(\{rk\}_{i=0}^{r-1}\right)$, and bootstrapping key $(bk)$. The encryption keys are utilized for data encryption and decryption operations, whereas the evaluation keys are shared with the evaluator, who will be executing the CKKS computation. The multiplication key enables homomorphic multiplication, allowing the evaluator to multiply two encrypted quantities, while the rotation keys facilitate homomorphic rotation, enabling the rotation of an encrypted vector quantity by any integral rotation index $i \in \{0, \dots, r-1\}$. The bootstrapping key, on the other hand, is exclusively required for deep computational workloads that necessitate the refreshing of the noise in the encrypted quantities, ensuring the continued security and integrity of the computation.

#### *3.2.2 Data encoding and encryption*

CKKS provides two fundamental primitives for data encoding, defined as follows:

- ENCODE: takes as input real or complex vector **a** either $\in \mathbb{R}^n$ or $\in \mathbb{C}^n$ and returns a plaintext object $(a)$ that encodes the input vector.

- DECODE: takes as input a plaintext object $a$ and decodes it into the corresponding vector quantity **a** either $\in \mathbb{R}^n$ or $\in \mathbb{C}^n$, enabling the retrieval of the original encoded data.

For data encryption and decryption, CKKS provides two main primitives as follows:

- ENCRYPT: takes as input either $sk$ or $pk$ and a plaintext object $a$, and returns an encryption of $\overline{a}$, a.k.a., ciphertext $\overline{a}$.

- DECRYPT: takes as input $sk$ and a ciphertext $\overline{a}$ and returns the corresponding plaintext object $a$.

After encoding and encrypting their sensitive data, the user can transmit it to an untrusted evaluator for homomorphic computation. Upon completing the computation, the evaluator returns the encrypted results to the user, who can then decrypt and decode them to obtain the desired insights.

#### *3.2.3 Homomorphic data processing*

The CKKS homomorphic encryption scheme offers the evaluator the capability to perform specific operations on encrypted data without requiring decryption. This section details the three primary homomorphic operations supported by CKKS:

- Homomorphic Addition—$\text{EVALADD}(\overline{c}_1, \overline{c}_2)$ : performs homomorphic point-wise addition of the underlying encrypted vectors yielding ciphertext $\overline{c}_{\text{add}} = \text{Encryption}(\text{Encoding}(\mathbf{v}_1 \oplus \mathbf{v}_2))$. Furthermore, CKKS inherently supports homomorphic subtraction using the same principle.

- Homomorphic Multiplication—$\text{EVALMUL}(\overline{c}_1, \overline{c}_2, evk)$ : performs homomorphic point-wise multiplication of the underlying encrypted vectors yielding ciphertext $\overline{c}_{\text{mul}} = \text{Encryption}(\text{Encoding}(\mathbf{v}_1 \otimes \mathbf{v}_2))$. The multiplication key $evk$ is used for noise maintenance.

- EvalRotate($\bar{c}$, $i$, $\rho$, $rk_i$): performs cyclic rotation of the encrypted message vector by an amount $i \in \mathbb{Z}^+$ in direction $\rho \in \{0 = \text{left}, 1 = \text{right}\}$, generating a ciphertext that encrypts the rotated vector. This operation disrupts the the ciphertext structure and the rotation key $rk_i$ is used to restore the original structure.

It is important to note that both EVALADD and EVALMUL support a mixed-mode operation, where one input argument can be in plaintext while the output remains encrypted. Specifically, when using EVALMUL with one plaintext input argument, the computation is significantly faster compared to when both input arguments are encrypted.

## 3.3 SVM

SVMs are powerful supervised machine learning algorithms widely used for classification and regression tasks. While both classification and regression involve learning from a labeled dataset, this section will primarily focus on their application in classification problems. We begin by providing a brief overview of the training process employed to generate the SVM model parameters, followed by a detailed description of the SVM inference process. The latter is a computational procedure that is specifically implemented in CKKS, and it is this process that enables the homomorphic encryption and secure computation of SVM-based predictions.

### *3.3.1 SVM training*

As mentioned previously, the presented system requires the server to have a pre-trained model. This model can be realized through various approaches, including the utilization of public domain data, which is freely available and accessible, which eliminates concerns regarding data privacy. Another common approach is the use of synthetic data, which is artificially generated to mimic real-world data, providing a viable substitute for the sensitive dataset. Furthermore, non-private segments of the dataset can be utilized, comprising data from participants who have explicitly consented to open-source their information, a common practice observed in genome studies where individuals willingly share their genetic data for research purposes (e.g., [35]). The resulting pre-trained model is used as an input to the privacy-preserving SVM inference protocol. The subsequent paragraphs describe formally the training process, which involves utilizing a subset of the evaluation dataset, designated as the training dataset, to train and fine-tune the SVM model's performance and accuracy.

SVM training can be described as follows. Given an input dataset comprising $m$ data points, each characterized by $n$ features, which can be represented as a matrix $\mathbf{X} \in R^{m \times n}$. In addition, a label vector $\mathbf{y} \in \{+1, -1\}^m$ is associated with the dataset, where each entry $y_i$ indicates the class to which data point $\mathbf{X}_i$ belongs. Given a chosen kernel function $\mathbb{K}$, a SVM classifier can be trained to identify the optimal separating hyperplane between two classes.

Several widely utilized kernel functions exist for support vector machines, each serving distinct purposes. The identity function, which maps inputs to themselves, is primarily employed in linearly separable problems due to its simplicity. Conversely, for non-linearly separable problems, more complex kernel functions are employed. In such cases, the polynomial kernel, Radial Basis Function (RBF), also known as the Gaussian kernel, and the Sigmoid kernel, a smooth and continuously differentiable function, are commonly utilized to facilitate non-linear transformations and enhance the SVM model's descriptive capacity.

The training process of a SVM model involves determining the optimal hyperplane that best separates data points into different classes. This is achieved by optimizing the model parameters to maximize the margin between the classes while minimizing the misclassification error. To achieve this, SVM employs quadratic programming and Lagrange multipliers. This mathematical formulation transforms the problem of finding the optimal hyperplane into a constrained optimization problem. The solution to this problem yields the model parameters, including the weights and bias of the hyperplane.

The training algorithm learns the following model parameters:

- set of support vectors $\{SV\}_0^{l-1}$ which is a subset of $\mathbf{X}$.
- the coefficients vector $\boldsymbol{\alpha} \in \mathbb{R}^l$ which can be interpreted as weight factors assigned to the support vectors, influencing their contribution to the decision boundary.
- the intercept (or bias) parameter $b \in \mathbb{R}$.

We conclude our discussion on SVM training at this point, as our system assumes the availability of a trained SVM model's parameters as input. Omitting the mathematical description of SVM training for the sake of brevity, we instead refer interested readers to consult dedicated SVM resources for a comprehensive understanding of the training process [36].

### *3.3.2 SVM inference*

The SVM inference function is of paramount importance in our system. Specifically, the evaluator is tasked with evaluating a given SVM model on encrypted data points provided by the user. Consequently, the server performs an encrypted evaluation of the SVM inference function, which necessitates a detailed description of this function. The SVM inference function is responsible for computing the prediction output of the SVM model on the encrypted data points, and its secure evaluation is crucial for maintaining the confidentiality of the user's data.

During SVM inference, our primary objective is to evaluate the decision function, as presented in Eq. (1). The kernel function $\mathbb{K}$ poses a challenge when it is chosen as RBF or Sigmoid. In contrast, a polynomial kernel function is inherently compatible with the CKKS computational model and does not present any difficulties. To address the challenges associated with RBF and Sigmoid kernel functions, we can employ polynomial approximations over a predefined range, which have demonstrated excellent performance in various studies [12, 13, 37–39].

$$c(\mathbf{x}) = \text{sign}\left(\sum_{i=0}^{l-1} \alpha_i y_i \mathbb{K}(\langle \mathbf{x}_i, \mathbf{x} \rangle) + b\right), \text{where } \mathbf{x}_i \text{ is the } i\text{-th support vector.} \quad (1)$$

The decision function presents an additional challenge in computing the *sign* function, which is a non-arithmetic operation. To address this, we can draw on a similar strategy employed for handling the kernel function, approximating the sign function as a polynomial. Alternatively, the sign function can be computed on the client side upon returning the SVM insight. In our approach, we opt for the former method, approximating the sign function as a polynomial to facilitate its evaluation within the decision function. Notably, for SVM regression tasks, the sign function is not required, thereby eliminating this challenge altogether.

## 4. System implementation

This section outlines the implementation details of our system. We begin by introducing the dataset employed for evaluation purposes, followed by an overview of the tools utilized in our implementation.

### 4.1 Evaluation dataset

We evaluated our system using Dal's Credit Card Dataset [40], a comprehensive collection of credit card transactions and user information. This dataset contains transactions made by European cardholders in September 2013, spanning two days, with a total of 284,807 transactions, of which 492 are fraudulent.

#### *4.1.1 Data preprocessing*

Due to privacy concerns, the dataset is not publicly available in its raw format. Instead, a preprocessed version is provided, which has undergone Principal Component Analysis (PCA) to extract the most informative features. The PCA transformation retains only the features that show a high correlation with the response variable, a class label indicating whether each transaction is fraudulent (Class 1) or legitimate (Class 0). This preprocessing step helps to reduce dimensionality and improve model performance.

It is in these particular situations where privacy-preserving machine learning analysis prove to be paramount. Traditional data preprocessing techniques can compromise data quality, potentially limiting the accuracy of the analysis. Furthermore, these techniques often lack cryptographic security, making it possible for unauthorized parties to invert the preprocessing and recover the original dataset [41]. To address this concern, it is essential to adopt cryptographically secure systems that can process encrypted raw data without sacrificing privacy.

#### *4.1.2 Dataset characteristics*

The dataset comprises only numerical data, making it suitable for machine learning-based fraud detection. The dataset is extremely unbalanced, with a fraud rate of approximately 0.17%. This imbalance is a common challenge in fraud detection, as fraudulent transactions are typically rare compared to legitimate ones. The dataset characteristics are summarized in **Table 1**. It comprises 28 predictor features, denoted as $\{V1, \ldots, V28\}$. These features represent the transformed variables resulting from the PCA preprocessing technique, with the exception of two original features:

1. *Time*: The timestamp of each transaction, which was not subjected to PCA transformation and is retained in its original form.

| Attribute | Value |
|---|---|
| Number of Features | 28 |
| Type of Classification | Binary (1: fraud, 0:legitimate) |
| Number of Samples | 284,807 |
| Number of Fraudulent Samples | 492 |
| Number of Legitimate Samples | 284,315 |
| Feature Type | Numerical |
| PCA Transformed Features | 26 |
| Original Features | 2 (Time, Amount) |

**Table 1.**
*Dal's credit card dataset characteristics [40].*

2. *Amount*: The transaction amount, which was also exempt from PCA preprocessing and is present in the dataset in its raw form.

The inclusion of these two original features, alongside the 26 transformed features, provides a comprehensive set of predictors for modeling and analysis.

## 4.2 Implementation

We used three key open-source tools to develop our privacy-preserving credit card fraud detection system. We utilized Python's scikit-learn's SVM package [36], which provides an efficient implementation of SVMs for both training and inference. We also employed the FHSVM framework [15], an FHE-based privacy-preserving SVM inference engine, enabling secure and private predictions on encrypted data. Lastly, we used the OpenFHE framework [42] which includes an implementation of CKKS that is required by FHSVM. Below, we describe this computational infrastructure in more detail and how they are utilized to build a privacy-preserving credit card fraud detection system.

### *4.2.1 Scikit-learn SVM*

We employed the Python sci-kit-learn library's SVM package to train an SVM model on the credit card dataset. The comprehensive training methodology, including data preprocessing, feature selection, model configuration, and extraction, is shown in **Figure 2**. Below, we detail each step in the training procedure.

#### *4.2.1.1 Dataset processing*

To prepare the dataset for model training and evaluation, we performed the following processing steps. The dataset was randomly partitioned into training and testing sets, adhering to a ratio of 80% for training and 20% for testing. This split ensures that the model is trained on a substantial portion of the data while reserving a sufficient amount for evaluation purposes. The random partitioning helps maintain the integrity of the dataset's distribution, reducing the likelihood of bias in the training process. We also excluded samples with missing values to enhance the reliability and accuracy of our analysis.

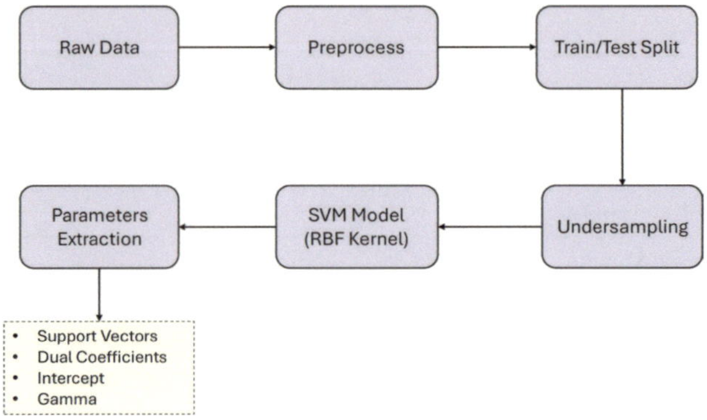


**Figure 2.**
*SVM training workflow.*

### *4.2.1.2 Model training*

Given the dataset's inherent class imbalance, we adopted an undersampling approach to create a balanced training dataset. This involved maintaining the entirety of the fraudulent samples, while randomly sampling an equal number of legitimate transactions from the dataset. By doing so, we ensured that the model was trained on a dataset with an equal number of instances from both classes. It should be noted that undersampling was only applied to the training dataset. During model evaluation, the entire testing dataset is used without undersampling.

To address the critical nature of accurately detecting fraudulent transactions, we implemented a cost-sensitive approach by assigning higher penalties to false negatives than false positives. Specifically, we penalized missing a fraud more heavily by modifying the SVM's class_weight parameter to 0:0.75, 1:0.25. This adjustment ensured that the model prioritized the accurate detection of fraudulent transactions.

Furthermore, we selected the Radial Basis Function (RBF) kernel for the SVM model due to its superior performance in capturing non-linear relationships between the predictor variables and the response variable. Given the complexity of the relationships between predictor and response variables in our dataset, the RBF kernel's ability to model non-linear patterns made it the preferred choice for our SVM. Preliminary experiments with other kernels reinforced this decision. Detailed SVM model parameters are presented in **Table 2**.

| Parameter | Value |
|---|---|
| Kernel | RBF |
| Penalty C | 1.0 |
| Gamma | scale |
| Probability | True |
| Number of Support Vectors | 114 |
| Class weight | 0: 0.75, 1: 0.25 |
| Decision function shape | OVR |

**Table 2.**
*SVM model summary.*

#### *4.2.1.3 Model evaluation*

Following the training phase, we conducted a comprehensive evaluation of our model's performance using a range of standard metrics. These metrics provide insights into the model's ability to accurately detect fraudulent transactions while minimizing false positives. The evaluation metrics employed include:

1. *Precision*: Measures the proportion of true positives (correctly identified fraudulent transactions) among all positive predictions made by the model.

2. *Recall*: Quantifies the proportion of true positives among all actual fraudulent transactions in the dataset.

3. *Classification Accuracy*: Calculates the overall proportion of correctly classified transactions (both fraudulent and legitimate).

4. *F1-score*: Harmonizes precision and recall into a single metric, providing a balanced measure of the model's performance.

5. *Area Under the Receiver Operating Characteristic Curve (ROC-AUC)*: Assesses the model's ability to distinguish between fraudulent and legitimate transactions.

#### *4.2.1.4 Exporting the model parameters*

We have successfully developed a high-performing SVM model, capable of accurately classifying transactions as fraudulent or legitimate. To facilitate the secure evaluation of this model on encrypted data, we extract its key parameters, including support vectors, gamma value, dual coefficients, and intercept, and store them in plain text files. These extracted parameters will be utilized by the FHSVM module to enable the homomorphic evaluation of our SVM model on encrypted input samples.

### *4.2.2 FHSVM framework*

The FHSVM framework enables the secure evaluation of an SVM model on encrypted input samples, utilizing the CKKS FHE scheme to compute the decision function in Eq. (1). This framework facilitates the classification of transactions without compromising data confidentiality.

As mentioned previously, the decision function involves basic arithmetic operations on real numbers, which are inherently supported by the CKKS scheme. However, the kernel and sign functions require special handling, as they are not supported by CKKS. To address this, the FHSVM framework substitutes these functions with polynomial approximations, ensuring accurate computations.

To implement the FHSVM framework, two critical parameters must be defined:

1. The range over which the Radial Basis Function (RBF) and sign functions are evaluated, ensuring accurate polynomial approximations.

2. The degree of the polynomial approximations required to accurately represent the RBF and sign functions.

| Parameter | Value |
|---|---|
| Ring Dimension | $2^{16}$ |
| Multiplicative Depth ($d$) | 13 |
| Desired Compute Precision ($\sigma$) | 59-bit |
| Security Level ($\lambda$) | 128-bit |
| Bootstrapping | Disabled |
| Secret Key Distribution | Ternary |

**Table 3.**
*CKKS parameters used in our privacy-preserving credit card fraud detection system.*

It is important to note that increasing the degree of polynomials and expanding the evaluation range can lead to more accurate polynomial approximations of the RBF and sign functions. However, this enhancement comes at a cost, as it requires the use of larger CKKS parameters, which can significantly degrade performance. To achieve a balance between accuracy and efficiency, careful optimization of these parameters is necessary to tailor them to the specific requirements of the problem at hand. In our case, we have found that evaluating the RBF and sign functions over a range of $-16$ to 1, with a polynomial degree of 13, provides an optimal trade-off between accuracy and performance. Through rigorous experimentation, we have validated these parameters and present them below as the optimal values for our dataset.

### *4.2.3 OpenFHE*

OpenFHE is a comprehensive, open-source FHE library that provides a robust implementation of various FHE schemes, including the CKKS scheme. As a versatile and efficient backend, OpenFHE enables the secure evaluation of complex mathematical operations on encrypted data. In the context of our system, OpenFHE plays a crucial role as the underlying FHE library for the FHSVM framework, facilitating the secure evaluation of CKKS operations.

As a result of our system requirements, we have carefully selected the following CKKS parameters to ensure optimal performance and security. **Table 3** shows the cryptographic parameters used in instantiating CKKS in OpenFHE. The polynomial ring used for encryption is set to $2^{16}$. The multiplicative depth is set to 13, indicating the maximum number of multiplications allowed during homomorphic evaluation. We have chosen a security level of 128-bit, providing robust protection against known attacks. The scale precision is set to 59-bit, ensuring accurate fixed-point arithmetic operations. As bootstrapping is not needed for our system, it is disabled to optimize performance, and the secret key distribution follows a ternary scheme. These carefully chosen parameters enable our system to achieve a balance between security, accuracy, and efficiency.

## 5. Results

In this section, we present the results of our experiments evaluating the performance and security of our privacy-preserving SVM inference system using the CKKS FHE scheme. We first report the results of training our SVM model in the clear. We then present the results of our homomorphic inference experiments, including the accuracy and performance overhead of encrypting and decrypting our data. Finally, we evaluate the security of our system, verifying that our encryption parameters achieve the desired level of security and that our homomorphic inference process preserves the privacy of our input data.

### 5.1 Training results

To establish a baseline for our privacy-preserving SVM inference, we first trained our SVM model in Python clearly. This allowed us to evaluate the model's performance on our dataset without any encryption overhead. We report the results of this training process, including the model's accuracy, precision, recall, F1 score, and other relevant metrics.

**Table 4** characterizes the classification quality of our SVM model when evaluated on the testing dataset. The model achieves a precision of 0.9988, recall of 0.9971, and accuracy of 0.9971, demonstrating its ability to accurately detect fraudulent transactions. Moreover, the F1-score of 0.9977 and AUC of 0.9834 further validate the model's robustness. Notably, the balanced accuracy of 0.9283 highlights the model's effectiveness in handling class imbalance. Overall, these metrics indicate that the SVM model succeeds in distinguishing between legitimate and fraudulent transactions.

### 5.2 Homomorphic inference results

With our SVM model trained, we then proceeded to evaluate its performance under homomorphic encryption using OpenFHE's CKKS implementation. This involved encrypting our input data, performing inference on the encrypted data, and then decrypting the results. We report the accuracy and performance overhead of this homomorphic inference process, comparing it to the clear-text inference results.

**Table 5** characterizes the performance of the SVM model's homomorphic inference. The most time-consuming operation is the SVM decision function evaluation, taking approximately 5.21 seconds, which is roughly 86% of the total inference time. This suggests that optimizing the decision function evaluation could significantly improve overall performance. In contrast, sample encryption and decryption are relatively fast, taking less than 0.2 seconds combined. The sign function evaluation takes around 0.82 seconds, which is a reasonable overhead considering its importance in the inference process. The computation precision of up to 4 decimal digits (13 bits) indicates a good balance between accuracy and efficiency.

| Metric | Value |
|---|---|
| Precision | 0.9988 |
| Recall | 0.9971 |
| Accuracy | 0.9971 |
| Balanced Accuracy | 0.9283 |
| F1-Score | 0.9977 |
| Area Under the Curve (AUC) | 0.9834 |

**Table 4.**
*Characterizing the SVM model performance.*

| Operation | Time (sec) |
|---|---|
| Sample Encryption | 0.146 |
| SVM Decision Function Evaluation | 5.214 |
| Sign Function Evaluation | 0.816 |
| SVM Inference Total Evaluation Time | 6.030 |
| Sample Decryption | 0.054 |
| Computation Precision | Up to 4 decimal digits (~13 bits) |

**Table 5.**
*Characterizing the SVM model homomorphic inference performance.*

Potential performance optimizations can significantly enhance the efficiency of our privacy-preserving SVM inference solution. One approach is to offload the sign function computation to the client, who can process it in the clear. By doing so, we can drop approximately 0.816 seconds from the overall computation time. Furthermore, it's essential to recognize that in SVM regression tasks, the sign function evaluation is not required and can be entirely eliminated.

We emphasize here that encryption imposes a substantial performance overhead on private SVM inference, significantly amplifying runtime by four to five orders of magnitude. While plaintext SVM inference completes in mere milliseconds, the equivalent encrypted operation demands several seconds of computation. This dramatic slowdown is attributable to the inherent complexities of operating within the encrypted domain using FHE. Furthermore, the approximate nature of CKKS computations results in a notable reduction in computational precision to 13 bits, a stark contrast to the double-precision standard prevalent in plaintext calculations (52 bits). Despite this limitation, we verified that 13-bit precision is adequate for our specific use case and potentially applicable to a broader range of scenarios.

## 5.3 Security evaluation

Our FHE-based privacy-preserving fraud detection system assumes a semi-honest threat model. The semi-honest threat model, also known as the "honest-but-curious" model, is a security framework commonly assumed in FHE protocols. In this model, both the server and client are assumed to follow the protocol correctly, executing the agreed-upon steps without deviations. However, they are also curious and may attempt to infer additional information from the data they receive or observe during protocol execution.

Crucially, the semi-honest model assumes that the server and client do not collude with each other and do not actively attempt to cheat or manipulate the protocol. Their malicious behavior is limited to learning more information than is explicitly provided by the protocol.

Thus, the primary security goal of FHE under the semi-honest model is to prevent the server from gaining any significant knowledge about the data beyond what is intentionally revealed by the protocol. This implies that even if the server attempts to analyze or intercept the encrypted data, it should be unable to deduce sensitive information. By operating within the semi-honest threat model, FHE offers a robust security guarantee, ensuring that even curious parties cannot compromise data confidentiality.

To ensure the security and privacy of our homomorphic inference process, we conducted a thorough security evaluation. This involved analyzing the encryption parameters used in OpenFHE's CKKS implementation to verify that they achieve the desired security level (128-bit) against known attacks. We also confirmed that the homomorphic inference process preserves the privacy of the input data, as demonstrated by the inability to recover original data from ciphertext.

It is crucial to acknowledge that current FHE schemes lack robust security guarantees, specifically Chosen-Ciphertext Attack 2 (CCA2) security and verifiable computation. This vulnerability allows a malicious server or interceptor to manipulate ciphertexts by performing computations on them, potentially disrupting the service by providing incorrect results. Furthermore, FHE inherently lacks verifiable computation security, leaving the client unable to verify whether the server has performed the intended computation. Hence, FHE operates ideally under the honest-but-curious threat model, relying on legal bindings or incentives to enforce honest behavior among participating parties.

In addition, FHE schemes are susceptible to side-channel attacks if not implemented correctly, as demonstrated in recent studies [43, 44]. These findings highlight the need for enhanced security measures and rigorous implementation to ensure the integrity of FHE-based systems.

### 5.4 Discussion

Our results demonstrate the feasibility of privacy-preserving SVM inference via FHE but also highlight the trade-offs between accuracy, performance, and security. In this discussion, we summarize our key findings, explore the implications of our results for practical applications, and identify avenues for future research to further improve the performance and security of homomorphic inference.

#### *5.4.1 Predictive performance*

The SVM model exhibits remarkable predictive performance, achieving high accuracy and precision in detecting fraudulent transactions. In addition, the model demonstrates robustness across different evaluation metrics, including F1-score, AUC, and balanced accuracy.

It is important to note that we view SVM training and SVM inference as essentially orthogonal processes. This independence means that any optimizations or improvements made to the training process, aimed at enhancing the classifier's performance, will not impact the homomorphic SVM inference functionality. Advancements in training techniques, such as kernel selection, regularization, or data preprocessing, can be explored and implemented independently without affecting the encrypted inference pipeline. This decoupling of training and inference enables flexibility and future-proofing, allowing for continuous improvements in classification accuracy without compromising the security and privacy benefits of homomorphic inference.

#### *5.4.2 The importance of privacy-preserving MLaaS*

A significant challenge in our research was the unavailability of raw data due to stringent privacy regulations. Sensitive data owners often preprocess data using techniques such as PCA before sharing it, which can potentially compromise data integrity and limit the effectiveness of machine learning models. While PCA can reduce dimensionality, it also inherently discards information which impacts the model performance. Furthermore, the vulnerability of PCA-processed data to inversion attacks raises serious concerns about data privacy [41]. This highlights the importance of cryptography-based privacy-preserving technologies such as FHE which facilitates data analysis on encrypted raw data. This not only safeguards sensitive information but also enables comprehensive data utilization providing valuable insights without compromising privacy.

### *5.4.3 Scalability*

We tested the SVM inference on a commodity laptop, which provided valuable insights into the model's performance under typical computing conditions achieving 6 seconds overall inference latency. However, it is likely that utilizing a high-end server with advanced processing capabilities, increased memory, and optimized hardware configurations could significantly enhance the performance of the SVM inference. Such a setup could potentially reduce the computation time, especially for the most time-consuming operation, the SVM decision function evaluation, and improve the overall efficiency of the homomorphic inference process. Moreover, a high-end server could also enable the processing of multiple SVM queries, larger datasets, more complex models, and increased precision levels, making it an attractive option for applications requiring high-performance secure computations.

## 6. Conclusions

In conclusion, this paper has demonstrated the feasibility and effectiveness of implementing privacy-preserving SVM inference using the CKKS FHE scheme. We successfully enabled SVM inference on encrypted data samples, ensuring the confidentiality of sensitive information even when processed on untrusted servers. Our comprehensive evaluation on a large-scale credit card fraud detection dataset showcased remarkable predictive accuracy and reasonable inference latency of nearly 6 seconds, highlighting the practicality of our approach.

The significance of this work lies in its ability to bridge the gap between machine learning and privacy-preserving computing, enabling organizations to harness the power of SVM inference without compromising data privacy. As the demand for secure computing solutions continues to grow, our implementation serves as a vital step toward realizing the full potential of FHE in real-world applications.

Future research directions may focus on optimizing the performance of homomorphic SVM inference, exploring alternative FHE schemes, and expanding the scope of privacy-preserving machine learning applications.

## Conflict of interest

The authors declare no conflict of interest.

## Author details

Ahmad Al Badawi
Department of Homeland Security, Rabdan Academy, Abu Dhabi, United Arab Emirates

*Address all correspondence to: ahmad@u.nus.edu

## References

[1] Cortes C, Vapnik V. Support-vector networks. In: Machine Learning. Vol. 20. Boston: Kluwer Academic Publishers; 1995. pp. 273-297

[2] Suthaharan S, Suthaharan S. Support vector machine. In: Machine Learning Models and Algorithms for Big Data Classification: Thinking with Examples for Effective Learning. New York, NY: Springer; 2016. pp. 207-235

[3] Pisner DA, Schnyer DM. Support vector machine. In: Machine Learning. Amsterdam, Netherlands: Elsevier; 2020. pp. 101-121

[4] Pavlidis P, Wapinski I, Noble WS. Support vector machine classification on the web. Bioinformatics. 2004;**20**(4): 586-587

[5] Battineni G, Chintalapudi N, Amenta F. Machine learning in medicine: Performance calculation of dementia prediction by support vector machines (svm). Informatics in Medicine Unlocked. 2019;**16**:100200

[6] Altan A, Karasu S. The effect of kernel values in support vector machine to forecasting performance of financial time series. The Journal of Cognitive Systems. 2019;**4**(1):17-21

[7] Alanazi A. Using machine learning for healthcare challenges and opportunities. Informatics in Medicine Unlocked. 2022; **30**:100924

[8] Singh G, Gupta R, Rastogi A, Chandel MDS, Ahmad R. A machine learning approach for detection of fraud based on svm. International Journal of Scientific Engineering and Technology. 2012;**1**(3):192-196

[9] Jha J, Ragha L. Intrusion detection system using support vector machine. International Journal of Applied Information Systems (IJAIS). 2013;**3**:25-30

[10] Voigt P, Von dem Bussche A. The eu general data protection regulation (gdpr). In: A Practical Guide. 1st ed. Vol. 10, No. 3152676. Cham: Springer International Publishing; 2017. pp. 10-5555

[11] Domingo-Ferrer J, Farras O, Ribes-González J, Sánchez D. Privacy-preserving cloud computing on sensitive data: A survey of methods, products and challenges. Computer Communications. 2019;**140**:38-60

[12] Gilad-Bachrach R, Dowlin N, Laine K, Lauter K, Naehrig M, Wernsing J. Cryptonets: Applying neural networks to encrypted data with high throughput and accuracy. In: International Conference on Machine Learning. United States: PMLR; 2016. pp. 201-210

[13] Al Badawi A, Jin C, Lin J, Mun CF, Jie SJ, Tan BHM, et al. Towards the alexnet moment for homomorphic encryption: Hcnn, the first homomorphic cnn on encrypted data with gpus. IEEE Transactions on Emerging Topics in Computing. 2020;**9**(3):1330-1343

[14] Bajard J-C, Martins P, Sousa L, Zucca V. Improving the efficiency of svm classification with fhe. IEEE Transactions on Information Forensics and Security. 2019;**15**:1709-1722

[15] Al Badawi A, Chen L, Vig S. Fast homomorphic svm inference on encrypted data. Neural Computing and Applications. 2022;**34**(18): 15555-15573

[16] Al Badawi A, Hoang L, Mun CF, Laine K, Aung KMM. Privft: Private and fast text classification with homomorphic encryption. IEEE Access. 2020;**8**:226544-226556

[17] Chan FM, Al Badawi AQA, Sim JJ, Tan BHM, Sheng FC, Aung KMM. Genotype imputation with homomorphic encryption. In: Proceedings of the 6th International Conference on Biomedical Signal and Image Processing. New York, NY, USA: Association for Computing Machinery; 2021. pp. 9-13

[18] Blatt M, Gusev A, Polyakov Y, Goldwasser S. Secure large-scale genome-wide association studies using homomorphic encryption. Proceedings of the National Academy of Sciences. 2020;**117**(21):11608-11613

[19] Geva R, Gusev A, Polyakov Y, Liram L, Rosolio O, Alexandru A, et al. Collaborative privacy-preserving analysis of oncological data using multiparty homomorphic encryption. Proceedings of the National Academy of Sciences. 2023;**120**(33): e2304415120

[20] Gentry C. Fully homomorphic encryption using ideal lattices. In: Proceedings of the Forty-First Annual ACM Symposium on Theory of Computing. New York, NY, USA: Association for Computing Machinery; 2009. pp. 169-178

[21] Hesamifard E, Takabi H, Ghasemi M, Wright RN. Privacy-preserving machine learning as a service. Proceedings on Privacy Enhancing Technologies. 2018;(3):123-142

[22] Tanuwidjaja HC, Choi R, Baek S, Kim K. Privacy-preserving deep learning on machine learning as a service—A comprehensive survey. IEEE Access. 2020;**8**:167425-167447. DOI: 10.1109/ACCESS.2020.3023084

[23] Graepel T, Lauter K, Naehrig M. Ml confidential: Machine learning on encrypted data. In: International Conference on Information Security and Cryptology. New York City, United States: Springer; 2012. pp. 1-21

[24] Kim M, Song Y, Wang S, Xia Y, Jiang X, et al. Secure logistic regression based on homomorphic encryption: Design and evaluation. JMIR Medical Informatics. 2018;**6**(2):e8805

[25] Blatt M, Gusev A, Polyakov Y, Rohloff K, Vaikuntanathan V. Optimized homomorphic encryption solution for secure genome-wide association studies. BMC Medical Genomics. 2020;**13**:1-13

[26] Rovida L, Leporati A. Transformer-based language models and homomorphic encryption: An intersection with bert-tiny. In: Proceedings of the 10th ACM International Workshop on Security and Privacy Analytics. 2024. pp. 3-13

[27] Chen T, Bao H, Huang S, Dong L, Jiao B, Jiang D, et al. The-x: Privacy-Preserving Transformer Inference with Homomorphic Encryption. arXiv preprint arXiv:2206.00216. 2022

[28] Bergamaschi F, Halevi S, Halevi TT, Hunt H. Homomorphic training of 30,000 logistic regression models. In: Applied Cryptography and Network Security: 17th International Conference, ACNS 2019, Bogota, Colombia, June 5–7, 2019, Proceedings 17. Springer; 2019. pp. 592-611

[29] Park S, Byun J, Lee J, Cheon JH, Lee J. He-friendly algorithm for privacy-preserving svm training. IEEE Access. 2020;**8**:57414-57425

[30] Nandakumar K, Ratha N, Pankanti S, Halevi S. Towards deep neural network training on encrypted data. In: Proceedings of the IEEE/CVF Conference on Computer Vision and Pattern Recognition Workshops. New York City, U.S.: Institute of Electrical and Electronics Engineers (IEEE); 2019

[31] Paul J, Annamalai MSMS, Ming W, Al Badawi A, Veeravalli B, Aung KMM. Privacy-preserving collective learning with homomorphic encryption. IEEE Access. 2021;**9**:132084-132096

[32] Lee S, Lee G, Kim JW, Shin J, Lee M-K. Hetal: Efficient privacy-preserving transfer learning with homomorphic encryption. In: International Conference on Machine Learning. United States: PMLR; 2023. pp. 19010-19035

[33] Cheon JH, Kim A, Kim M, Song Y. Homomorphic encryption for arithmetic of approximate numbers. In: Advances in Cryptology—ASIACRYPT 2017. Cham: Springer International Publishing; 2017. pp. 409-437. ISBN 978-3-319-70694-8

[34] Regev O. On lattices, learning with errors, random linear codes, and cryptography. In: Proceedings of the Thirty-Seventh Annual ACM Symposium on Theory of Computing, STOC '05. New York, NY, USA: Association for Computing Machinery. ISBN 1581139608; 2005. pp. 84-93. DOI: 10.1145/1060590.1060603

[35] Haeusermann T, Greshake B, Blasimme A, Irdam D, Richards M, Vayena E. Open sharing of genomic data: Who does it and why? PLoS One. 2017; **12**(5):e0177158

[36] Chang C-C, Lin C-J. Libsvm: A library for support vector machines. ACM transactions on intelligent systems and technology (TIST). 2011;**2**(3):1-27

[37] Lee J-W, Kang HC, Lee Y, Choi W, Eom J, Deryabin M, et al. Privacy-preserving machine learning with fully homomorphic encryption for deep neural network. IEEE Access. 2022;**10**: 30039-30054

[38] Brand M, Pradel G. Practical privacy-preserving machine learning using fully homomorphic encryption. Cryptology ePrint Archive. 2023

[39] Hong S, Park JH, Cho W, Choe H, Cheon JH. Secure tumor classification by shallow neural network using homomorphic encryption. BMC Genomics. 2022;**23**(1):284

[40] Dal Pozzolo A, Boracchi G, Caelen O, Alippi C, Bontempi G. Credit card fraud detection: A realistic modeling and a novel learning strategy. IEEE Transactions on Neural Networks and Learning Systems. 2017;**29**(8): 3784-3797

[41] Kwatra S, Torra V. Data reconstruction attack against principal component analysis. In: International Symposium on Security and Privacy in Social Networks and Big Data. New York City, United States: Springer; 2023. pp. 79-92

[42] Al Badawi A, Bates J, Bergamaschi F, Cousins DB, Erabelli S, Genise N, et al. Openfhe: Open-source fully homomorphic encryption library. In: Proceedings of the 10th Workshop on Encrypted Computing & Applied Homomorphic Cryptography. 2022. pp. 53-63

[43] Aydin F, Karabulut E, Potluri S, Alkim E, Aysu A. Reveal: Single-trace side-channel leakage of the seal homomorphic encryption library. In: 2022 Design, Automation & Test in Europe Conference & Exhibition (DATE). New York City, United States: IEEE; 2022. pp. 1527-1532

[44] Aydin F, Aysu A. Exposing side-channel leakage of seal homomorphic encryption library. In: Proceedings of the 2022 Workshop on Attacks and Solutions in Hardware Security. 2022. pp. 95-100

Chapter 11

# Recognizing Heat Exchange Crisis Using the SVM ALG

*Viktoria Sheshukova*


## Abstract

This article discusses the use of support vector machines to recognize a heat transfer crisis. A heat transfer crisis during boiling is the phenomenon of a sharp deterioration in heat transfer on a heat transfer surface, leading, as a rule, to a rapid increase in its temperature.


**Keywords:** VVER, reactor diagnostic systems, heat exchange crisis, heat transfer crisis, support vector machine

## 1. Introduction

Among the world's developments of supercritical pressure reactors, a single-loop thermal design with a near-critical temperature at the entrance to the core and significantly higher than critical at the exit from the core (CSR1000, HPLWR, VVER-SKD-1700, etc.) prevails [1].

One of the most common types of reactors is the PWR type reactor—pressurized-water power reactor (in Russia, it is VVER). PWR (**Figure 1**) technology uses a double-circuit nuclear steam-producing vessel installation with a thermal neutron reactor, in which the coolant and moderator is ordinary water under high pressure (up to 16.0 MPa) and temperature up to 324 degrees (these are data for the VVER-1000 reactor).

The reactor core has a complex structure with a large number of fuel assemblies and regulators operating under stressful conditions (**Figure 2**) [2].

The coolant, in direct contact with fuel assemblies, becomes radioactive. Therefore, it is closed in the first sealed circuit and does not leave the power unit (red-orange circulation in the **Figure 1**).

Primary coolant is in orange, and the secondary coolant (steam and later feedwater) is in blue.

Due to the fact that the water is under high pressure, it does not boil, despite the high temperature of 324 degrees. Boiling of water in a VVER, especially in the primary circuit, is an extremely undesirable process, because boiling can lead to deterioration and/or cessation of heat transfer from the fuel element, which can cause burning of the pipeline wall and further depressurization of the primary circuit. This problem is called heat transfer crisis.

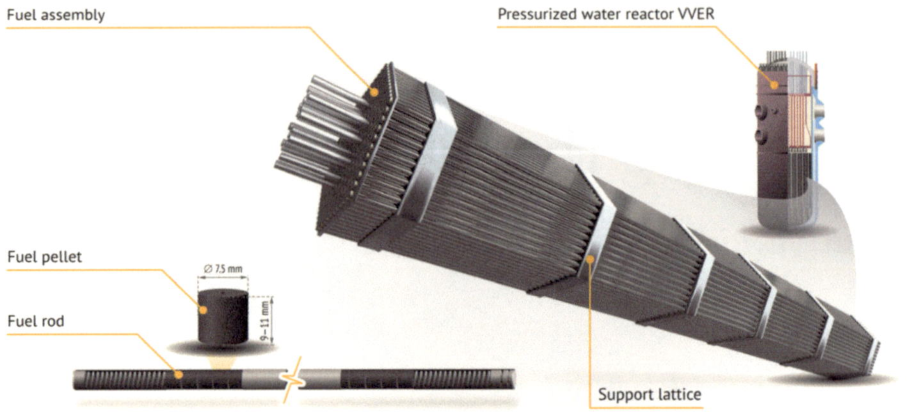


**Figure 1.**
*Fuel assemblies. Source: https://www.energyencyclopedia.com/en/nuclear-energy/nuclear-fuel/fuel-assembly.*

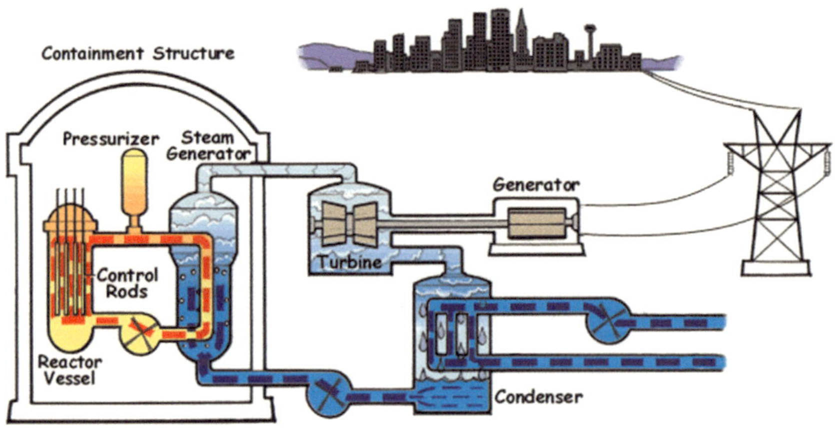


**Figure 2.**
*Pictorial explanation of power transfer in a pressurized water reactor. Source: https://en.wikipedia.org/wiki/Pressurized_water_reactor.*

High temperatures of the coolant and its large heating in the core lead to multi-pass circulation patterns, and a strong change in density leads to complex designs of fuel assemblies. Coupled with the complexity of heat transfer processes in the region of pseudophase transition, questions arise regarding the thermal reliability of the core.

Heat transfer regimes in the near-critical region have pronounced specificity, determined by the sharply changing properties of water in the vicinity of the pseudophase transition. In addition, as studies have shown, the specificity of heat transfer during supercritical pressure in a pipe differs from the multi-rod geometry of a fuel assembly, primarily in the boundaries at the beginning of the degraded heat transfer mode.

The danger of an accident with depressurization of the primary circuit is as follows. When it occurs, the sealed primary circuit is destroyed, the cooling of the fuel matrix is disrupted (**Figure 3**), and a steam-water mixture is released into sealed

**Figure 3.**
*Consequences of the heat transfer crisis (burnout of fuel rod walls). Source: http://nrcki.ru/.*

rooms, which poses a potential danger to the integrity of the containment shell. Thus, there is a possibility of destruction of all safety barriers [3].

The margin before a heat transfer crisis is the most important parameter in determining the thermal reliability of a reactor. Therefore, it is necessary to be able to determine the critical power as accurately as possible for various operating modes [4].

Determining the laws of the heat and mass transfer process in fuel assemblies is impossible without conducting experiments on a multi-rod beam, the parameters of which are as close as possible to the parameters of the active zones of the supercritical pressure reactors being developed.

An algorithm for early detection of a heat transfer crisis was developed for a shipboard nuclear power plant with a water coolant. We choose Support Vector Machines (SVM) for the prediction of a heat transfer crisis.

In the context of heat transfer crisis recognition, SVM can be utilized to classify different instances of heat transfer crisis based on features like temperature, pressure, flow rates, and so on. The theoretical basis of SVM lies in the concept of finding the optimal hyperplane that best separates the data points in a high-dimensional space.

In the context of heat transfer crisis recognition, SVM works by mapping the input data into a high-dimensional feature space using a kernel function, such as a radial basis function (RBF) kernel. It then aims to find the hyperplane that maximizes the margin between the classes, effectively separating normal heat-transfer situations from crisis situations.

References to previous studies supporting the use of SVM in anomaly detection tasks in heat transfer systems can be found in research papers such as Ref. [5]. This work used SVM accurate prediction of convection heat transfer coefficient of nanofluids through circular pipes. The main emphasis was placed on the modeling of emergency situations. However, the research has not paid enough attention to the real experimental data.

In this work [6], SVM was used to detect faults in heat exchanger systems. However, the study did not consider heat transfer crises as a specific type of anomaly, which could be useful in preventing serious problems in thermal installations.

This study [7] used SVM to diagnose faults in heat exchanger networks, but it did not analyze in detail the crisis situations that may be critical to the safety and reliability of heat transfer systems.

These studies demonstrate the successful application of SVM in anomaly detection and fault diagnosis in heat transfer systems, highlighting its effectiveness and practicality in real-world scenarios.

## 2. Experiment description

Thus, a heat transfer crisis is called the cessation of heat removal from the heating element. The precursors of the crisis are bubbles formed on the hot surface (subcooled boiling); as the power increases, the number of bubbles increases, and they begin to unite into a single space, forming an air cushion that prevents heat removal (saturated boiling) (**Figure 4**).

Since the fuel rod is located in the fuel assembly, we cannot measure and control the temperature of the fuel rod wall directly. Accordingly, we need indirect methods, for example, the acoustic method.

The surface temperature of the heat-releasing wall, even under conditions of cooling with a subcooled liquid, becomes much higher than the saturation temperature, but despite this, there will be no boiling. This is facilitated by the high flow speed, its hydrodynamic stability, underheating of the core, and the minimum amount of gas dissolved in the liquid. Heat removal is necessary during the operation of these devices, in which thermal energy can be dissipated up to $1{\cdot}10^4$ kW/m$^2$. To meet complex heat dissipation requirements, the development of new cooling technology for heat fluxes with enormous values is essential [8].

The effect of an advanced change in the characteristics of the acoustic signal, compared to a jump in the temperature of the wall of the fuel rod, allows for early diagnosis of a crisis and heat transfer.

An algorithm for early detection of a heat transfer crisis was developed for a shipboard nuclear power plant with a water coolant. The research was carried out at the IPPE stand SVD-2. The SVD-2 stand of the State Scientific Center of the Russian

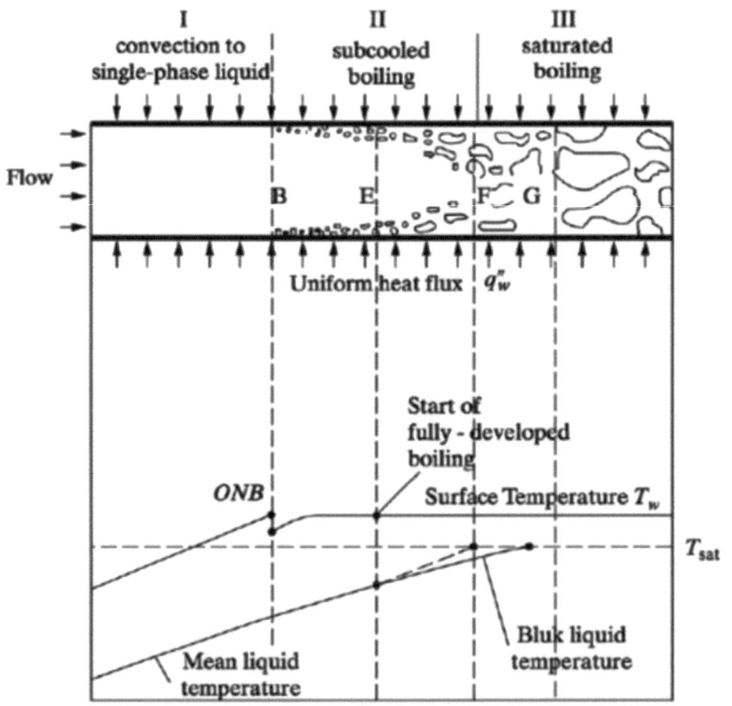


**Figure 4.**
*Types of heat transfer mode, flow image, and pipeline wall graph. Source: Bui A. et al. Statistical modeling support for calibration of a multiphysics model of subcooled boiling flows.*

Federation IPPE includes three circuits. The heat from the main circuit is transferred by the intermediate circuit to the circulating water supply circuit, from which the heat in the drip cooling tower is transferred to the atmospheric air.

The SVD-2 stand is a unique three-circuit installation (**Figures 1** and **2**), essentially a model of a water-cooled nuclear power plant under pressure. Stand intended for conducting studies of heat transfer, heat transfer crisis and hydrodynamics in stationary and dynamic modes on full-scale models of fuel assemblies in height (19, 25, 37 fuel rod simulators) of water-cooled reactors to justify improved fuel assembly designs.

The high-pressure stand makes it possible to carry out a safety justification for the use of nuclear fuel at VVER NPPs, to study thermal hydraulics and the heat transfer crisis in full-scale assemblies of VVER fuel rods at a pressure of up to 25 $MPa$ and an energy release power of up to 10 $MW$, and to simulate accidents. With coordinated operation of both loops, a coolant flow rate of up to 70.0 $\frac{m^3}{h}$ is provided for one experimental device.

The appearance of the stand can be seen in **Figure 5**.

The stand is designed for studies of heat transfer, heat transfer crisis, and hydrodynamics on full-scale models of fuel assemblies of water-cooled reactors and other experimental devices. The main circuit contains three loops:

- High-pressure loop
- Medium-pressure loop
- Natural-circulation loop

Integral equipment and major components of the stand are a cooling tower for design capacity, power supply, pumping unit, and so on. Main characteristics of the SVD-2 high-pressure stand are given in **Table 1**.

**Figure 5.**
*High pressure stand. Source: https://www.ippe.ru/facilities/thermal-physics/heat-hydraulic-water/17-high-pressure.*

| Parameter | SVD-2, three loops | | |
|---|---|---|---|
| | High pressure | Medium pressure | Low pressure |
| Power, MW:<br>• Stand<br>• Work area | 12<br>11 | 12<br>11 | _<br>_ |
| Pressure, MPa | 26 | 20 | 8 |
| Flow, m3/h | 35 | 35 | 8 |
| Pump pressure, MPa | 1.5 | 1.5 | Natural convection |
| Temperature at the entrance to the work area, °C | 450 | 350 | 240 |
| Temperature at the outlet of the work area, °C | 500 | 450 | 280 |
| Reactor installation height, m | 10.0 | 10.0 | 10.0 |

**Table 1.**
*Main characteristics of the SVD-2 high-pressure stand.*

The high-pressure loop makes it possible to conduct experiments on forced circulation of the coolant in a closed loop with heat removal by an intermediate loop. It should be noted that the equipment of the stand ensures research in the field as the stand is equipped with an automated system for collecting and processing experimental information, designed to receive and accumulate information from sensors of experimental devices.

The acquisition system includes a 12-channel multiplexer and an analog-to-digital converter, providing up to 100 thousand measurements per second [9].

Algorithms for diagnosing regimes with boiling coolant and heat transfer crisis, including the onset of a crisis under non-stationary conditions, have been developed for transportable and ship-based reactors with water coolant. The correct operation of the algorithms was verified by indirect (heat balance disturbance) and direct (measurement of vapor content, control of fuel rod wall temperature) methods in independent series of experiments.

## 3. Experimental data

The experimental section was a square profile rod inscribed in a cylinder with a diameter of 7.0 mm—simulating fuel element. **Figure 6(a)** shows a cross-section of a fuel rod indicating the position of eight thermocouples for measuring the temperature of the wall of the fuel rod located around the perimeter.

The mode was set as three main parameters P, G, T:

- Pressure - P
- Flow - G
- Outlet temperature - T

Of course, the critical power also depends on other additional parameters, such as:

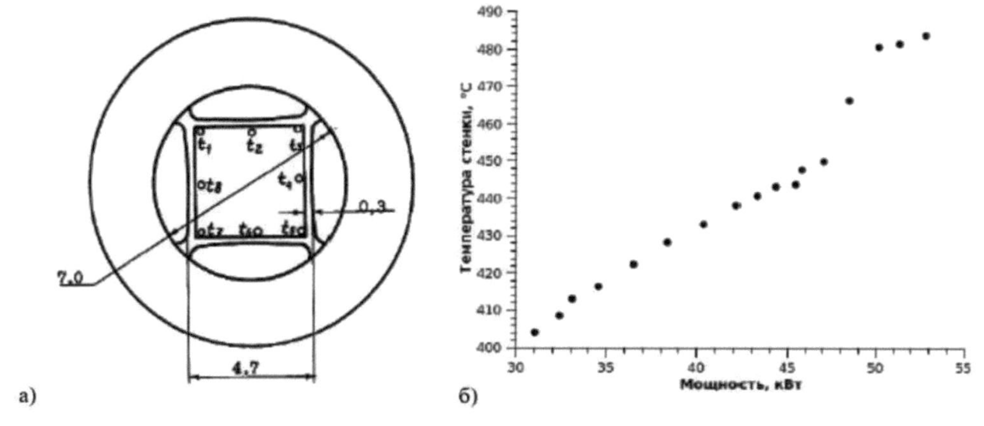


**Figure 6.**
*Experimental determination of critical power on the SVD-2 stand: (a) Cross-section of fuel rod and location of thermocouples, (b) Dependence of fuel rod wall temperature on power. Source: Skomorokhov A. O. Multivariate statistical diagnostic methods anomalous states of nuclear power plants.*

1. Length of heated area
2. Power distribution by height
3. Chemical composition of the coolant
4. Smoothness of the fuel rod surface
5. Channel geometry, and so on.

However, in this experiment, they are not of decisive importance.

The power value was set to be obviously less than the critical power for the given conditions. Further, the power value increased in steps of about 1 kW. The next power at which a jump or pulsation of the wall temperature was observed was defined as the critical power.

**Figure 6(b)** shows that up to a certain value, the fuel rod wall temperature linearly depended on the increase in power, but at a certain value (48 kW), there was a jump in the fuel rod wall temperature (heat transfer crisis), associated with the formation of a vapor film in the heated area.

For each experimental point, when the parameters reached steady-state values, a spectral analysis of the acoustic signal was carried out. Power spectral density (PSD) was estimated in the range 0.25–50 kHz with a frequency resolution of f = 250 Hz. Thus, each PSD was set with its own values at 200 equidistant frequencies, which were used as initial signs when developing a diagnostic algorithm. A total of 20 modes were implemented, for which 175 spectra were evaluated. The spectra measured at moments after the temperature jump in the wall of the fuel element belonged to the "heat transfer crisis" class [3].

In this work, the Jupyter Notebook command shell was used for interactive data processing in Python. This tool can work not only with Python but also with other programming languages: Julia, R, Haskell, and Ruby. It is often used for data science, statistical modeling, and machine learning.

| | 49 | 199 | 57 | 135 | 61 | 114 | 12 | 223 | 73 | 527 | ... |
|---|---|---|---|---|---|---|---|---|---|---|---|
| **count** | 172.000000 | 172.000000 | 172.000000 | 172.00000 | 172.000000 | 172.000000 | 172.000000 | 172.000000 | 172.000000 | 172.000000 | ... |
| **mean** | 198.395349 | 142.947674 | 83.686047 | 58.44186 | 90.988372 | 62.517442 | 94.267442 | 64.110465 | 266.930233 | 500.081395 | ... |
| **std** | 348.490942 | 177.769325 | 133.844045 | 82.57325 | 178.546830 | 93.795938 | 195.781620 | 100.340674 | 655.620572 | 1204.653979 | ... |
| **min** | 7.000000 | 8.000000 | 7.000000 | 7.00000 | 7.000000 | 7.000000 | 7.000000 | 7.000000 | 7.000000 | 7.000000 | ... |
| **25%** | 28.000000 | 48.000000 | 16.000000 | 16.00000 | 16.000000 | 16.000000 | 12.000000 | 12.000000 | 19.000000 | 31.000000 | ... |
| **50%** | 76.500000 | 85.000000 | 32.000000 | 30.00000 | 32.000000 | 28.000000 | 24.000000 | 24.000000 | 36.000000 | 63.000000 | ... |
| **75%** | 158.000000 | 157.000000 | 90.000000 | 53.00000 | 61.250000 | 62.000000 | 53.000000 | 53.000000 | 119.000000 | 252.000000 | ... |
| **max** | 2438.000000 | 1058.000000 | 933.000000 | 487.00000 | 1453.000000 | 569.000000 | 1453.000000 | 572.000000 | 4336.000000 | 8402.000000 | ... |

*Source: own development.*

**Table 2.**
*Initial data.*

Let us look at the general approach to machine learning:

1. Data processing - deleting or interpolating empty cells;

2. Dimensionality reduction - uninformative and interfering features are discarded;

3. Dividing the data into training and test sequences;

4. Training the model on the training set - choosing optimal parameters;

5. Prediction on a test sequence;

6. Evaluation of the results obtained.

The source data, which consist of 172 rows and 200 columns (**Table 2**), are loaded using the read_csv library of pandas:

The 30 most informative diagnostic features among the measured set of spectra were identified using the chi2 test.

For the selected features, a decision rule was constructed using the support vector machine [8–12].

## 4. Math SVM

SVM is a powerful machine learning algorithm that is chosen over other algorithms for heat transfer crisis recognition for several reasons, especially in the context of robust classification tasks like anomaly detection in complex systems. Here is a detailed justification for selecting SVM over other algorithms:

1. Effective in high-dimensional spaces - SVM is effective in high-dimensional spaces, which is crucial for analyzing complex systems like heat transfer crisis recognition where multiple features and parameters are involved. SVM can construct decision boundaries in high-dimensional spaces efficiently, which is beneficial when dealing with a large number of features in heat transfer systems.

2. Good performance with limited data - SVM can handle small datasets effectively, making it suitable for tasks where data might be limited or where the number of positive examples (crisis situations) is relatively small compared to normal instances. This is often the case in anomaly detection scenarios in heat transfer systems where crisis situations are rare.

3. Optimal margin - SVM aims to find the hyperplane that maximizes the margin between classes, which helps in achieving good generalization performance. In the context of heat transfer crisis recognition, having a clear margin between normal and crisis situations is important for accurate classification.

4. Robust to overfitting - SVM is less prone to overfitting, especially when the regularization parameter C is appropriately tuned. This is crucial for maintaining the model's performance on unseen data, which is essential in real-world applications like heat transfer crisis detection.

5. Kernel trick - SVM can efficiently handle non-linear decision boundaries through the kernel trick, allowing it to capture complex relationships in the data without explicitly transforming the features. In heat transfer crisis recognition, where the relationship between variables may not be linear, the kernel trick can be beneficial.

Let there be a training sample:

$$(x_1, y_1), \ldots, (x_m, y_m), x_i \in \Re^n, y_i \in \{-1, 1\} \quad (1)$$

The support vector machine constructs a classification function F in the form

$$F(x) = sign(\langle \boldsymbol{w}, \boldsymbol{x} \rangle + b) \quad (2)$$

where.
$\langle , \rangle$ - is the scalar product,
$w$ is the normal vector to the separating hyperplane,
$b$ is an auxiliary parameter.
Those objects for which $F(x) = 1$ fall into one class ("norm"), and objects with $F(x) = -1$ into another class ("crisis").
Any hyperplane can be specified as

$$\langle w, x \rangle + b = 0 \quad (3)$$

for some $w$ and $b$ [for a two-dimensional space, this will be a straight line (**Figure 7**)].
The next step is to select $w$ and $b$ that maximize the distance to each class—this distance is equal to $\frac{1}{\|w\|}$ (**Figure 8**).

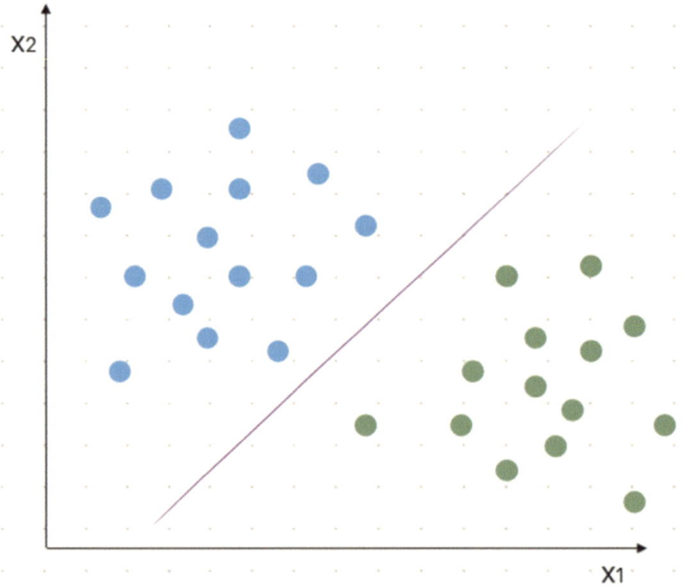


**Figure 7.**
*SVM illustration.*

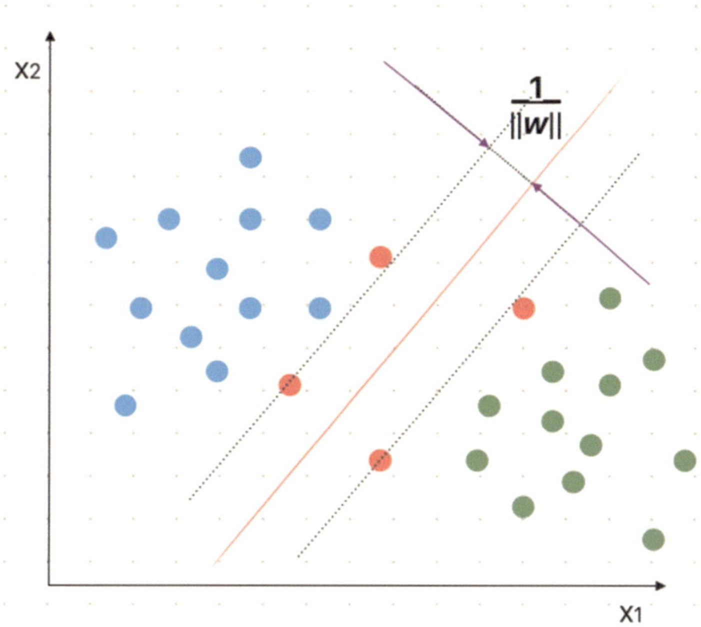


**Figure 8.**
*Support vectors.*

The vectors closest to the separating hyperplane are called support vectors. In **Figure 8**, they are marked in red.

Support Vector Machine (SVM) is a powerful machine learning algorithm for classification and regression problems. Let us compare support vector machines with other classification methods:

1. Logistic regression:

   - Logistic regression is a statistical method for predicting the likelihood of an event occurring.

   - SVM tries to find the optimal separating hyperplane, while logistic regression models the probabilities of assigning objects to certain classes.

2. Decision trees:

   - Decision trees build a sequence of questions to classify objects.

   - SVM is based on finding the optimal hyperplane for separating classes in feature space.

3. k-nearest neighbors (k-NN):

   - k-NN classifies objects based on neighbor classes in feature space.

   - SVM strives to find the widest possible separating hyperplane.

4. Naive Bayes classifier:

    - Naive Bayes classifier is based on the principle of Bayesian probability.
    - SVM examines support vectors, that is, data points located on or close to the separating hyperplane.

5. Neural networks

    - Neural networks model complex nonlinear relationships between input and output data.
    - SVM works well for medium to large-sized data with relatively few examples.

So, support vector machines stand out for their ability to perform well in high-dimensional spaces and have good generalization ability. However, the choice between classification methods depends on the specifics of the data and the requirements of a particular task.

## 5. Executive mathematical notation

The initial data was a matrix of $173 \times 200$, and the ratio of the "norm" and "crisis" classes was 109 and 64, respectively. Examples of DMAs belonging to different classes are presented in **Figure 9**.

Although support vector machines often produce good model quality, they are very sensitive to parameter settings and data scaling [13].

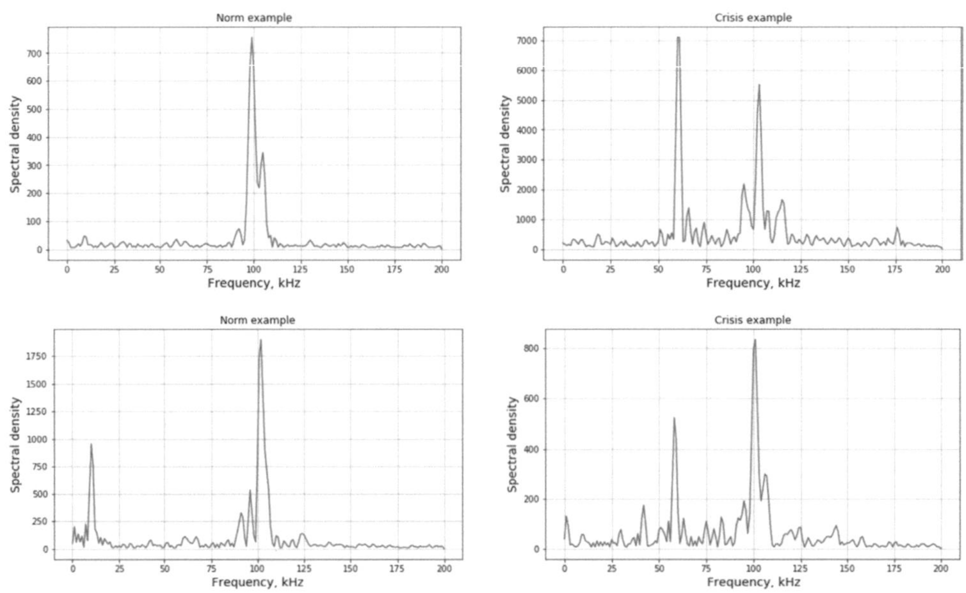


**Figure 9.**
*Examples of "norm" and "crisis."*

| Class | Norm | Crisis |
|---|---|---|
| Norm | 17 | 2 |
| Crisis | 1 | 15 |

**Table 3.**
*Results of heat transfer crisis recognition.*

One way to solve this problem is to scale all features so that they all have approximately the same scale. A common scaling method for kernel SVM is to scale the data so that all features take values between 0 and 1 [14].

To identify boiling, the scikit-learn library of the python programming language was used, with the Jupyter software shell [14–16]. To find the optimal separating hyperplane, the following parameters were selected for the SVM classification method:

*kernel*: kernel type used in the algorithm; the following kernel types are available: "linear," "poly," "rbf," "sigmoid," and "precomputed."

*degree*: degree of the polynomial kernel ("poly"), not taken into account for other kernels.

*gamma*: coefficient for kernel types: "rbf," "poly," and "sigmoid." The default value is "auto," which is calculated as 1 N, where N is the number of features. Also, gamma can take the value 'scale' =1 N.

*coef0*: independent kernel function coefficient, only significant in "poly" and "sigmoid" kernels.

*C*: error penalty parameter.

We will build the model for classification based on the support vector machine. To select model parameters, we will use the *GridSearchCV* module from the sklearn package. The classification results are shown in **Table 3**. The highest accuracy belongs to the model with the RBF kernel, as well as in the problem of predicting the critical thermal load.

Model parameters: $C = 10; coef0 = 1; gamma = 0.5$.

Thus, the accuracy on the testing set was 91.4%.

Thus, let us compare our results with other different classification methods, like K-Nearest Neighbors, Random Forest Classifier, GaussianNB AdaBoost Classifier, and MLPClassifier. The confusion matrix is displayed below **Table 4**:

The accuracy of the K-Nearest Neighbors method on the testing set was 82.9% (**Table 5**).

The accuracy of the MLPClassifier method on the testing set was 68.6% (**Table 6**).

The accuracy of the Random Forest Classifier method on the testing set was 74.3%. Of course, these results can be better after fine-tuning parameters more and detailed consideration.

| Class | Norm | Crisis |
|---|---|---|
| Norm | 23 | 3 |
| Crisis | 3 | 6 |

**Table 4.**
*Confusion matrix for K-nearest neighbors.*

| Class | Norm | Crisis |
|---|---|---|
| Norm | 22 | 4 |
| Crisis | 7 | 2 |

**Table 5.**
*Confusion matrix for MLPClassifier.*

| Class | Norm | Crisis |
|---|---|---|
| Norm | 24 | 2 |
| Crisis | 7 | 2 |

**Table 6.**
*Confusion matrix for random forest classifier.*

The obtained result for SVC can be considered satisfactory for solving the task at hand—recognizing a heat transfer crisis at such a complex diagnostic object as a nuclear power plant.

## 6. Conclusion

The margin before a heat transfer crisis is the most important parameter in determining the thermal reliability of a reactor. Therefore, it is necessary to be able to determine the critical power as accurately as possible for various operating modes. The effect of an advanced change in the characteristics of the acoustic signal, compared to a jump in the temperature of the wall of the fuel rod, allows for early diagnosis of a crisis and heat transfer.

This paper examined the use of support vector machines for the problem of recognizing a heat transfer crisis using the python programming language and its sklearn library. The radial basis kernel was chosen as the kernel function.

The successful application of SVM in the recognition of heat transfer crises can significantly improve the safety of nuclear reactors through early detection of potentially critical situations.

The development of automatic monitoring systems that use the developed SVM model to recognize heat transfer crises will make it possible to quickly detect potential problems and take measures to prevent them. The results obtained can be used to optimize the operation of nuclear reactors, improve energy efficiency, and prevent situations that could lead to downtime or emergency situations.

The developed models can be used to train personnel in recognizing and preventing heat transfer crises, which will increase the level of safety and operational efficiency of nuclear reactors.

Overall, the research results on heat crisis recognition using SVM can have a significant impact on the design, operation, and safety of nuclear reactors, contributing to more efficient and safe operation of power systems. Therefore, further research in this area could bring significant benefits to both the academic community and the nuclear energy industry.

## Author details

Viktoria Sheshukova
Obninsk Institute for Nuclear and Power Engineering, Obninsk, Russia

*Address all correspondence to: victoriariabtceva@gmail.com

## References


[1] Schulenberg T, Leung L. Supercritical water-cooled reactors. In: Handbook of Generation IV Nuclear Reactors. Woodhead Publishing; 2016. pp. 189-220

[2] Marguet S. The Technology of Pressurized Water Reactors: From the Nautilus to the EPR. Springer Nature; 2022

[3] Skomorokhov AO. Multivariate Statistical Methods Diagnostics of Anomalous States of Nuclear Power Plants: Abstract. Dis. For the Job Application Scientist Step. Doc. Tech. Sciences. Obninsk: Skomorokhov Alexander Olegovich; Obninsky Institute of Atomic Energy; 2003, 2011. 43 p

[4] Website of the Institute of Physics and Energy named after A.I. Leypunsky. Available from: https://www.ippe.ru/facilities/thermal-physics/heat-hydraulic-water/17-high-pressure

[5] Safdari Shadloo M. Application of support vector machines for accurate prediction of convection heat transfer coefficient of nanofluids through circular pipes. International Journal of Numerical Methods for Heat & Fluid Flow. 2021;**31**(8):2660-2679. DOI: 10.1108/HFF-09-2020-0555

[6] Muthukrishnan S et al. Support vector machine for modelling and simulation of heat exchangers. Thermal Science. 2020;**24**(Part 1B): 499-503

[7] Tudón-Martínez JC, Morales-Menendez R, Garza-Castañón LE. Fault diagnosis in a heat exchanger using process history based-methods. Computer Aided Chemical Engineering. 2010;**28**:169-174

[8] Belozerov VI. Research of critical heat flows in small-diameter channels, news of higher educational institutions. Nuclear Energy. 2021;**3**:44-57

[9] Mogilner AI, Skomorokhov AO, Shvetsov DM. On the problem of noise spectra classification in nuclear power plant operation diagnostics. Nuclear Technology. 1981;**53**(1):8-18

[10] Bzdok D, Krzywinski M, Altman N. Points of significance: Machine learning: Supervised methods. Nature. 2018;**5**:5-6

[11] Wu X et al. Top 10 algorithms in data mining. Knowledge and Information Systems. 2008;**14**(1):1-37

[12] Ramaswamy S, Rastogi R, Shim K. Efficient algorithms for mining outliers from large data sets. ACM SIGMOD Record. 2000;**29**(2):427-438

[13] Skomorokhov A, Nakhabov A. Support vector machines in A+. ACM SIGAPL APL Quote Quad. 2004;**34**(4): 8-17

[14] Muller A, Guido S. Introduction to Machine Learning Using Python, Guide for Data Scientists. O'Reilly Media, Inc.; 2017

[15] Settouti N, Bechar MEA, Chikh MA. Statistical comparisons of the top 10 algorithms in data mining for classification task. International Journal of Interactive Multimedia and Artificial Intelligence. 2016;**4**:46-51

[16] Python. Available from: https://www.python.org/